D0671398

LOGGERS OF THE BC COAST

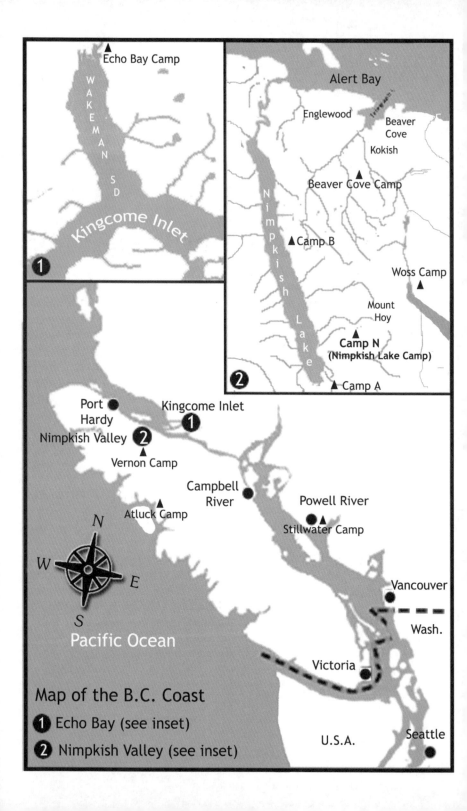

Map of the B.C. Coast
1 Echo Bay (see inset)
2 Nimpkish Valley (see inset)

LOGGERS OF THE BC COAST

HANS KNAPP

hancock

house

ISBN 0-88839-588-4
Copyright © 2005 Hans Knapp

Cataloging in Publication Data

Knapp, Hans
    Loggers of the BC coast / Hans Knapp.

ISBN 0-88839-588-4

    1. Knapp, Hans. 2. Logging—British Columbia—Pacific
Coast—History. 3. Lumber camps—British Columbia—Pacific
Coast—History. 4. Loggers—British Columbia—Pacific Coast—
Biography. 5. Pacific Coast (B.C.)—Biography. I. Title.

SD537.52.K52A3 2005   634.9'8'092   C2004-904886-4

All rights reserved. No part of this publication may be reproduced, stored
in a retrieval system or transmitted, in any form or by any means, electron-
ic, mechanical, photocopying, recording, or otherwise, without the prior
written permission of Hancock House Publishers.
Printed in South Korea — PACOM

Editor: Mary Scott
Production: Mia Hancock
Cover design: Rick Groenheyde
Front cover photo: The author walking a felled 227-foot sitka spruce, Atluck Camp, 1965.
Courtesy of Erik Cook and Peacock Postcards.
Back cover photo: Skidder crew with steam yarder, 1934. *Photo courtesy of BC-WCB.*

*We acknowledge the financial support of the Government of Canada through the
Book Publishing Industry Development Program (BPIDP) for our publishing activities.*

Published simultaneously in Canada and the United States by

HANCOCK HOUSE PUBLISHERS LTD.
19313 Zero Avenue, Surrey, B.C. V3S 9R9
(604) 538-1114 Fax (604) 538-2262

HANCOCK HOUSE PUBLISHERS
1431 Harrison Avenue, Blaine, WA 98230-5005
(604) 538-1114 Fax (604) 538-2262
Web Site: www.hancockhouse.com *email:* sales@hancockhouse.com

CONTENTS

ACKNOWLEDGMENTS

Special appreciation goes to my wife for her unwavering support and effort spent in scrutinizing the many drafts of the manuscript. Further, a note of appreciation to our son who typed and prepared the entire manuscript as it took shape over a ten-year period, and to our daughter who suggested the appropriate title for this book. Finally, a special thankyou goes to Jeff Keller for his assistance in editing and helping shape the structure of this work into its final form.

DEDICATION

To all the great loggers of their time.

PREFACE

This book is intended as a tribute to all the untold men who toiled in myriads of coastal logging camps in an effort to make a living. Logging was the spearhead of the forest industry in British Columbia, and has been a significant source of employment during the province's last 100 years. Despite this significant contribution to the rovince's economy and history, little has been written, and even less published, about the countless men who worked in the woods along the rugged British Columbia coast. What is missing from many publications is an accurate description of the loggers themselves: who they were and how they worked, lived, talked and cursed. All the capital in the world cannot fall a tree by itself or transport it to the mills without the skilled and industrious hands of the men in the logging industry.

These days, men no longer flock from northern Europe to work in the woods along the beautiful shores of British Columbia. The many jobs are no more; gone too are the big logging camps. What was once a way of life for thousands of men is now a thing of the past.

The contents of this book were written as they were experienced, by a native of Austria who spent his lifetime working as a timberfaller, in various logging camps on the British Columbia coast from 1950 to 1993.

HANS KNAPP
West Vancouver, B.C.
Autumn, 2004

Chapter 1

The Newcomer

From Austria To Wakeman Sound

On April the 8th, 1951, I left my native Austria to make a life for myself in British Columbia. I traveled first to Le Havre, in France, and from there to Québec City on a ship of the Cunard line. Within days I had made my way to Renfrew, Ontario, and had already found two jobs; the first in a lumberyard, sorting lumber for fifteen cents an hour, the second washing dishes in a restaurant.

The restaurant was Greek, but the kitchen staff, a mother and her grown-up son, had come from Poland to Canada as "displaced persons" after the war. When they learned that I was from Austria they expressed their resentment in the strongest terms. One night the son followed me into the washroom and unleashed a barrage of ethnic slurs about Germans. I had heard enough, so I punched him out. When the manager learned of the incident she gave me a raise.

No raise, however, could have kept me from my destination. I had already given notice at the lumberyard, and held firm to my decision, despite the promise of ten cents more an hour. The foreman seemed eager to keep me, and even sought to discourage me from leaving.

"In Vancouver," he admonished, "people carry an umbrella everywhere they go. Why? Because sometimes it rains for forty days!"

I left as planned, with five dollars in my pocket and a ticket for Vancouver on the Canadian Pacific Railway, and arrived, in spite of the foreman's warnings, on a brilliantly sunny day toward the end of May. It had been a long trip. Taking my meagre baggage from the overhead compartment, I headed for the station exit. Looking around, I saw others getting off the train in similar straits to mine:

no home, no job, little money. Our prospects were unknown, and our chief asset was the simple courage we needed to fend for ourselves in this unfamiliar city.

The streets of Vancouver were bustling and noisy. It was the first time I had seen so many people of so many different colours and races, and the first time I had heard the unfamiliar sounds of the many languages they spoke. There were people from the Orient in colourful dresses and headgear, women and girls looking like paper dolls, as dainty as in fairy tales. There were Native Indians, and dark men in turbans. And, of course, there were loggers.

For loggers, Vancouver was the hub of the universe. It was from here they were hired out to the hundreds of logging operations all along the B.C. coast, on Vancouver Island, up to the Queen Charlotte Islands and beyond. A newcomer, standing forlorn in the street, looking for work with hardly a word of English, faced some formidable challenges. For some, the future was decided by the subtle ways of chance. A few, for example, were recognized and helped by fellow countrymen, but I was not one of those. Since I did not speak the language well, and since I had no trade or special skill, fate pointed its fickle finger to the woods.

It was in the woods that I spent the next forty-two years of my life. During that time I worked and lived with hundreds of men, many of them so memorable that their looks, gestures, accents, and even their words are etched on my memory with perfect clarity. As I look back over the years it seems that the men I worked with are clamouring for attention, both as individuals, and as a group of pioneers in the process of being forgotten. Their stories, often tragic, occasionally triumphant, will be lost forever if my pen is still.

The majority of B.C. coast loggers came originally from Scandinavia, Finland, Scotland and Poland. Whether they arrived in British Columbia overland by train or on a sailing ship, most had several things in common. Few had any formal education, or had learned a useful trade by which they could make a living in this pioneering country. Many were from large families with little hope for the future. One thing more drove the majority: in our hearts dwelled an unbending will to survive and succeed.

With such an attitude half the battles waiting in the future were already won. Some challenges, however, took more than will to conquer: sickness, terrible injuries and accidental death were always just behind the next tree. No new immigrant to the coast could be aware of these unpleasant facts. Only as life went on, and through bitter experience, could such a person become wise.

The camps were full of single and married men, some very

young, others no longer youthful. Parents, brothers, sisters, and kinsmen had for the most part been left behind. So too friends, schoolfellows, and even sweethearts. Some burned all bridges behind them, vowing never to return. For the married man who left behind a family, to be sent for at a later date, it was a particularly trying time. For some it took many years to be reunited. For others, dreams fell by the wayside. Most, though, stuck to their resolutions. With only a few, notable exceptions, they were good, God fearing men.

Having arrived in Vancouver, I found myself applying for work at The Loggers Agency, one of the logger hiring outfits near the old skid road. Most hiring offices looked somewhat alike: well-worn doorknobs and chafed door panels, wooden floors worn down from heavy work boots studded with hobnails, and one or two long, high counters behind which stood lean, cranky-looking men.

Somewhere on the dilapidated wall was the ever-present clock, next to enlarged pictures of early logging scenes: bearded men holding long-handled axes, standing beside huge trees half-felled, or beside teams of oxen in tandem hauling logs along a "skid road." From the ceilings hung old-fashioned lamps to light up the room during the dreary months of winter, when little or no sunlight would find its way through the narrow, soot-covered windows. Occasionally there was a safe in the office, in which were kept cheques or letters for loggers with no fixed mailing address. Elsewhere stood the unavoidable black telephone, and the filing cabinet in which loggers' records and addresses were kept.

The agencies not only hired the loggers, they kept a personal work record of each man. On a card it would state: "Back anytime," or "NOT wanted back," depending on the degree of satisfaction the company in question had derived from the hire. It also held names of individuals being blackballed by companies all up and down the coast of British Columbia, for violent offenses against fellow workers, or for willfully damaging company equipment.

Perhaps the most prominent features of the hiring offices were the large signs, almost like school blackboards, which hung on the walls. These signs named the various logging companies for which the agency did the hiring, and the positions for which companies required men. The signs read like this:

O'BRIEN LOGGING: STILLWATER
* *

1   HIGHRIGGER

| 1 | HOOKTENDER |
| 4 | CHOKERMEN |

KELSEY BAY LOGGING
****

2	SETS OF FALLERS
1	HEADCOOK
2	BOOM-MEN

ALICE LAKE LOGGING
****

2	LOGGING-TRUCK DRIVERS
1	ROADMAN
1	SCALER

In the years to come I learned that the agencies, and the rules they enforced, had evolved over time, and were actually more sophisticated, and a little more humane, than they once had been. (For more on the logging agencies, the early days of logging, and the rise of the IWA, see Appendices 1 and 2.)

Within days of applying at the agency I was assigned to Echo Bay Logging's camp in Wakeman Sound, where I would work as a chokerman for forty-five cents an hour. I had only a few dollars left in my wallet to tide me over, and I needed an inexpensive place to stay till leaving for camp. Normally, loggers travelled to work on one of the boats which sailed the entire length of the B.C. coast. These boats serviced the different logging and fishing communities along its route, sailing in and out of the coastline's many inlets. Coming newly from Europe, I could only appreciate such a vast distance when I realized that the coastline of British Columbia would stretch, in European equivalents, all the way from Norway to Greece.

Boats from several shipping companies left Vancouver once a week for delivery of passengers, freight, mail, and other goods. While waiting in town for a ship to sail, a logger or would-be logger put his gear together, got drunk if he still had any money left to spend, or just waited for the boat to take him back to the woods, where he recuperated from his time in town and worked hard to make a new stake.

Eventually, I found myself in a drab, run-down room in the Blackstone Hotel, one of many lodgings in that part of town where loggers used to congregate. To eat, I frequented the numerous downtown cafés which were run by industrious Chinese people. The food (in restaurants such as the Greasy Spoon) was cheap, but wholesome and just what I needed. There would always be at least one other young man there, writing a letter, perhaps the first since his arrival in Canada, or sending a postcard back home to a waiting mother, wife or sweetheart. So far there had been little or no time to think about the past. The immediate needs had taken priority. In time I became oriented to my new surroundings, and ultimately the day arrived for me to board the boat which would take me one step closer to my destination.

The ships which took loggers to their jobs up the coast generally sailed out of Vancouver harbour around eight o'clock in the evening, when it was already dark during the cheerless winter months. Since I was looking forward to seeing the seacoast, the late evening departure from port came as a disappointment. Quite frequently, when an agency was sending out a number of newly hired men, an agent would be at the pier to make certain all men got on board, sober or drunk. Once on the wharf waiting for the gangplank to be lowered, I got my first really good look at what veteran loggers seemed to be like. They came singly or in pairs, carrying weighty suitcases or large cumbersome bags containing their gear. Some had a woman friend along to see them off.

It was easy to see that loggers were very different in outlook and behaviour from the rest of the people waiting to walk on board. The young, full of vigour, the older, slower, more patient, more sure of themselves. Some came singing, others in a quarrelsome mood, depending on the amount of rye they had managed to drink before leaving their hotels. They came in all shapes and sizes: big, tall, strong, slim, lean, sinewy and a few short and fat. Their clothing looked somewhat alike: woolen pants with jacket in winter, denim outfits the rest of the year, and a broad-brimmed rain hat, to keep the head dry in country where it can drizzle or pour for days and nights on end. On their feet they wore sturdy-soled, leather boots.

On every departure for the coast, there was at least one man, if not more, who had to be helped up the gang-plank and into his stateroom, which he usually shared with another fellow woodsman, quite often in the same pitiful, drunken shape. If he had not already gone "snakey" with hallucinations, he would eventually fall asleep and remain so for the rest of the day and night. The snakey ones were a nuisance, both on board and in camp.

Such were the scenes a logger saw at the beginning of his working days, and such were the scenes during his frequent trips to and from his holidays in town — provided he lived long enough to enjoy them. It has been calculated that a soldier had a better chance of returning alive and uninjured from any of the last two World Wars, than had a logger of working safely a lifetime in the woods.

Should a passenger have had the good fortune to be on a ship leaving Vancouver in the morning or the early part of the day, there were many magnificent scenes to behold. As one left Vancouver harbour, the last impression of the city was provided by the wide sweep of the vessel along wooded shores, before it passed beneath the Lions Gate Bridge. To the south lay Stanley Park, named after Lord Stanley, once Governor-General of Canada, who dedicated the park to the use and enjoyment of people of all colours, creeds and customs, in October, 1889. Past Stanley Park, the boat sailed into Howe Sound and soon after into the Strait of Georgia. Along the coast the mountains seem to spring right out of the sea, rising abruptly and steeply and covered with snow till late summer. Next the ship's bow pointed northwest, along the inside passage; to the North, British Columbia's mainland, to the South, Vancouver Island. At the time I had no knowledge of the area's rich history, but later these waters became known to me, not just as places I had often been, but as landmarks of bygone voyages of discovery.

Captain James Cook first sailed into North Pacific waters to land at Nootka, on the west coast of Vancouver Island, in the spring of 1778. Cook was seeking shelter and a suitable place to cut trees to replace spars and masts, broken during a rough voyage from New Zealand. He also needed fresh water, as well as wood for the galley stoves and for other repair work. Captain Cook and his crew are now generally credited with being the first Europeans to have "logged" on the coast of what is now British Columbia. Two of his lieutenants were later to gain fame of their own, Captain William Bligh, known for the mutiny that took place on his ship the "Bounty," and Captain George Vancouver, who first circumnavigated the island now named after him.

Captain Vancouver named many places after crew members or British admirals, e.g., Mt. Baker, Birch Bay, Puget Sound and Howe Sound. The Strait of Georgia he named after King George III. Others also left their mark. Active Pass, both busy and swift-watered, was named for the American survey ship "Active." The Spanish explorer of the same time, Jose Maria Narvaez, left names in his tongue sprinkled through the area; Cortez Island, Saturna Island (named after his flagship "Saturnia"), and on the west coast of Vancouver Island, Zeballos and Tofino.

As well, there are numerous Native Indian place names along

the coast. Tsawwassen is Salish, meaning "looking over the shimmering water." Nanaimo (sney-ne-mo) means "meeting of tribes." The once fierce Cowichans reigned over the east coast of Vancouver Island, and their war canoes raced up the passages of the Gulf Islands. So much for a brief history of the waters through which the loggers passed when travelling to and from camps. Of all this I was unaware, as I made my first journey up the coast.

As the ship cruised northwards, it passed surf-pummelled headlands, tranquil coves and dense forests where the wet kiss of the sea lingered. Arms of the ocean that provide arteries for tugboats towing log booms, also bring the warming "Kuroshio," or Japan current. Therefore temperatures in coastal winters seldom dip below freezing for any length of time, which helps to make year-round logging possible.

Vancouver Island and the more northerly Queen Charlotte Islands are remnants of a sunken mountain chain, and bear the brunt of drenching storms from the sea. The retreat of Pleistocene glaciers chiselled the landscape with a sculptor's discernment, leaving the corrugated coast a maze of bays and deep fjords into which roaring rivers discharge. Also carved were lovely forested isles, to which seagulls return to sleep at night. And to all this the spectacular Coast Mountains raise a green-robed backdrop.

Soon we passed splendid Jervis Inlet, Texada Island, and the bustling town of Powell River on the "Sunshine Coast." Here can be observed the most resplendent sunsets on the entire B.C. coast. At the northern end of the Strait of Georgia, nine miles north of Campbell River, the boat approached the dangerous Seymour Narrows. Here, with its treacherous current, swirling eddies, and the turbulent tide-rips off the twin peaks of "Ripple Rocks," the Narrows has claimed numerous ships and lives since it was first charted in 1792 by Captain George Vancouver.

Despite the blasting of Ripple Rock on April 5, 1958, the Seymour Narrows are still considered by many seamen the worst hazard to marine navigation on the B.C. coast. It's of interest to note how the tops of the dreaded Ripple Rocks were eliminated. A shaft was driven from shore and under the seabed to the twin peaks. An area of the shaft was then filled with an enormous amount of high explosives and detonated. The resulting shock waves equalled the force of a small earthquake — the largest non-atomic manmade explosion to that date.

The sea, not normally a logger's forté, makes most woodsmen uncomfortable, especially a stretch of dangerous water like Seymour Narrows. I stared from the port-hole of my state room while the vessel waited out the oncoming tide. The moonlight shone on swirling eddies, strong enough to suck up a large log or a tree as if it were a toy. Many a logger was given the creeps by the sight of such turbulent tide-rips.

Having passed the treacherous currents of the Seymour Narrows, the boat might make stops in Toba Inlet or the winding Knight Inlet to discharge passengers, and to unload freight or goods that people there had ordered. Between Johnstone Strait and Queen Charlotte Strait lies a little island where the old Indian settlement of Alert Bay is strategically located, right opposite the Nimpkish (Cla-anch) River on upper Vancouver Island. This is an important river for the coastal Indians, since it holds the great fish runs, on which many in the past depended, and still depend.

Most boats halted at Alert Bay. A supply base for handloggers, fishermen, trappers and prospectors on this part of the coast, Alert Bay was also widely known for its ancient Indian village. It was here that I saw my first community "longhouse," which the Indians used to build in former days. I found the local totem poles fascinating, although I did not understand the meaning of the strange carvings. The shoreline here was dotted with tiny dwellings, and everywhere all kinds of boats were tied up on the sandy beach. Friendly natives smiled at strangers; children and dogs chased each other on the road along the seashore.

Once in a while a man would stagger up the road from the Bayside Hotel, which for years contained the only bar far and wide. In the ideally located bay, fishermen worked on their old boats or did repair work on their fishing nets. An azure sky, snowy mountains in the distance, green hills and the fresh smell of the sea made this one of the most unforgettable places on earth.

Nearby, almost adjoining Cormorant Island (on which Alert Bay is situated), lies Malcolm Island, where since the turn of the century a tightly meshed Finnish settlement of roughly 800 souls has existed. The name of the community is Sointula, meaning "harmony," a most befitting title for this peaceful colony. Sointula has given B.C. many fearless fishermen and top-notch loggers. Malcolm Island was also, I learned, just across from my destination, Wakeman Sound on the mainland.

On my first cruise up the coast I stood for hours on deck, struck with awe. The scenery was overwhelming. As far as the eye could see grew tall timber of the finest quality. The sea teemed with salmon, and with fishing boats. Wherever the shore allowed, driftwood washed in by the tides simply piled up on the beach. As a newcomer from Europe, where wood is precious and often scarce, such a sight represented enormous wealth.

I ogled the gulls, the pageant of comely isles, and the chorus line of killer whales cavorting in the ship's wake. Wings set, a bald eagle soared, sole owner of an endless sweep of sky. Lordly white mountain goats peered down from precipitous cliffs. A wolf howled in the not-too-far distance, sending a shiver up my spine. Wilderness is still the spell of B.C., and beauty is the province's birthright.

Cruising at a steady pace, the vessel ploughed through the fields of kelp that drift along with the tide. Early settlers homesteading along the coast used kelp as fertilizer in their garden plots, for it contains all the minerals the soil needs to grow good, rich vegetables. On nearly every one of the major inlets and islands, men, with the help of their wives and children, have tried to homestead, to wrest a living from the generous land. But the weather and the isolation doomed most of their attempts. Only one industry besides fishing had a good chance at survival, and that was logging.

From the deck I could see the scars on the steep hillsides above the shore where handloggers had done their work. Theirs was the simplest way to log, although backbreaking and exceedingly dangerous work. In many cases, handlogging was a family business. Men would sail up in a boat or a skiff with all their equipment aboard, set up a tent camp, use local trees to build a lean-to or a log cabin on skids (runners), which could then be floated to the next logging site. These could be called the first float camps, of which there were so many in later years.

The handloggers would select their place of action with great care. The timber had to be of the right quality to be readily sold on the log market, and of the right size to be handled. There had to be nearby running water, a stream or creek that would not dry up during a hot, dry summer, and a sheltered bay or cove, where they could shore their logs in bagbooms, till they could sell them to a log broker or a sawmill. Some did well, others only made a living.

The handlogger's tools consisted of axes, crosscut saws, sledge hammers, slender long steel wedges for falling trees, shorter, wider ones for bucking the timber into logs, an oil can and the essential "Gilchrist jack." The task at hand was to fell the trees in such a manner as to land them in the sea. This was done by falling smaller trees or saplings crosswise or parallel to the shoreline. Such transversely felled trees would act as a skid over which larger trees would slide down into the bay. The steeper the hillside, the further up the handloggers could cut timber.

It was quite a sight to see a tree leave the stump, touch the ground far down the hill, the top break off and the trunk or remaining portion shoot downhill at ever-increasing speed. Then it would hit the tidewater with great force, arch out of the sea like a geyser, then drop back into the water to settle with the waves it had created. And it was a rare and spectacular thing to see, when a tree by some odd chance landed on its broken end, butt up in the air, like a flagpole standing on its top, balancing precisely for a split second, then falling over to continue downhill.

On less steep ground, trees tended to hang up behind stumps, rocks, or get stuck with the top buried in the ground. To get these logs into the seawater was extremely hard, perilous work, and it took a great toll on handloggers throughout the years. These men logged in pairs on the slopes of many rough inlets. At various times, there were several thousand handloggers labouring on the coast of British Columbia.

Another common sight along the craggy B.C. coast were the "A-frame" shows. This was an unsophisticated way of yarding logs off a hillside. A raft was built of sturdy, durable logs, such as red cedar, spruce or fir, upon which an A-frame was erected and a donkey (the engine for a yarder) placed behind it. The raft was securely anchored and would float, rise and fall with the tide. It also could be towed to new areas to do its job over again. A-frame shows were often run by "gyppos," who built their living shacks on shore, or on floats nearby. The remains, tumbled down huts and rusty machinery, can still be seen, a reminder of how some of today's "giants" started out in logging.

Of course, where there were logbooms, there had to be tugboats to tow them, and anywhere one sailed on the B.C. coast, sooner or later one would meet one of the trusty coastal tugboats with its valiant crew, towing any size log-boom behind it. From a distance, one of these daring workhorses of the cruel sea looked like a dot pulling a dash.

From the deck, I could only marvel at all the new experiences I was eagerly absorbing. The vessel passed numerous islands, where cottages nestled behind sandy beaches, blue smoke lazily curling up from their chimneys into the clear summer sky. Once in a while you could see a horse near the shore, or several goats, to provide the islanders with their milk, and children waving frantically at the passing ship. Not to be missed were the clotheslines, strung from one sapling to another, on which the family wash was hung to dry in the fresh breeze. Conspicuously absent were cars and trucks. Instead there were boats, skiffs, canoes, dugouts and kayaks pulled up on the beach; the standard modes of transportation for people living along the coast.

A-frame with Donkey. Coastal Logging, 1980.
Courtesy of Douglas-McIntyre.

What a first-time traveller to these waters could not very well know, is that Indian habitations, as well as other outposts, are always on the sheltered side of the land, away from the dreaded south-east winds. The frequent storms which last from late fall to spring whip the ocean to a grey-green tempest, with high waves pounding far into shore. The white man learned from the natives to build his cabin in the lee of the land, so as to face the sun most of the days of the year. This reduces the need for light and heating during cheerless winter months. It also lifts the spirit of human beings, when a rare ray of sunshine falls through a hole in the low rain clouds and lights up the room. It lends truth to the age-old saying: "Face the sun and the shadow will fall behind you."

Along the route were strategically located lighthouses, flashing their beams out into the night. Those pretty lighthouses, painted a spotless white with a distinctive red roof, situated on a green patch or a wave-pounded rock, are visible from a great distance. At these lighthouses a keeper normally lived with his family, and tended to his important duties to the mariners.

Somewhere on that journey I saw my first clear-cut. I was appalled at its enormous size, which disfigured the coastal slopes along the ship's route. Where natural regeneration had not yet occurred, one could see huge areas completely denuded of greenery, with blackened stumps and rock outcroppings poking forth from steep slopes. It was amazing to me how much wood had been discarded, for lack of value on the open market.

Sailing up the coast was an excellent time for observation and reflection. While staring at the sky from the deck of the ship, I also heard the occasional noise of a seaplane engine, long before the aircraft itself came into sight. At other times, the sound of the motor would be audible almost simultaneously with the appearance of an aircraft overhead. This happens often along the narrow inlets into which bold pilots fly year-round. It is alleged that flying along the B.C. coast is one of the most difficult and challenging jobs for seaplane pilots. With strong, unexpected crosswinds, high mountains, up-drafts, air pockets, dense fog, low clouds, poor visibility in heavy rain or mist, it is indeed a Herculean task to fly the B.C. coast.

Seaplanes played a vital role in transporting injured or sick loggers in and out of isolated camps, especially in those areas where a supply boat did not call. Loggers used to relate to each other hair-raising stories of trips they made in those small planes, either flying into a camp to start work, or being flown out to the nearest hospital. It is difficult to believe the dilemmas the pilots had to overcome when trying to land in stormy weather in restricted bays, often clogged with log booms. Taking off again presented new difficulties, especially with a hurt logger strapped down on a stretcher. It was, in most cases, a race against time.

Tales were told of men hanging on to the tail section of the plane, while the pilot revved the engine to the necessary RPMs so it could take off fast on the short, restricted stretch of water and clear the log booms in front. Often the pilots just barely succeeded, cheered on by men standing on shore with crossed fingers. Yes, those were lion-hearted pilots and brave or desperate passengers. Pilot dedication greatly exceeded the lowly pay they received.

But most of these facts I could never have known, as I stood on deck watching the coast slip by. And at times, when the coast was blanketed in the thick fog that could be encountered any time throughout the year, even the sound of the floatplanes was muted beyond recognition. One heard only the monotonous sound of the ship's foghorn as it blared into the milky void.

Whereas I spent that trip taking in everything around me, storing it away in my mind, marvelling at the bounty of this large, rich, beautiful country, the typical old-timer stayed below deck, his perceptions blunted over the course of years. Sometimes he'd venture on deck to get his bearings, look at the weather, utter a profanity, and disappear again below deck to his stateroom. There he'd join his roommate, if he had one, and continue talking about whatever they were talking about before he went on deck. Customarily there would be a bottle of rye on the folding table, and each would light a smoke or take a pinch of snuff.

Should the experienced traveller happen to travel alone, or be by himself in the room, he would flop down on whatever there was to lie on. Usually he had a hangover or some sort of headache that needed nursing along, or the events of his visit to Vancouver, or plans for the next one, to be sorted out in his numbed mind. If he wasn't thinking about the latest trollop who had relieved him of his hard-earned stake, he was dreaming of the upcoming job which he planned to hang on to a little longer than normal, so he could save up a new stake, get out of the hole, back up on his feet again as a tough old logger should. By now he may have felt hungry, and was waiting for the steward to sound the gong to announce dinner or supper, served in the dining room. He stood up, not always steadily, looked into the mirror on the wall, straightened himself up as well as he could and marched to the dining-room, endeavouring not to bump into any other passengers, especially the ladies.

The steward led him to a table, most likely with a group of his peers, and he sat down awkwardly, obviously ill at ease in these unaccustomed surroundings. While studying the menu he tried to figure out what some of the dishes might be. Patiently, the steward stood at his side and waited for his order. Finally, he made up his mind and ordered something, although often not sure what would come. Accustomed to camp life, loggers were used to seeing the food on a platter first, and then deciding what to have. Struggling to eat politely with knife and fork, he was glad for the tea or coffee at the end of the meal. Unfortunately, at the last moment he spilled whatever he had in his cup because his hands were so shaky from alcohol. He stood up, thinking to himself:

"I'd better get the hell out of here before I spill more — or worse, before the steward asks me to leave."

Actually, things did not always run as smoothly for the steward working in the dining room. There were occasions when a logger made a nuisance of himself, although, as a matter of fact, it was an unwritten law that loggers never bothered women or children. Should a man unintentionally overstep himself around women or children, then in most cases he apologized. Loggers have invariably been very peculiar in this regard. No matter how rough they were amongst themselves, they knew where to draw the line in public. Credit is due for loggers who were unfairly labelled as troublemakers when in town.

By now the ship had made several more stops on its route up the harsh coast. The scene never varied much. People knew the approximate time the boat was due and were waiting for her on the dock with much excitement. As the ship drew close there came a long, loud blast from the bridge, announcing her arrival to the people on shore. And then she would round the corner of a bay, already slowing her engines for docking. Everyone waiting for the ship to land had been looking forward to it for a reason of his own. The old man puffing away on his pipe expected his weekly newspaper. Women waited for children's things they had sent for from a mail order catalogue. Others expected parts or pieces of machinery. Somebody else looked for the disembarkation of newly hired loggers coming from town.

First in line, the passengers went ashore. Next came the exchange of the "Royal Mail" bags. After that the cargo was unloaded. People on ship and shore would trade a few pleasantries and tell each other the latest news. The bay, like so many others, would be filled with log booms to be towed to their destined mill.

Seagulls flying noisily overhead would be scrambling for a

catch. A boy sitting at the edge of the mooring would be attentively engaged with his fishing gear. The ship, having finished its call to port, eased out into the channel to continue northward right up to Skagway. People on shore waved till the vessel faded in the distance. The weekly ship was the lifeline to isolated communities on the long B.C. coast.

A logger could disembark anywhere on this lengthy route from Vancouver, B.C. to Skagway, Alaska. A man taking a boat up coast on his original trip knew only the name of his destination, written out on the hiring paper. If there was a map on board that indicated the route the vessel would sail, the newcomer surely studied it anxiously. Apprehensive about missing his place of disembarkation, he would, at the earliest opportunity, start making inquiries about how long it would take for the boat to get there. The newcomer of those days had, as a rule, little or no command of the English language, and any sensible enquiry or conversation cost the immigrant a tremendous effort.

Assured by the ship's crew that his destination would be announced in advance, the newcomer felt somewhat more at ease. He strolled around the rolling boat, or climbed up on deck to delight in the beauty of nature. It was conceivable that, having sailed a day or so, the boat was nearing the first-timer's terminus.

At one of those tiny, coastal ports of call, the loggers on-board were given distressing news. An exceptionally dry spring and hot summer had already turned the forests into tinder. Fires were raging out of control, and logging operations had been brought to a halt by a province-wide shutdown.

The news was devastating. I had next to no money, and no place to go. Fortunately, The Logging Agency sent word that there was work at the Powell River paper mill, should I choose to find my way there. I had little choice.

The following three months were the worst in my life. The pulp grinding room where I worked was noisy and hot. Every week our shifts were rotated, from morning shift to afternoon, from afternoon to night, from night to morning. My body grew tired from the constant disruption.

Worse yet, the whole time I spent in Powell River I don't recall having a square meal. My pay, twenty-five cents an hour, was pitiful, and every penny I wasn't forced to spend on room and board I sent home to Austria, as I had promised to do when I left home. My father's wagon-building business had been bombed during the war, and our family was struggling to survive. For my first two years in

Canada I kept nothing for myself.

In September, after three months of unrelenting sunshine, the blessed rain came, washing away the soot of summer's conflagrations, and releasing me from the Hell of the Powell River mill. With enormous relief I boarded the very next boat for Echo Bay.

Arrival

The moment I'd been waiting for arrived. The vessel sailed slowly up a fjord-like inlet, where precipitous cliffs rise abruptly from the sea. Standing on deck by the ship's railing, ready to shoulder my rucksack, I beheld with dread those high, dark peaks around me. Bewildered, I told myself that this was a fitting place for mountain goats — but not for me.

The vessel came to a gentle halt; the holding rope was thrown out onto the narrow dock to hold the ship securely. A gangplank was rolled into place by the crew. Because the tide was low, the walkway looked almost as steep as the cliffs. With some relief I noticed another would-be logger filing in behind a group of women and children, so I brought up the rear and walked steadfastly down onto firm land. So far, so good!

A burly looking man in faded work garments and an old rain hat stood at the end of the narrow dock, where a small tugboat was tied up. Perceiving two forlorn looking lads, obviously greenhorns, both of us outlandishly dressed, he walked towards us, certain that we were the fellows he was waiting for.

"Hello, boys," he called, "are you coming to work for Echo Bay Logging?"

"Yes," I replied. The man beside me, a Swede named Thor, only nodded his head.

"I'm Sam," said the man, "and I'll get you to camp."

All three of us walked to the tugboat and Sam helped us put our gear on board.

"Would you boys mind helping me load the freight and mail for the camp?" he asked. This did not take long, and then we were ready to leave. Sam started the engine, untied the holding line, swung out into the middle of the channel and steered the boat past a boom of logs being towed to the mills down south. Joining Sam in the pilothouse, Thor asked how far it was to Wakeman Sound, and how long would it take to get there.

Sam answered with a patient smile, thinking back many years to the day he first arrived in camp. Then he turned to me and asked how long I had been in Canada, and how I liked it here. I replied in my halting English that I'd just arrived in B.C. and was on my first job in the woods as a chokerman. Not knowing what a chokerman's job was, I tried to find out from Sam.

"Be patient, son," het old me. "By this time tomorrow — you'll know."

Thor stayed with Sam in the wheelhouse, while I went out and sat down among the boxes of freight piled at the stern end of the deck. I watched the passing shoreline, the low sun shining warmly on my back. My thoughts came vividly while I gazed into the boat's wake.

Even as a young boy I had wanted to come to the shores of that country where the sun sets in the Western Ocean. I remember a school teacher telling the class about Canada, and its most westerly province, British Columbia, where the forests and mountains were vast and huge, and the coastline lay on the Pacific Ocean. That was when I decided to go to this distant land. I had only basic schooling, no trade or any other special skills, but I possessed a good, sound practical sense, and an unbending will to succeed in life.

As I reminisced, the "Chack Chack" (the name of the little tug we were riding), had neared its destination.

"Sam," I asked, "could you please explain the meaning of "Chack Chack?"

"Yes, son," answered Sam, yelling over the noise of the engine to make himself heard, "'Chack' is the Indian name for bald eagle. Have you seen one yet? The adults are about three feet high, with a wingspan of seven feet."

"No," I replied, "but I certainly would like to."

"You'll have lots of opportunities," Sam assured me, "especially when the salmon swim upriver to spawn." Sam reflected a moment before continuing. "I personally think 'bald eagle' is the wrong name for them. They're not bald at all — their heads are covered with white feathers. You can tell young eagles by their dark grey tail feathers, but when they're adults their tail feathers are as white as their head feathers."

As the little boat chugged through the cold, deep waters of the inlet, Sam continued his natural history lesson, punctuating his sentences with hand gestures to help us understand what he was saying. "Eagles mate for life," he told us. "Once they've chosen a suitable tree for their nest, normally a big old tree with a good fork in the top, they start building on it with dry branches, and twigs from evergreens. I've watched a pair of them from this tug for years, and every year their nest gets bigger — they can be twelve feet high and nine feet wide. In early spring the female lays her eggs and sits on them for forty to forty-five days. One year the eaglets hatched three weeks earlier than usual because the fish run out at sea was also that much sooner. Just goes to show how nature works.

"By the time the salmon runs start the eaglets are ready to fly. It's quite something to watch eagles fish for salmon. I saw one almost get drowned, pulled under by a large fish it hooked with its talons. They have big, strong beaks and claws for catching and tearing apart their prey, and if an eagle misjudges the size of a fish, it can get pulled under by the weight."

As I learned in the months to come, people and eagles are not the only ones that come to the rivers to catch fish in the fall. Black bears, and, in this part of the country, grizzly bears as well, hunt from the river banks or stand in the shallows and throw fish out of the water with their large paws.

"Salmon always return to the same river where they were hatched," continued Sam. "When they're young they go out to sea, where they stay for four years. Then they come back to the same river where they were born to spawn and die — provided they don't get caught in a fisherman's net, or eaten by an eagle or a bear. And as far as I know," he concluded, "nobody really knows yet where the salmon go once they put out to sea."

While Sam talked, Thor and I simply listened. Seldom can a teacher better command the attention of his pupils than Sam did then. In the direction the Chack-Chack plied a revel of icy peaks appeared, ribbing the horizon. In my mind, I dubbed them "the Shining Mountains," for they presented the eye with a dazzling and abiding majesty. In the distance we could make out a logging road as it wound a path through peak-lined, glacier-carved valleys. The road rose half as high as the spires that reached into the sky, but height is merely a measure — it was the splendour of the scene that took our breath away. Not every day can one see a sky so blue, waterfalls so high and powerful, or glaciers so brightly turquoise. Such was the scenery that awaited the loggers arriving at Wakeman Sound.

The Chack-Chack rounded a bend, revealing the head of the inlet and the end of the journey. To one side, what appeared to be quite a large river emptied out into Wakeman Sound. Opposite it were the booming grounds. Along the rocky shore a sturdy pier made of huge logs served as a landing for boats, and for other multifarious purposes. Upon it stood a big shed with no doors, wide open on the sheltered side. There was a light breeze blowing up the inlet from the Northwest, just enough to lightly ripple the sea. The tide was incoming and high. Sam slowed the Chack-Chack down and made a gentle landing. One of several fellows waiting on the pier helped us grab our gear and climb onto the rough planked dock. A dusty old supply truck with a greenish wooden box on it was parked nearby. One of the men, Scotty the Loudmouth, shouted to the newcomers:

"Hey, fellows, where do you come from? Have you got a snort with you?"

"It's none of your God damn business to know," answered Thor good-naturedly.

"All right now," said Sam, "let's get things moving here." He started unloading what had been taken earlier from the coastal steamer.

As at any other transfer point, first to go off were the mailbags, then came the rest of whatever there was headed for the camp. Bill, who drove the freight truck and did other odd jobs besides, loaded it all onto the back of his flat deck. Sam looked once more over his little tug, making sure she was fastened down securely to the floating ramp, before getting into the cab next to Bill. Scotty and his gang helped Thor and me get our gear onto the rear of the flat deck, then one of the boys signaled to Bill to let him know that they were all ready to leave. Bouncing wildly, we hit the gravel road, leaving a cloud of dust behind.

"It's only about one mile or so to camp," said Scotty to the newcomers, who were already wondering how far they would have to ride in this rickety old rig.

Soon the truck came to an abrupt halt; we had arrived. Everyone jumped out and shook off the dust from his journey. It was a large yard we were standing in, and since it was Sunday, the only day of rest for loggers, there were all kinds of men standing around, gaping at the newly arrived "slaves" from town. And slaves we all were, whether we admitted it or not, because all of us were fettered to the woods by invisible chains. As an old Swedish saw filer would later tell me:

"Once a man has spent five years in a logging camp, he will always return to it, no matter how hard he tries to break away. Men have always tried to get away from the woods, but they nearly all come back within a short period of time."

Out of the staring onlookers limped an elderly man with a dreary look on his face. It was Hank the Finn, the head bullcook in camp, responsible for delegating much of the camp's daily housework, and for showing new men to their living quarters. It was in this capacity that he accosted Thor and me, asking what kind of work we had come to do, in order to place us in the appropriate bunkhouses.

Hank told me to remain where I was while he placed Thor in

one of the huts farther down the line. This interval gave me time to get a fleeting look at my new environment. From what I could see it appeared to be a fairly large logging camp, located partly on a flat stretch of land, the remaining portion standing on a gentle slope, all facing southwest.

Similar to army barracks, the men were housed in row upon row of bunkhouses. The houses were uniform, built of rough lumber, and if they had ever been painted, the colour had faded to nothing after many years' exposure to extreme sunshine and pounding rain. What immediately attracted my attention was that every hut was built upon large, sled-like runners. At this time I could not have guessed the reason — only later did I realize that once an area has been logged off, the whole camp would be moved away. Thanks to the runners, the camp buildings could be hooked up behind a "cat" and towed to a new location.

Another thing I found odd were the wooden planks upon which I stood. They were about one foot wide and two inches thick, forming a three-feet wide sidewalk which interconnected throughout the camp. Those plank walks served two purposes. First, they kept the mud out of the camp buildings; second, they helped the bullcook when he lugged firewood in a wheelbarrow to the bunkhouses. The planks were severely worn from the caulks on the loggers' boots.

Soon I spotted Hank the Finn limping my way and gesturing at me to follow. At the top row of the farthest bunkhouses, Hank stopped in front of #19 and pointed to the entrance. Then he walked in, stopped next to a vacant bunk, and said:

"This is yours for the time being."

With these words Hank hobbled outside again. Absorbed in my thoughts, I remained motionless beside the bunk.

"Take heart, young man," said a cheerful voice behind me. "You'll get used to it." When I turned around I saw a white-haired man with the looks of a patriarch reclining on a bunk.

"You just came in on a boat?" the old man asked.

"Yes," I answered, and took this as an opportunity to introduce myself.

"And I am Thom," he replied. "I take it you came here to set chokers?"

"That's right," I said, feeling better for the old man's friendly intonation. Pointing at my gear, he asked:

"That's all you have with you?"

"Yes."

"Well, then you'll need logging boots and work clothes for tomorrow. The commissary will be open tonight after supper. You go there, give the timekeeper your hiring slip, and he'll let you take what you need so you can get to work. Pretty soon it will be suppertime, and afterwards we'll go down to the commissary together. I need some snuff for the coming week."

I sat down on the edge of the bunk, the only place there to sit on. Thom put away a pair of steel-rimmed reading glasses, along with an old worn book with a darkish cover. Probably a Bible, I thought, and I was right. Like so many of his Polish countrymen, Thom was Catholic and deeply religious. On the wall above the bunk was an old apple box which served as a shelf, and there Thom put his things.

I took a look at Thom. He was of medium height, but powerfully built, raw boned with a big head, prominent nose, large ears, deep blue eyes and no beard. His forearms and wrists were unusually strong and wide, as were his hands. Thom wore a light woolen shirt with a pair of old trousers. On his feet, which were also large, he wore a pair of boots, their shape and colour indescribable.

Turning my scrutiny to the inside of the hut, I perceived how crude it all was. The bunkhouse must have measured about forty feet long by fifteen feet wide. Entering the door, one faced a wood burning heater on the opposite wall. There were eight bunks in all, four on each side, arranged so that the foot ends faced each other. At each end of the hut was a window of medium size, and there was one more window behind the heater, the stovepipe of which ran straight up and out of the roof. The hut had no ceiling, only rafters, full of cobwebs. The rafters served to hang work clothes, and through them one could see right up to the shake roof.

The bunkhouse floor was made of rough lumber, as were the walls. There was neither table, nor chair, nor bench to sit on. Whenever a man had any writing to do, however seldom, he sat on his bunk, his knees drawn up, a short piece of board across them to serve as table. Beside each bed there was an low watt electric lamp, and there was another lamp hanging from a rafter in the center of the hut. Loggers were not supposed to have more belongings in camp than their work clothes, and for these there was no need for a locker. The whole room was permeated with an intense smell of sweaty clothes, leather boots and stale tobacco smoke.

While making these initial observations, I was visited by the first pangs of doubt. Never had I seen anything so primitive as the accommodations before me, nor was I mentally prepared for such a sight. For a moment I felt like taking the next boat back to town. But then I remembered Thom's reassuring words: "Take heart, you will get used to it." Strengthened, I pushed further thoughts of

25

retreat out of my mind. Thom must have noticed the desperate expression cross my face, because he tried to offer further comfort.

"Believe me," he said, "you could have fared worse than what you see here."

Other than Thom and I, there was only one more person present in the bunkhouse. He was an old man, well over seventy, lying on his bunk and smoking a short pipe. Thom gestured toward the old man:

"He's the bullcook for this row of bunkhouses. His name is old Tompkins, and he's hard of hearing."

The occupants of the remaining bunks were not in at the moment. Having recovered from my initial misgivings, I stowed my gear under the bed and lay down on my back, staring at the rafters above me. Thom kept on talking, but I could little understand what he said — my English was still too limited. An hour must have gone by before Thom got up from his bunk:

"It's nearly supper time. Let's go to the cook shack to eat."

I followed my new friend out the door and tramped towards the cookhouse at the far end of the bunkhouse rows. The cookhouse squatted on its runners, a gigantic, low wooden building with two wide entrances, one on each side. In front of each entrance waited a throng of hungry men, not that they appeared undernourished.

At 5:30 p.m. sharp the doors opened. From the south side door appeared a shrimp of a man with a wide grin on his face. He walked up to one of the support beams, from which a triangular piece of steel was suspended on a short strap of strawline. He beat this make-shift gong with a short hunk of iron, making a pleasing sound which carried the call to supper throughout the entire camp.

"He's the head flunky," said Thom, "and he does that every day to announce meal times. Some men refer to it as the 'old guthammer.'" Thom walked toward the head flunky, saying, "Handy, here's a new chokerman. Got a good table for him?"

"We'll see what's available," Handy replied, and told me to follow him.

Once inside, I faced an immensely large mess hall, where tables stood beside tables, all hurriedly occupied by hungry loggers. Handy led me to the far end of the dining-room, far from the kitchen. There, at one of the last tables, he assigned me a seat.

"Remember this table and your seat," he warned, "or you'll get in trouble by taking someone else's place."

Most of the men had already sat down on the long benches and turned their plates over. At each table sat eight men, four on either side. For every man there was a plate, a cup, a spoon, a knife and a fork. The food was brought from the kitchen on large platters by a flunky who had to look after four or more tables. The farther away a table was from the kitchen, the harder the flunky had to work. Most of the time they were forced to run, full or empty platters balanced on their outstretched forearms. It was hard work to fill so many hungry mouths, especially for the flunkies who had to dash the whole length of the mess hall.

To begin with, the tables were laid out with large platters of food, and one great tea or coffee pot per table. After that, it was the flunky's job to refill the empty platters as long as there was demand. If anything wanted was out of reach, one asked politely: "Please pass the bread," or whatever it was one desired. Small talk at the table was discouraged. There were so many different languages spoken at the camp that a free-for-all discussion at dinnertime would have turned the cookhouse into a madhouse.

To my relief, I liked the food. My first dinner consisted of swiss steak with potatoes, salad, fruit, fruit juice and tea. It was good, plentiful and wholesome. And, fortunately, there was "No Smoking" in the cookhouse. The fellows around me were mostly young and agreeable, and I looked forward to getting to know them better. Glancing over the dining area, I noted that the proportion of elderly men to young ones was about equal. I was surprised to notice how quickly everyone, regardless of age, ate, got up and walked out.

As I later found out for myself, good cooks are hard to get in isolated camps, and even harder to keep. Either they have personal troubles of one kind or other, or the men they feed drive them away by being unreasonable in their demands.

A logger coming from town, broke and hungry, will usually eat anything without grumbling — at least until he fattens up. He'll eat hearty and work hard until he gets out of the hole. Then, in most cases, discontent sets in, and there is nothing easier than to complain about the grub and nag the cook, who already has a hard time pleasing 180 or more diverse palates. It made no difference when discontented loggers quit, or got themselves fired, there were always new men coming up the line.

The worst were those who couldn't afford a bowl of soup in town, yet complained the loudest at the full table in camp. In many ways, the cook's job was the most thankless one in a logging camp.

Having greatly enjoyed my first meal in camp, I got up and sought my way back among the rows of bunkhouses. Thom was already there, sitting on the edge of his bed, waiting to show me the location of the washroom nearest our bunkhouse.

From the outside, the washrooms were little different from the bunkhouses, except that they were longer, had narrow windows, two entrances at the front, and one exit near each end. Inside were two long rows of tables with small aluminium washing bowls. At the back stood the shower stalls, as well as a voluminous, wood-fired boiler, where the wash water was heated. At the other end stood several washtubs for soaking and scrubbing clothes. Also at the rear were the toilets, that is to say, the place where a thin pole was all that kept a man from falling down the hole behind and below him, the interior of which was sprinkled with lime to mitigate the stench.

Having shown me the washroom, Thom suggested that we go to the commissary and hand my hiring slip over to the timekeeper. There we met Thor, who was tagging along with Scotty.

"The foremost thing you need," said Thom, "is a pair of caulk boots. I strongly advise you to try out a pair of Paris boots. The reasons for this are as follows: Paris's latest design, with their snug-fitting arches and well-balanced heels provide proper support. These boots are comfortable and minimize stress and fatigue when you wear them all day long. Keep in mind, your feet have fifty-two bones, thirty-eight muscles and two hundred fourteen ligaments." I couldn't help but wonder where Thom got all his knowledge, since he had no proper schooling. Later I found out that it was all printed on the side of each Paris shoe box.

Thom continued on with the subject of boots:

"Trust your feet to the best! Paris Boots are made in Vancouver. They last a very long time, retain their shape, and can survive harsh conditions and even periods of neglect. Believe me, I can testify to that, because I have worn every brand of logging boot that has been manufactured so far."

Convinced, I motioned to the storekeeper to find a pair of Paris boots in my size.

"Next," said Thom, "you will need woolen socks, woolen shirts, a pair of strong denim trousers with suspenders, and a pair of good leather gloves to protect your hands." When handling chokers, he explained, wire rope cable, or other equipment which is liable to prick and scrape your hands, a good pair of gloves was indispensable.

"Now you need rain gear," said Thom. "Here I advise you to stick with old 'Bone Dries' — a Pioneer brand. Good woolen underwear will keep you warm and dry in weather conditions such as snow, rain, sleet and wind, all very common along the B.C. coast during the wet period from autumn to spring. Wool will keep you warm even when it's wet, because it's an organic fibre. It absorbs sweat and does not feel clammy on your body."

Now that I was outfitted with proper clothes, Thom turned his attention to the finer points of living.

"Have you got soap and towel with you?" he asked. "Now is the time to get them, along with a few bars of laundry soap. Also get yourself a can of boot grease or wax oil to preserve the leather of your caulk boots, to keep them watertight. You will also need a lunchbox, with a thermos bottle."

The storekeeper, Cecil, piled the wares onto the large counter in front of us. Since there was nothing more that I needed for the present time, Cecil began to tally the items.

"The cost of these goods, along with the fare from town to here will be deducted from your pay," said Cecil, who also doubled as timekeeper, and with these words he motioned for me to sign at the bottom of the purchase list. Thom got himself the tin of Copenhagen snoose he had come for and we left with our arms full.

As we came out of the commissary, there was a long line-up of men waiting for Cecil to hand out the mail and newspapers that Sam had delivered earlier in the afternoon. As we passed the line of impatient loggers, we were the subject of jeers:

"Sucker! Sucker!"

"Don't pay them any attention," said Thom. "They mean no harm."

Back at the bunkhouse, I realized the good fortune I'd had in meeting Thom, and thanked him kindly for his assistance.

"Don't mention it," he told me. "Some day you do the same and give in kind."

By now, the rest of the inmates had come in and were sitting on their bunks, opening their mail or reading the newspapers.

"You'd better get yourself some rest," urged Old Thom. "A good night's sleep so that you'll be ready for whatever the day might have in store for you tomorrow. It won't be easy, let me tell you. I will wake you when I get up at five. This gives us enough time to get dressed, go to the washroom and to the lunchroom to make our lunch. Breakfast is at six, and after that comes marshalling time."

Thom began to undress, slowly hanging some of his worn-out clothes on a nail in the wall, other garments he put on top of the foot end of his bed. I did likewise, as did others in the bunkhouse, and a short while later, all lights were out.

I had a difficult time falling asleep. The bed I was in felt strange, and gave off a peculiar smell. Finally weariness overcame the complaints of my senses, and I drifted into slumber.

On the Job

Next morning, I awoke from the touch of a heavy hand on my shoulder. A voice in the still, dark room said:

"Son, it's time to get up."

It was good Old Thom again, making sure that I didn't sleep in, and that I rose in time to face the day's challenges. I got out of bed, dressed, and followed Thom to the washroom, where several of the old-timers were already sitting on the pole over the manhole. While washing myself, I looked out the window and saw the first light of dawn appearing in the sky. It promised to be a nice, sunny day.

Having finished in the washroom, I went back to the bunkhouse, grabbed my lunchbox, and walked with Thom to the lunchroom, a separate building next to the cookhouse. At this time of day it was as busy as a beehive.

One long wooden counter extended the whole length of the room, and was loaded with lunch meat, bread, butter, cheese, lettuce, pies, honey, peanut butter, marmalade, etc. At the far end stood coffee urns and large teapots for the men to fill their thermoses. Behind the counter, the lunch maker was engaged in his duties. On one side of the long front wall, opposite the lunch counter, were shelves on which ready-made sandwiches were laid out. On each shelf was printed the kind of sandwich available, such as ham, beef, egg, etc. These ready-made sandwiches served the lazy ones well — those who had a difficult time getting up in the morning, and consequently were always late and in a great rush. Each man put what he liked into his lunchbox or paper bag, filled his thermos, and left for his bunkhouse again to wait for the breakfast bell.

Breakfast was punctually announced by the ringing of the guthammer at 6:00 a.m. Characteristically at mealtime, there was a throng of men assembled at both side entrances to the cookhouse, waiting for the doors to open. The flunky, who was in charge of opening the out-swinging double doors, always had a hard time getting the second wing open, because the impatient loggers would push against it from the outside. No matter how much the flunky cursed them, this scene never changed. Then, at the sound of the gong, the rest of the men came hurrying from all directions.

Thom's table was just next to the entrance door, so he had an easy time of it, whereas I had to push through the throngs to the far end of the dining-hall to get to my table. Breakfast consisted of normal camp fare, such as bacon and eggs, toast, flapjacks, porridge, coffee and milk.

It was incredible to witness the great haste with which the men ate their morning meal. Just as fast as they came in to eat, they darted out again. As I was soon to find out for myself, everyone was under pressure from the time he got up until the time he took off his logging boots after work. What was the mighty rush for? In short: all and everything revolved around the drive for logs, logs, and still more logs. The very reason for our existence was to get those logs out of the woods by any means — as fast and as many as humanly possible. This deplorable atmosphere carried over into every aspect of camp activity, and even to the off hours. It was, and still is, the chief cause of logging accidents.

Back at the bunkhouse, Thom showed me how to lace up my new caulk boots properly. He demonstrated the "logger's tie," which is designed to prevent the laces from inadvertently releasing themselves. He explained how to break the new boots in, so that they wouldn't hurt my feet too much during the first few days. I was now dressed, except for the hard hat which would be issued to me in the first aid shack by the first aid attendant.

Ready to go, we picked up our lunchboxes and left for work. Thom led me to the marshalling yard, and left me there with woods foreman Pat, better known as "Squinty." I could not help but notice how appropriate the nickname was. Not only did Pat squint, he always had a nasty grin on his long face. His movements were cat-like, and whenever he talked to the men he had a habit of tilting his head to one side. As I learned soon enough, hardly anyone in camp liked Squinty, owing to his slyness. On top of everything, he had a terrible, squeaky voice with which he screeched his orders at the men. In this abrasive and rattling manner he directed me to the first aid shack to get my headgear — a safety helmet.

In order to get to the first aid shack, I had to cross the marshalling yard. While doing so, I perceived how sizable an area it was, and how trucks of all shapes and sizes were lined up along one edge of its perimeter. At the shack, Ernie, the first aid man, gave me a choice between two helmets, a round one with a canvas brim, the other brimless. The first one came in either brown or white, the other only in white. I chose the helmet with the brim, because it seemed it would give me better protection against rain, whereas the other looked like a chamber pot without the handle, and I could already imagine the rainwater trickling down my neck.

Returning to the yard, I was dispatched to see Hjalmer the skidder foreman, commonly known as "Blondie." The marshalling yard was full of loggers milling around or boarding crummies. Blondie told me to get onto No. 9 crummy, and I did so. All those vehicles looked alike; old and run down. The cab of No. 9, where the driver and two passengers sat, was occupied by Blondie and two engineers.

Behind the cab, on a flat deck, was an enclosed wooden box, similar to the box on a moving van. There was one narrow, wooden bench along each wall, and a wider bench in the middle, extending the full length of the van. The men sitting on the middle bench sat back to back and faced the men sitting on the opposite bench. Inside the van was a cord strung along the ceiling as a means of signalling the driver in the front of the cab.

By the time I made my way to Crummy No. 9 it was almost loaded, and I had to sit at the rear end of the vehicle, which was wide open to the elements. At first, I welcomed the prospect of fresh air and scenery, but as the truck got under way, all the dust from the gravel road came whirling in to envelope us. We sat passively with our lunchboxes on our lap. Few, if any of us, talked or joked during the long, rough ride. Blondie was driving, and he spared no horses. The men at the rear were bounced around, and at times caromed off the low ceiling with their heads. By the time we arrived at the work site we were very shaken up.

No sooner had the crummy stopped than the fellows jumped out and shook off the dust. Meanwhile, Blondie came around and introduced me to the crew I'd be working with: the skidder foreman, one donkey puncher, one loading engineer, one chaser, one head loader, one second loader, two hookers, the first hooker on the bullhook, and the second hooker behind. With each hooker were two chokermen, one backrigger with his two chokermen, and one lonely whistle punk. (For explanations of logging terminology, see the Glossary of Logging Terms, beginning on page 178.) In other words, Bus No. 9 transported the entire crew for operating the skidder high lead yarding and the logging site.

Also riding bus No. 9 was the cold deck crew, whose job it was to haul the logs that were too high up the slope for the sky line. They included one hooker, one engineer to operate the cold deck yarder, one chaser, one rigging slinger, two or three chokermen and one whistle punk. This small crew was cold decking on the far side in advance of, and above, the skidder setting.

That morning, like all mornings, we began the day with a long hike up a sheer slope, knowing that we faced a treacherous descent at quitting time. Blondie parked the crummy outside the landing, facing camp and ready in case of emergency — a safety precaution of his own. The donkey puncher (yarding engineer) and loading engineer walked straight from the crew bus to their own machines, to start them and warm them up before work commenced. All the rigging men placed their lunchboxes at the rear of the yarder before climbing the hill from which they were yarding. Thoughtfully, one chokerman had brought along two water bags for the day. These he left by the lunches. Also at the rear of the yarder was an army type stretcher with wool blankets and a large first aid kit.

Promptly at 8:00 a.m. the yarding engineer blew the starting whistle — one long toot. As soon as the rigging men were at the job site and ready for yarding, the first hooker would let the whistle punk blow two shorts, which let the engineer know that he could send out the rigging.

The landing crew went about its accustomed activity. Romolo, the chaser, got busy at his large, wooden splicing block. The whistle punk gathered up the extension cords for his whistle wire and headed up the hill. Old Dad came heaving up the steep road with his brute of a logging truck, pulling noisily into the landing. This coincided with a tremendous roar as the yarding and loading engines started up. Clouds of acrid, dark blue smoke belched from their large exhaust pipes.

Overhead, the rigging dangled from the skyline and clanked, and the wooden loading heelboom screeched fiercely as the loading engineer swung it back and forth to test its movement. To my unaccustomed ears, it seemed as though all hell had broken loose. I could not have heard a word if anyone had spoken. On the landing, communication between men took place by hand signal. For every move or action there was the appropriate gesture. That was the only way to communicate in the landing. The constant uproar made life particularly difficult for the chaser, who had to listen for the infernal yarder signals, which let him know what additional equipment to send out with the rigging.

I was overwhelmed by my first sight of the huge wooden spar with its cumbersome rigging. The spar tree must have measured three feet or more in diameter at the base, where it rested on a pad made from a log mat. I had no way of estimating the height of the towering spar, but it seemed to reach far up into the clear sky. From it hung a confusion of wires, cables, large blocks and guy lines.

From the top of the spar tree a thick wire cable, called the skyline, extended about 1,500 feet or more to the back spar, where it was securely anchored. The higher the spar the farther out we could reach to yard. On top of the skyline rode the carriage, back and forth. The spar was similar to the hub of a wagon wheel, from which the roads to be logged radiated like spokes out to the back spars.

While taking a break for a drink of water, I counted twenty-four guy lines securing the spar. It amazed me that anyone could stand such an enormous tree on end and use it to drag other enormous logs around a mountainside. I knew that the words "spar" and "rigging" came from the sailing ships, but how had they come to be applied to logging? The answer to that was provided by an old hooktender. It was the Finnish loggers who pioneered wooden spar trees down in the swamps of Louisiana, and from there it spread to the Pacific-Northwest, right up to Alaska.

The previous week one of the young chokermen on the skidder had quit, and I was assigned to fill the vacancy. My work partner was Bruce, the second hooker, who told me:
　"Just call me 'Red.'"
A most befitting name it was. Bruce was a freckled redhead with a beard to match. Red proved to be one hell of a nice fellow, right from the start. He took me under his care and instructed me in the ways of my new job. Above all, Red made sure that I was always thinking about safety.

I was lucky to have come under the wing of a conscientious and experienced hooker, who cared for the safety of his crew. The first thing Red impressed on me was this:
　"At all times stay in the clear — get out of the 'bight!' Stay on the outside, that is, of the moving lines. This is the ground rule, the foundation upon which all our safety is based."

Next, Red taught me how to walk logs safely, so as to stay up on my feet.
　"For your feet to get the best grip on a log," he instructed, "walk with your feet at an angle to it." This is not an easy thing to do for a greenhorn, especially on a steep hillside like the one we were working. Red also instructed me in the proper setting of chokers, and warned of specific hazards of the turn (a "turn" is a log, or a group of logs, being pulled into the landing).

A choker consists of three parts: the cable, the bell and the knob. The cable was anywhere from fifteen to twenty feet long, and its thickness depended on the size of the log being hauled. It was my job to pass the cable under the thick end of the log, and then to place the bell (a loop in the cable) around the knob, to make it fast. When this was done (no mean feat, depending on the thickness of the ground cover, the steepness of the hill and the diameter of the log), I would signal the all-clear and the yarder would haul the choked log off to the landing.

Starting that very day, I also learned to distinguish the different species of timber we were yarding, such as the renowned "Douglas

Rigged up skidder tree pulling logs into the landing.
Courtesy of BC WCB.

fir" (named for Scottish botanist David Douglas who explored the Pacific-Northwest in 1825), red cedar, hemlock and balsam. The sizes of the logs we yarded were enormous, and kept me constantly amazed. Never before had I seen trees as tall and large as here on the B.C. coast.

"What makes them grow so big?" I wondered. And later, I reasoned: "It must be the weather." In time I learned that I was right. The size of the trees was due to the incredible, perhaps (at least to a logger) excessive amount of rain that falls on the B.C. coast.

The whistle for quitting time came as an enormous relief that first day on the rigging crew. The ride back to camp was much like the ride to the setting: rows of silent men sitting on wooden benches with lunchboxes on their laps; lips and eyes shut tight against the dust; jolted by every pothole and jostled together by every turn of the road.

As soon as the crummy stopped in the marshaling yard, the men jumped out and headed for their bunkhouses. Next stop, the washrooms, to clean up for supper. Dinner was much like breakfast — the food wolfed down and newcomers ignored. After dinner the men chatted in their bunks, and then, one by one, the older loggers first, they fell asleep.

As I lay in my bunk that evening I felt my all-consuming determination bolstered by a sense of hope. What I had left behind in Austria was far, far worse than anything I might encounter in Echo Bay. Here, by the labour of my hands, I could prove myself, make money to send home, and eventually forge a life.

The day's work had been busy, but not too physically demanding. The men in general were a mixed lot, but old Thom, Red, and others on my crew were friendly and helpful. I drifted into peaceful sleep. Little did I know that there were many days to come that would make my first day on the job seem like a blissful holiday.

Chapter 2

Autumn

Indian Summer

I worked in various logging camps over the years; Wakeman Sound until '54, then the O'Brien Logging camp at Stillwater for a year, then Canfor's camps in the Nimpkish Valley (Camp A, Camp N, Vernon, Atluck and Woss camps). In general the camps were much alike, built along standard lines with only minor variations.

Life quickly became a monotonous and unending cycle of work, meals and sleep. There was little to do in the evenings, and I refused to be drawn into wastrel pursuits such as drinking and gambling. We had no radios in camp, but once a week newspapers would be shipped up from Vancouver. I had no interest in seven-day-old news, and didn't bother to read them. Much less frequently mail would arrive from Austria, but during my early years in the woods even the fifteen cents it cost to send a letter constituted financial hardship for my family.

After dinner there was generally little to do but lie on my bed, stare at the ceiling, or read the books that were shipped to me on a regular basis by the Victoria Public Library. With each shipment came a list of available titles. When I packaged the books for their return to Victoria, I included the list with a few choices ticked off. Mostly I read books on European history, or the works of authors such as Sigmund Freud and Thomas Mann. It was in this manner that I profited from my free time, by expanding my education and teaching myself to read and write English.

As time rolled by I came to understand that the most important constants in the life of a logger are dictated, not by accommodations, or even by food, but by the weather. Often, the memories of my life in the woods run together according to season, since one day of work in the blistering heat, driving rain, or heavy, wet snow, is much the same as another, regardless of the passage of time.

I had arrived in Wakeman Sound during a long Indian summer, a period of mild, dry weather, accompanied by a generally hazy atmosphere, which, Red informed me, is the best time of the year for loggers and logging. No more, said Red, were the days as oppressively hot as they had been during the summer, the nights were also cooler, and the torture of the mosquitoes mercifully abated.

In the earliest part of the forenoon we worked in the shade of the high mountain. Then, slowly, the sun came rising over the crest and the heat became noticeable. By 10:00 a.m. everyone yearned for cool, clear water. Jimmy, the first hooker, called for one of the waterbags which Sandy, the chokerman, had left by the yarder. Romolo the chaser fastened a two-gallon bag of watertight canvas to the bullhook and sent it back out with the chokers. No sooner had the rigging stopped overhead and been partially lowered, choker cables swinging wildly and chokerbells ringing loudly, than the men were there. Jimmy undid the waterbag, took a long, deep drink, and passed it on to his chokermen. Red was the last to get a swig.

The whistle punk had to carry his own waterbag if he desired water throughout the day. His was a lonesome, monotonous but indispensable job. He linked the rigging crew to the yarding engineer via signals he transmitted from the hooker to the yarder. Right from the start when a new yarding road had been commenced, the whistle punk moved parallel with the rigging crew but at a safe distance away. It was his job to stay at all times in the clear, but close enough that he could easily understand the audible signals from the hooker. His electrical cord — called a "whistle wire" — was hooked up to the yarder, and he carried coils of 100-foot extensions with him. Usually he sat on a stump, hunched over, holding the transmitting device in one of his hands, always alert, because there was no room for even a single mistake.

As the men gulped water and wiped the sweat off their brows I took the opportunity to look at each of them in turn. Ken was the whistle punk, a young native lad from one of the many coastal Indian reserves. On first impression one would have thought he was a girl. He had raven black hair, no beard, and small hands and a slender build. The remarkable thing about Ken was the incredible speed with which he transmitted his signals. There was little space between each push of the button, a fact that exasperated engineer and chaser alike, who had to listen and decipher all day long.

The yarding engineer on the skidder was James, a quiet Scot who never said much to anyone, fully concentrating on his duties as he ran the big yarder. James was undersized, very skinny, with grey hair cropped short and covered with a threadbare engineer's cap. Forever with a cigarette holder and cigarette clenched between his strong front teeth, he kept both hands and feet busily engaged on throttle, levers and brakes. Every so often he would consult his old-fashioned railroad pocket watch, by which the rest of the crew set their time. James blew the starting whistle at 8:00 a.m., then at 12:00 noon for lunch and at 4:30 p.m. for quitting time. It was the last whistle of the day that almost everyone was anxiously waiting for.

Romolo, the chaser (no one knows how he got this name), came from a Polish-Ukrainian settlement on the Canadian prairie. He spoke with a strong Slavic accent in a voice that was both loud and harsh, and which reminded one of the sound of a worn-out gramophone needle. It can truly be said that not one of the entire skidder crew worked harder than Romolo did. He perpetually walked bent over forward, never having time for a minute's rest. (Owing to a bad accident in the landing where he worked, this good fellow eventually ended up in a wheelchair, through no fault of his own.)

Jimmy, the first hooker, came years ago from Newfoundland, and started out (like everyone else in the woods) as a chokerman. He was young, strong, with a robust and agile frame. In the morning he would lead the gang up the steep slope, striding far ahead of the next best man. At quitting time he would literally glide down the hillside in long leaps like a flying squirrel. Neither smoking nor chewing snoose, Jimmy would drive the entire crew hard in its quest for logs and still more logs, having neither mercy nor compassion for anybody or anything — not even for himself. He would charge through the brush, over logs and stumps, to wherever the chokers had to be set.

Fighting hang-ups was Jimmy's responsibility. Once the turn (a single, or several logs) was on its way into the landing, Jimmy would stand looking pensive, one foot resting on a log, his arms hanging loosely beside him, always whistling the same old tune — There Is A Little Shack Down By The Railroad Track — through the gap created by one of his missing front teeth. Jimmy's entire attention was given to the ingoing turn, his brown weasel eyes alert for any possible foul-up, always ready to stop the rigging or send signals down to the yarding engineer.

When yarding long distances it was customary to work with two sets of chokers. While one turn was on its way into the landing, the other set of chokers was attached to the nest turn, keeping everybody on the move constantly, yarding the maximum amount of logs per day. Should the in-going turn get hung up behind a stump or boulders, the chokermen hollered with glee: "Hooker business, hooker business!" Then Jimmy had to stop the rigging and rush to the hang-up, often halfway down the yarding road, where he would rush to change or reset the chokers. Sometimes it took him fifteen minutes or longer to get it all cleared up. This was practically the only reprieve the chokermen had during a day's work, and they relished it to the fullest. But should the hang-up have been caused through faulty or improper choker setting, then all hell would break loose — Jimmy was really good at taking out a piece of a man's hide if he wanted to do so.

As the morning progressed, everyone grew hungry and impatient. Shortly before noon, Romolo put all the lunchboxes into a gunnysack and sent them out with the rigging to the waiting men. At 12:00, right on the dot, James blew the long awaited whistle for lunch break, and the entire worksite quickly settled into quietness as each man took his much-needed rest. Hookers and chokermen alike looked around for a somewhat level spot on the sheer slope, a place to sit down in the shade of a big log to eat and rest. In no time the sandwiches had been wolfed down and the thermoses were empty.

As I ate my lunch I listened to the occasional conversation — conversations that would repeat themselves thousands of times over the next forty years: someone would comment on the beautiful bird's-eye view we had of the broad valley and distant inlet. Another man would assert that people in town would pay good money to enjoy such a magnificent view. And then the silence would settle in again, as we enjoyed our precious moments of peace and relaxation, greatly enhanced, said Red, by the autumnal absence of mosquitoes. This was, he said again, the very best time of the year for loggers.

At 12:30 sharp the shrill, piercing sound of James' whistle got the show into motion again. Brent, the loading engineer, with the help of the head loader, Norm, and his second loader, Sven, worked as a team to load logs onto the hi-balling logging trucks.

Norm stood on top of the truck's cab, facing the heel boom — a rectangular log frame attached to the spar by cables, used to move logs around on the landing. With hand signals only, Norm directed Brent to place the logs where they were needed. First he indicated a certain log from the pile. Then Sven took the massive tongs, which came down from the heel boom on a thick steel cable, and placed them around the selected log. Finally, Brent swung the log onto the truck, exactly where Norm wanted it.

Norm started out by filling the base of two sixteen-feet wide bunks, and from there he built the cradle into which the shorter logs were loaded. Higher and higher he piled the logs; when finished, the load resembled a one-storey house. Before any loaded logging truck could pull out of the landing, Sven had to stamp each log on both ends with a branding hammer, and chop off all protruding branches.

Blondie, the skidder foreman and a highrigger as well, kept on pacing up and down the landing. Tall, blonde and clean shaven, his jaw was constantly working — although what he was chewing was never ascertained. (It wasn't snoose, because there was no tell-tale lump in his cheek, he didn't spit, and his teeth were gleaming white.) As he paced, he planned his next moves. Blondie never hurried — he had his men to do that for him. He observed and watched the spar with its heavy rigging, from time to time taking corrective measures with the guylines. Out there Blondie was the "big wheel," ultimately responsible for the production, equipment and safety of the entire crew. Not too tall an order for a rigging hand such as trusty old Blondie.

The afternoon of an Indian Summer day can still get very hot. By mid-day the men working on the rigging were sweating freely, and Jim had no other choice but to call for Sandy's second waterbag from the landing. Romolo made sure it got there quickly, and it didn't take long until the hoary, moist, two-gallon bag was empty. While waiting to get a cool drink I heard a faint, distant honking, which caused most of us to tilt our necks back and lift our eyes skyward. The sound built to a cacophony as a large flock of Canada geese passed overhead in two long rippling lines that met to form a gigantic "V." On the night of a full moon, Red told us, the geese will keep flying for the rest of the night and probably the whole next day. Such a large flock of geese, he warned, coming so early from the north, bodes an early winter.

Thor, the fellow I'd come off the boat with, had not been as lucky as I had been. For one thing, his hooker, Double Drum Mike, was a cranky old curmudgeon with no patience for anything. The rigging slinger, Bible John, was more interested in preaching the gospel than in pulling the rigging, and Scottie the Loudmouth was of no great help to anybody.

Whenever there was hard work to be done, such as pulling the strawline or carrying a block up hill, through brush, over felled, bucked timber, Scottie would plead a weak back or some other ailment. What saved him from being fired was his personality. Scottie had a 24-hour grin and the gift of the gab, and his wit entertained the entire crew, regardless of where they happened to be. Scottie's voice carried across the show, with a broad Scottish accent that many a man had a hard time understanding. But when it came time to work, Scottie was utterly useless.

Any other fellow would have found himself fired at the earliest chance the hooktender had. Scottie, however, was not a stupid man. He knew just how far he could dare to let things go. Often, as he stood around avoiding work, he would recite from the lengthy poem "The Crying Hooktender," the last line of which says of the rigging: "Go ahead fast and come back slow, the whole side hill is a haywire show."

The Wood Yard

It wasn't long before I knew my way around the camp. Not too far away was the wood yard, where a small crew worked almost year round cutting firewood. Wood logs were hauled in from the woods and dumped there to be cut into twenty-two inch long blocks, which were hauled from the wood yard to the camp on a flat deck truck. The driver unloaded the truck at the end of each row of bunkhouses, after which the bullcooks wheeled the hefty pieces on a wheelbarrow to the bunkhouses, washrooms and drying rooms. There the wood was burned to warm the huts and to heat water.

Whispering Swede was more-or-less in charge of this department. He and Scissor Bill operated the drag saw with which they cut the different logs — mostly fir snags, although hemlock was frequently used too, since it burned quite well and gave lots of heat if the wood was very dry. A tremendous amount of firewood was needed to heat the entire camp from autumn to spring, and to a lesser degree in summer. Besides the drag saw operator, two or more stalwart wood splitters were employed. Two of the regular splitters were Old Thom and "Patchy." It was surprising the dexterity with which these two old timers swung the splitting axe and the ten-pound sledge hammer on top of the wide, steel, splitting wedges.

Patchy was quite a remarkable old man. For one thing no one but the office knew his real name. Year in and year out he wore patched-up clothes, which explains his colorful cognomen. He was of medium height and well built, but because of the work he did his body was bent forward. The top of Patchy's head was bald, and from his ears hung a garland of stringy, grey hair. With his bushy dark handlebar moustache, stern, grey eyes, and heavy long eyebrows, he portrayed a forbidding countenance. Few words escaped

Patchy's thin lips, and he never used profane language. Around his waist, to hold up his patched trousers, he wore an extremely wide black leather belt with a matching iron buckle. Behind his back the men would laugh: "With his belt he could tie up a bull." Patchy's footwear was something else for the fellows to laugh about. His large clumsy boots resembled the legendary seven-league boots.

There were, however, men in camp who saw more than the amusing in old Patchy, and I counted myself among them. Patchy was from Switzerland, not that far from my home in the Austrian Alps. By this time I was working as a hand faller, and it had been years since I had spoken in my mother tongue. One Sunday afternoon I went to see old Patchy in his bunkhouse. I found him sitting on the edge of his bunk, wearing only his aged pants while he mended his faded shirt. The sun shone warmly through the dusty window onto the old man's back. The skin of his chest hung down in folds, giving him an ancient appearance. I had only a brief, general conversation with Patchy, during which I instantly noticed his soft voice, and the pure Swiss dialect he spoke. He asked me where I came from and how long ago I had left there. We made small talk for a short while, but Patchy soon clammed up, concentrating on the long darning needle which he poked in and out of his worn-out shirt. After a while I departed in silence, wondering why the old man was so bitter and reticent. In a way, however, since I was also a loner, I felt that I understood the strange old man. One winter day Patchy vanished from camp and I never heard of him again.

Whispering Swede, on the other hand, was just the opposite of Patchy. His disposition was happy, and he radiated goodwill. Moreover, he spoke excellent English and liked to talk. The Whispering Swede was a giant of a man, but a gentle one. In the summertime, when everybody worked shirtless in the wood yard, his torso, covered in blond hair, stood out above all the others. At the back of his neck he had a lump the size of a fist, the result of an injury he received while still a new timberfaller on the B.C. coast. When he thought himself unobserved, he whispered constantly in Swedish, and quite frequently chuckled aloud. With so many other Scandinavians in camp, he had to whisper, or the others would have understood what was on his mind.

Habitually neat and clean, it was well known that the Whispering Swede spent a great deal of his off hours in the washroom. He could invariably be found either there or in the poker shack playing cards, or waiting for someone to show up for a game. The Whispering Swede possessed an enormous passion for poker. One never saw him wear patched or torn clothes. He could well afford new ones, because his take from playing poker always exceeded his wages. Several times he asked me whether I wanted to play a hand, since he knew that I was careful with my money, and therefore had a few dollars to my name. I told him I would, but only on one condition: that we play for marbles. The Whispering Swede just chuckled:

"There's no kick in that!"

The sad end for Whispering Swede came suddenly in 1952. One rainy winter day a turn of logs was hauled by cat into the wood yard, where Whispering Swede proceeded to unhook it. Something went wrong with the winch, and somehow, while he was bending over, he collapsed. Some said it was the cable that killed him, others claimed it was a heart attack, and a third group thought it was a combination of the two. They loaded him on a pickup truck, brought him to camp, and left him with the first aid man until arrangements were made to take the body out for burial. The RCMP were called, as they always were when a fatality occurred, to verify that it had been an accident.

The Blacksmith, his Helper, and the Slaughter of the Cats

Down the road from the wood yard, at the periphery of the large camp, was the location of the machine repair shop and the smithy. There Ed worked as the blacksmith, along with his trusty helper, Maki. No logging camp of any size at all could ever have functioned properly without a blacksmith, and a good one was worth his weight in gold. Ed was one of those: you named it, and reliable Ed would forge it. From strawline hooks to 120-pound loading tongs, it was all the same to Ed. His only true love was the smithy, and the moment he entered his noisy kingdom it was clear that he was home. In all the time I knew him, he never turned down a job as too difficult or large.

Ed fit the picture of a blacksmith: he was a tall, broad-shouldered man, and while at work he wore a protective leather apron. He stood in front of the forge, pumping a pair of bellows to make the iron in the fire white hot, then removed the glowing metal and hammered it into shape on the huge anvil. With black smudges on his striking face, dark, intense eyes, and white teeth gleaming from behind blood red lips, Ed resembled the living Lucifer.

Maki, his helper in the smithy, had a stupendous fondness for cats. To him they were almost as sacred as they once were to the ancient Egyptians. Wherever Maki walked in camp, he was followed by cats. Daily he fed about forty of them from a large bucket of kitchen waste. There were men in camp who did not share Maki's fondness for cats. As one angry logger said to me:

44

"All these lazy cats are good for is eating, sleeping and breeding."

Whenever the females were in heat (and it seemed they were in heat year-round) they made dreadful noises under the bunkhouses at night, which prevented the men from getting the proper rest they needed. Paradoxically, despite the multitude of felines, the camp was plagued by rats. Some of these rodents were the size of small cats, and they thrived beneath the camp's wood-planked sidewalks. The reason the cats did not hunt rats and mice was simple enough. They were too well fed from what Maki and other cat-lovers fed them from the cook shack. The rats, in turn, fed on the leftovers that the cats did not eat. What infuriated most loggers was the fact that those lazy cats were always catching birds.

Certain dogs in camp had a reputation for killing rats — they were not as afraid of them as the cats appeared to be — and one spring day a hawk swooped down among the bunkhouses and hooked a rat to the amazement of a group of spectators. But the cats couldn't be bothered with the rats. They were too busy eating the food that Maki and others gave them, or copulating in the daylight out in the open, often with groups of men standing around watching. It was disgusting, to say the least, to see young and old men gawking at the cats mating.

One day in the fall of 1953 the camp super declared a bounty on the cats for sanitary reasons. The bounty caught the attention of a driver named Terrible Ted, who was soon hounding down cats throughout the camp. A tall, lean man with a Roman nose, Terrible Ted was always in a hurry. He walked in long strides, carrying his head high and swinging his arms back and forth, saying:

"Trutt, trutt!"

His haste was so great that he never wore laces in his boots because it took too much of his precious time to do them up. He even unhinged the door on the driver's side of his gravel truck so he could get in and out more quickly. When driving, he hung on to the big steering wheel fiercely, as if he were trying to coax more power out of the old engine. Normally a somber man, he was just the opposite after a few drinks. Then his optimistic smile came out and he started to sing: Tra-ra-de-bums-de-ra...Tra-ra-de-bums-de-ra. Terrible Ted, who seldom talked to me when sober, always asked me to share a drink with him when he got tipsy. I, being a very unsociable person, always refused.

During the Second World War Terrible Ted had been a military policeman in the Canadian army overseas, which was where he picked up a taste for drinking and high living, as well as his nickname. When he left Canada for Europe, he was newly married and childless. After three years away from home, he returned to his wife to find her with two children. That ended his marriage abruptly. Eventually he found himself, like so many other former soldiers, working in the bush.

Once, having worked hard for a whole year in camp, Terrible Ted decided that he needed a holiday, so he ordered a seaplane to take him to Vancouver. Haywire John, a faller who also wanted to go to town, asked if he could accompany him and share the expense.

"Nothing doing," answered Terrible Ted: "I want to arrive in style." He also ordered a three-man band and a couple of whores to give him a big welcome on his arrival at the dock in Vancouver.

Terrible Ted's holiday in the city was a short one, a merry five days. During this time he passed himself off as a transportation foreman — gravel truck driver wasn't prestigious enough. The whores cleaned him out fast and he returned to camp flat broke, a year's savings gone down the drain. (And what did Haywire John do? He also ordered a seaplane for himself and left almost simultaneously for town. But Haywire John never made it back to camp; he got shanghaied in the city for another job.)

Perhaps Terrible Ted's profligate ways with money help to explain the energy with which he persecuted those cats. The worst slaughter was achieved in one of the washrooms where he managed to corner half a dozen or more which had been hanging around the huge water boiler where it was always warm. I happened to be having a shower that evening as Terrible Ted and his helper came storming through the door, shouting:

"Keep those doors shut!"

Terrible Ted had the wildest look on his face that one ever saw on a man. He worked himself into a frenzy as the cats tried to escape over the shower stalls. None of them escaped. There were blood stains and slaughtered cats all over the washroom. Later I saw Old George, a bullcook who looked after that particular washroom, carrying away the carcasses, one in each hand, holding them by their tails. Some of them were still kicking with their hind legs as he threw them into the wheelbarrow and hauled them to the dump. Those cats that survived the ugly purge remained out of sight for days. They must have taken to the neighbouring woods, or gone into hiding.

Highpocket

As time went by, I grew used to the life and the routine of living in logging camps. Every night after dinner men would sit or recline on their bunks, smoke, chew snoose, and chat. Many tall tales were told, there was lots of talk about women, and of course, there was endless talk about work.

Seldom a work day went by at Wakeman Sound, or at any of the many camps I lived and worked in, without an incident of one kind or other that adversely affected men, equipment, or both. Even daily occurrences such as getting pricked by a "jagger" in the hand or finger or leg were very painful. One frequently found men with jagger wounds in the washrooms after work, soaking an injured hand in a washbowl of warm saltwater. With a leg wound it was more difficult. Other common injuries included the usual cuts, bruises and twisted ankles a man sustains in the rough and tumble of a difficult day's work. Everyone got used to such minor injuries, and a greenhorn had to learn quickly. More serious injuries, or minor work-related adventures, were always the chief topic of conversation in camp when the men relaxed in their bunkhouses after work.

Much was made of the time, for example, when Flash Harry arrived in the landing at lunchtime with his logging truck, but minus his trailer. Harry hadn't noticed it bounce off, his mind miles away as usual.

"Damn, where in hell did I lose it?" he wondered out loud, scratching the back of his bald head. Just then Blondie, the skidder foreman, came around, noticed his predicament, and remarked in an extra loud voice so that all could hear:

"Flash Harry, you drive your truck the same way I fuck when I'm drunk!"

Then there was the story of Skookum Joe, a logging truck driver I met at the O'Brien logging camp at Stillwater, south of Powell River. Skookum Joe had just rounded a curve when he saw a wheel on the road in front of him, rushing ahead of him down the hill.

"Where in hell did that wheel come from?" he wondered, realizing almost at the same moment that it must be his own right-front wheel that had somehow come off. Although the story seemed amusing at the end of the day, it was a serious situation for Skookum Joe.

Episodes like this broke the monotony of the evenings in camp. Here was something harmless for all to laugh about, and laugh they did — even Skookum Joe and Flash Harry. More common, however, were the less amusing diversions that made the rounds after supper in the bunkhouses. One such story that captured our attention in 1953, was about Double Drum Mike, the hooktender, how he nearly lost his cold decker, and how HighPocket saved the day.

Double Drum Mike and his crew were in the process of moving

the cold decker up to a new setting. The hillside to be logged was unbelievably steep, and in some places badly broken up. The fallers had felled the timber more or less parallel to the slope of the ground, so the logs could act as skids for the sled of the cold decker to glide over.

Double Drum Mike, a stocky man with a nose like a blue potato, evaluated the terrain, planning the route up which he would take his machine. He checked every stump thoroughly before he hung the haulback block to it. It was by way of the block that the cold decker would propel itself forward under its own power via the main and haulback lines. On this occasion some of the ground was so abrupt that it seemed the cold decker might flip backwards. No great wonder Scottie called that hillside "a prime suicide show" the moment he laid eyes on it.

One Eyed Bill, the cold decker's donkey puncher, did his very best to stay on the steep, upward-slanting running board while he coaxed the yarder upwards in painful lurches. Impatient with the snail's pace at which the ascent was progressing, Double Drum Mike snorted to the crew that she was slower than the second coming of Christ, and slammed his double bit axe deep into a stump. Bible John, never one to curse or swear, resented Mike's unwarranted outburst of ill temper.

Charlie, the chaser, was having other thoughts. Shortly before moving onto this setting he had noticed that the mainline was worn and damaged in one place. He mentioned this to Mike, who brushed him off with the utterance:

"She'll be good for one more setting yet." Charlie, however, had his misgivings; he knew well the consequences of a severed mainline (or any other line) under tension.

Meanwhile, Double Drum Mike had ordered Scottie to carry the Tommy Moore block and a strap up ahead another 150 feet or so to a preselected stump, in order to have the strawline pulled through it. Scottie, the inveterate jester, had the misfortune that day to bungle it. This caused a new outburst from Mike, whose temper was getting short. Yelling over the mighty roar of the yarder he shouted to Scottie:

"Get lost, you son of a bitch, you are as useless as the tits on a boar. All you're good for is splitting wood for a diesel donkey!" (Diesel donkeys, of course, need no wood.) Albin and Joe, the remaining chokermen, hustled on for all they were worth, for fear of being bawled out too.

Meanwhile, the yarder crept uphill in fits and starts over logs and stumps. What everybody could see, but could not stop at the moment, was the dragging and chafing of the mainline over an out-

48

crop of rock. The mainline, taut to its utmost, severed with a hiss under the enormous strain of the yarder, and the line came whirling towards the yarder with a loud swish. Cut off from its lifeline to the stump, the cold decker began to slide backwards down the hill.

Consternation set in as the men watched One Eyed Bill hang on for dear life to the levers of the donkey — the cold decker gaining momentum by the second. A hard jolt pitched Bill off the yarder, down among the felled and bucked logs. He landed painfully on his side, and as he hit the ground the front end of the sled glided mercifully past him. Bill climbed to his feet and stood shakily on a log looking down the slope for his beloved yarder. In its wake it had left a trail littered with tools and other debris. Finally, for some reason as yet unknown, the yarder had slowed, and come shortly thereafter to its final halt.

Double Drum Mike came storming down the slope, stopping briefly to make sure Bill was okay, then continuing on toward the yarder. Others followed him one by one.

"Are you all right?" they asked One Eyed Bill.

"Must have bust my ribs," he answered, holding one hand to his injured side.

"You may consider yourself blessed," said Bible John, "it could have ended worse for you."

"You're right there," said Bill. "Anyhow, let's go see what shape she's in."

Double Drum Mike was already down by the yarder, and what he saw there he did not like one bit. What had brought the yarder to a halt was spending its momentum as it slid across a fairly level bench on the hill. In shape, the bench resembled a ski jump, ending in a long, sheer drop, over which yawning rift one third or better of the yarder now protruded. To top it all off, the whole yarder was tilted over to one side at a precarious angle.

"How in hell are we ever gonna get her back in from that?" said Mike.

"If ever there was a cliffhanger," said One Eyed Bill, "this has got to qualify. One thing's for sure, no one's getting me out there to run her back in." He pointed to the yarder. "Look closely: she's leaning right over where one has to stand to operate the levers. The only good luck we had is that the engine stalled on her way down."

Since there was nothing anyone could do at the moment, the men gathered up everything that had fallen off the sled and left in the crummy for camp. Dan, the camp super, was madder than a nettled hornet when he heard what had transpired up on the cold decker show. It was lucky for Double Drum Mike that Charlie the chaser had not yet tattled about the damaged mainline, or the super would have blown a fit. Word spread from bunkhouse to bunk house that evening, and for once, all the men had the same subject to talk about.

"How will they save the yarder?"

The question was on everyone's tongue. Some very heated discussion took place, and the topic kept most of the camp busy until bedtime.

Skidder Crew with Steam Yarder. Narrows Inlet Camp, 1934. Courtesy of Workers Compensation Board.

Gone, by this time of the year, were the sunny days that everyone liked and enjoyed. The last vestige of Indian summer was giving way to cloudy skies and rain. One knew autumn had arrived when every day became a "Bone Dry Show" — a day when loggers wore their "Bone Dries" to keep them from the rain.

Miserable weather affects everyone adversely, and is responsible for an increase in accidents and lowered productivity. In addition, men's tempers are inclined to wear thin beneath the weight of a barometric low pressure system.

When a man wakes on a cool, wet morning to hear the rain dripping off the shake roof, and when he comes to the chilly conclusion that the bullcook has not yet lit the fire in the bunkhouse heater (which he is supposed to attend to at four in the morning), then he might well shiver beneath his thin blanket and feel very nearly beaten. An older man might wake to the miserable sensation of every bone in his body aching, his muscles still tired from the previous day's exertions. Such physical discomfort is inevitably made worse by a sinking of the spirits and vitality. There is nothing to cheer about when one has to face up to yet another miserable, wet morning of logging.

The next day, Dan the super, Squinty the woods foreman and Double Drum Mike, hiked up to the stranded cold decker to size things up for themselves.

"She sits in a mightily awkward position," said Squinty. "How the devil can we ask or expect anyone to step out there and pilot her back in? It's the next thing to suicide, the way I figure it."

Dan remained pensive. He had one great hope, an ace up his sleeve:

"Highpocket. If he can't do it, no one else can. We need a man who knows how to operate a yarder who won't lose his nerve. Yes, Highpocket's the man — provided he's willing to take the job."

Highpocket, in the meantime, was working with Haywire George's crew to set up a new spar. Highpocket was no ordinary logger or highrigger. His rare talent and abilities made him a legend in camps along the coast. Furthermore, he was a man no one could ever have missed in a crowd of a thousand loggers. About six-and-a-half feet tall, his head always stood out above the crowd. When seating himself at a cookhouse table he would approach his chair from behind, then lift his left leg over the back of the chair and sit down.

Everything about this remarkable man was strikingly long. When he walked, it was in long, slow strides. His arms were lengthy and powerful, and his hands and fingers were well formed and also elongated. His somewhat narrow, high head was topped off by blondish hair, and his clean face was graced by deep blue eyes and an ever ready smile.

Highpocket possessed an indefinable something that words cannot adequately describe. He spoke very slowly with a clear ringing voice, and was never ruffled or in a hurry, no matter what took place around him. Highpocket radiated tranquility, both on and off the job. It was a pleasure and an experience to watch him don his climbing gear and work his way up a tree chosen for use as a spar. Every move he made appeared so effortless that one could almost believe there was nothing to being a highrigger. But Highpocket, like all the best highriggers, possessed profound skill, unsurpassed judgement, and plenty of endurance for dangerous work under severe weather conditions.

Certainly, Highpocket was using his physique to the very best advantage as he climbed the chosen spar tree, meticulously chopping away the branches until he reached the spot where he intended to top the tree — some one hundred feet above the ground. His long arms gave him tremendous leverage as he swung his double bit axe.

"Never work with a dull axe," he'd say to anyone who cared to listen, and true to his word, he honed his topping axe carefully, taking great pains to always keep it sharp. One would never have dared to reach for Highpocket's axe — even when he wasn't around.

Finally Highpocket reached the desired height, sized up the lean of the tree top once again, and began to hack out an undercut in the direction he wanted the top to fall. The process took time: the tree was a tall, old fir, and the top of the spar was in the neighbourhood of twenty-two inches. In time, one final stroke of the axe severed the last bit of holding wood in the center of the tree trunk, and the top heeled over gracefully and fell to the ground, causing the spar to sway wildly. The moment the top was clear of the trunk, Highpocket drove his axe into the top of the spar, using it to brace himself during the violent sway. He swung on the top of the spar till the last quiver, enjoying the towering feeling of a job well done. Then, as was his custom, he granted himself a moment of rest, folding his long body over the freshly cut top. As he breathed in the fresh air and looked on the setting he told himself, as he often told others:

"The world looks a lot different from my point of view."

It was from this recumbent position that Highpocket spotted Dan, who had arrived in his pickup in time to watch the top fall. Highpocket signaled the chaser that it was time for the engineer to let him down on the pass line. Back on the ground, he climbed out of the pass chain, undid the safety belt and climbing rope, loosened his climbing irons (spurs) and walked in slow measured steps over to Dan.

"What's new?" he asked with his customary smile.

"You know darn well what kind of a bind I'm in with that cold decker hanging out over the cliff," snorted Dan.

"Ah," said Highpocket with a smirk. "Is it really that bad?"

"No," answered Dan. "It's a lot worse. You wanna come have a peek for yourself?"

"Why not?" said Highpocket.

In such a calibre of a man had Dan, the camp super, placed his entire hope for saving the cold decker. And the dependable Highpocket was not about to be the one to disappoint him, provided that the job could be performed with a reasonable margin of safety.

Dan and Highpocket followed the trail the cold decker had left behind as it worked its way down to the bench where it came to a halt. Dan stood to the side while Highpocket carefully surveyed and appraised the situation. He said nothing as Dan outlined some ideas for retrieving the valuable machinery. Highpocket thought some more, then declared his own plan. Dan promptly agreed with the proposed scheme.

"All right, then," said Highpocket. "It's too late to start doing anything today, so let's get on with it first thing tomorrow morning."

That evening news spread through the camp about the next day's project. One could hear it repeated again and again in the grubby old bunkhouses as the fellows chatted before bedtime. All of them, to a man, wished they would be able to observe what promised to be a rare performance.

The drenching rain of the previous days had slackened off somewhat during the night, and by morning the weather had begun to improve. Double Drum Mike, with his full contingent of men and trusty old Highpocket with them, left camp that morning for the place of action far up on the hillside. Scottie was no longer with them; he had finally been fired. A character known only as "Step-and-a-half" took his place on the rigging, and an unforgettable character he was.

Step-and-a-half arrived in camp almost directly from jail, carrying only the worn-out clothes on his back. Several loggers recognized him from other camps, and the rigging men were quick to remember his nickname, created, without a doubt, in honour of Step-and-a-half's peculiar gait.

Forever a hard working chokerman, it was hard to tell Step-and-a-half's age. He was small and very skinny and usually had several weeks' stubble on his oval face. One of his upper front teeth was missing, and his thin, dark hair, which he combed with his fingers, went straight back over his skull. He carried his egg-shaped head high and tilted slightly backwards, so that he appeared always to be gazing at the sky. When he spoke, which was seldom, his voice sounded high pitched and disjointed.

Apart from Step-and-a-half's obvious shortcomings, he was a tolerable enough fellow who never bothered anybody or gave cause for trouble. In addition, he possessed one talent for which most men in camp admired him: woodcarving, which was done with his only possession — a single bladed pocket-knife. After supper and on weekends one could see him sitting on the edge of his bunk with a piece of wood or fir bark on his lap, his short legs dangling loosely, his active hands unceasingly shaving and scraping. From the proceeds of his handicraft he bought for himself the tobacco he smoked in camp. In any event, Double Drum Mike got more work out of Step-and-a-half than he could have from two Scotties. Indeed, he proved himself to be all right from the start on that mad cliff-hanger job.

Following the group's arrival at the stranded cold decker, Highpocket took charge.

"We'll have to long-splice the damaged mainline," he told the men. "Next, the haulback block has to be hung on a stump at the correct angle and distance from the yarder so as to counteract the dangerous side lean of the sled."

For additional safety, the anchor stump on which the haulback block hung had to be tied top and bottom with back twisters to two sturdy stumps a short distance away. Prior to starting the yarder, all the lines and cables had to be pulled by hand, meaning lots of hard bullwork for the entire gang. Once everything was ready and in its proper place all the men got clear. Only Highpocket and Double Drum Mike remained on the scene.

Cautiously, Highpocket worked his way out onto the heavily tilted running boards next to the levers of the cold decker. With steady hands he started up the engine. An ear-splitting roar shattered the early forenoon; black smoke belched out of the exhaust pipe: Highpocket was warming up the cold engine. The cold decker shuddered as he put the heavy line drums into gear and started reeling in the spent lines, preparing them for the final move.

Double Drum Mike positioned himself in such a manner as to be able to observe what Highpocket could not see from the slanted cold decker, and to relay information via hand signals on which the Highpocket relied. If not for the din of the yarder, one might have thought that the world had grown deadly quiet.

All eyes were fixed on the cold decker, and on the courageous man working the levers with both hands and feet. As the line drums reeled in the lines the yarder began to creep toward safety. In moments, Highpocket overcame the crucial point of no return, and moved the cold decker onto safe ground.

To the cheers and wide grins of Dan, Double Drum Mike, and all the crew, Highpocket shut down the engine and stepped off the sled. He gestured to One Eyed Bill, whose chest was taped over the broken ribs he'd received from his tumble two days ago:

"She's all yours again," said Highpocket. "However, I suggest you put a new mainline on her before you move her any farther up this steep slope."

That meant hard work again for everyone alike, pulling strawline from the road up to the yarder in order to drag up a new mainline. Thereafter, everything was normal again, just as it was on any other day on a cold deck show. That evening at suppertime Highpocket seemed to stand taller than ever. Dan, the super, surprised him with a well-deserved financial reward for his accomplishment. What would logging outfits do without men the equal of Highpocket? In truth, they would not exist. That is why they need loggers just as much as they need the timber they log.

A Kick in the Pants

Some men, like Highpocket, were the subject of bunkhouse discussions for reasons they could be proud of. Others, like poor Slippery, were not accorded the same respect.

Slippery was a likeable chap with, seemingly, no enemy in the world to cloud his happy-go-lucky days in camp. Smallish of stature, he had a round head with fine sandy blonde hair, although signs of premature baldness gave him an older appearance than he deserved in his early twenties. A good portion of Slippery's off hours was spent shaving and sprucing up in the washroom. Although not addicted to tobacco, he delighted in a bottle of rye whenever it was available to him. Somewhat given to exaggeration in his amiable talk, especially when he'd been drinking, he could fool many a willing listener. Forever beaming, displaying shiny white teeth and a ruddy complexion, Slippery walked in big strides, arms swinging wildly, leaning forward as if he were walking into the wind. One could hear his loud and cheerful voice from far away.

Slippery drove a logging truck at Wakeman Sound, and it was plain to see that he loved his job. No one cared better for his rig than he did, and he was always eager to bring in an extra load to give production that much desired boost. (The camp super could never get enough logs on any given day of the year. Some loggers nearly worked their hearts out trying to satisfy the demand, but it was like trying to fill a barrel without a bottom.)

Regrettably, Slippery was pursued by tough luck more than any other driver in camp. On several occasions, when meeting another truck on a narrow logging road, Slippery drove too far out on the soft shoulder. Consequently, the wheels of one side of his truck would slip off the road and get stuck. When the truck was loaded, the situation became a real problem. When asked by his fellow logging truck drivers what caused him to drive off the shoulder, his standard reply was: "The road was slippery." Hence his unfortunate nickname.

One fateful spring day in the late afternoon, Slippery came driving down a steep grade with his huge load of boomsticks just a trifle too fast. Precisely in the middle of a switchback, he met his buddy Terry coming full steam uphill for his final load of the day. The road was still wet from the melting of the last remnants of the high snow bank along the hauling road, thus there were no telltale clouds of dust, such as often warn logging truck drivers that they are approaching each other. Furthermore, the timing of where they should have met along the route had been mixed up because of trouble at the landing, where for a short time no logs had arrived for the loader to stack onto Slippery's truck.

Both drivers entered the abrupt hairpin curve at the same time, and neither was aware of the other till the moment when they came into each other's view. To make matters worse, Slippery was blinded for a crucial moment by the setting sun behind Terry's truck.

"Jesus Christ," screamed Slippery, as he applied the powerful air brakes. What else could he do? There was no place to maneuver his big rig, unless he chose to go over the edge of the road — which would have meant certain self destruction.

The brakes on Slippery's truck functioned well, almost stopping the wheels from turning. The heavy tires on the tractor and trailer bit deep into the wet gravel. Terry could see clearly what was coming straight towards him, and in no time at all he brought his truck to a stop.

Slippery, however, kept on skidding towards him. Steam from the water-cooled airbrakes rose up behind the mud-dripping wheels. Slippery could not slow his truck enough to prevent the unavoidable head-on collision. A terrific shudder from the colossal impact permeated both cabs as they meshed. Logs from Slippery's high load shot forward, pushing the steel-plated water tank for the cooling of the brake drums down, over, and against the back of the cab, which in turn buckled forward. This squeezed Slippery tightly behind the steering wheel, nearly crushing his chest.

Terry's position was much worse. The uppermost logs from Slippery's load shot like missiles into Terry's cabin. His forehead was badly cut by flying splinters of windshield glass, and he was jammed-in behind the wide steering wheel. Terry could not move at all, and was bleeding from deep cuts. The pain became unbearable;

loss of blood combined with shock made him almost faint.

First to arrive at the scene of the accident was the crummy with the bull gang. Shatterrock was the rigger, and was also in charge of the rig-up crew. He quickly sized up the situation and began shouting orders to his stunned men. It was lucky for the two trapped drivers that of all the vehicles on the road it happened to be the bull gang crummy that came along. These were the only men who carried their tools with them, the tools that were used to rig up spar trees. Without such tools no one could have freed the two drivers from their steel trap.

With the aid of a Gilchrist jack, crowbars and sledgehammers, the bull gang frantically went to work. Shatterrock decided that Terry should be freed first, before he lost too much blood. It was Shatterrock who struggled with the jack under the loose logs, in doing so exposing himself to the danger of being crushed. Gingerly, the logs were moved enough out of the way to allow the men to pry open the mangled door.

The next problem was to get Terry out from behind the steering wheel that held him tight. Panting and sweating from the exertion, the men finally pulled the driver from the wreckage and bandaged up the gash on his forehead with a field dressing from the crummy. Slippery, in the meantime, was screaming at the bull gang to get him out of there fast. Once again, Shatterrock took it upon himself to take on the risky job of jacking up the enormous logs. This done, it still took a while to pry apart the wreck, which was folded up like an accordion. Slippery looked pale, was obviously in shock, and could not be calmed down. Once they pried open the crushed door the men managed to wrestle the steering column to one side. No one needed to help Slippery out. He scrambled through the gap under his own power and ran down the road in the direction of camp. As he disappeared around the bend the bull gang could hear him screaming:

"Jesus Christ! Jesus Christ!"

By now it was nearly quitting-time on the slopes, and crummies from logging sites farther up were driving back to camp. No vehicle could get past the two trucks, which took up just about the entire width of the narrow road. The men, including Terry and Shatterrock's bull gang, had to walk for miles down to camp.

Next day, the two wrecked logging trucks were towed down to camp and left on the sideline. Both badly shaken-up drivers took a few days off from work, only to return behind the wheels of two more logging trucks.

Another of Slippery's mishaps occurred when he broke down with a full load of logs in the middle of a high, narrow bridge. What happened was this: the ridge — that is, the part of a logging truck that connects the trailer to the tractor — broke loose, and the two became separated; not too unusual an occurrence in itself. Part of Slippery's front load had spilled onto the decking of the bridge. This blocked all further traffic over the bridge, which happened to be on the main hauling road.

Slippery climbed down from his rig to survey the extent of the damage. Scratching his head, mumbling "Jesus Christ," and pacing back and forth, he saw another loaded logging truck pull up to the blockade.

"It's Jolly Good," sighed Slippery, relieved to see a friendly face. Jolly Good was British, and had received his nickname by preceding almost everything he said with the words: "jolly good." Jolly Good shut off his engine so the two drivers could hear each other better above the noise from the rushing creek below.

While the two talked and joked, a pickup truck came to a halt behind Slippery's back. Inside was no other than Slippery's half brother Mallory, who functioned as a "sidekick" in the operation.

"What happened here?" shouted Mallory in a raucous voice.

"You can see for yourself," replied Slippery, a little red in the face.

Mallory clambered along the edge of the decking, trying hard not to fall down into the foaming, cascading creek. He took a good look at everything and crept back out again. Slippery, who was starting to feel a little uneasy, shifted from one leg to the other as Mallory came up behind him.

"You stupid cocksucker!" hollered Mallory. "Couldn't you have found a better spot to break down?" So saying he booted poor Slippery square in the rear of his pants.

By next day, nearly every man in camp had heard about the way this unfortunate fellow had been kicked in the rear for having had the bad luck to break down where he did. And indeed, it was quite a job to get the truck and logs removed from the high bridge in order to open it up for traffic again.

Arne the Bull

One summer day Slippery had been hauling logs from the high-lead yarding site, where Arne — universally called The Bull — was tending hook. Arne originated from the far north of Norway, and was quite young at the time he came to British Columbia. His first job in B.C. was the usual one for an immigrant, namely, setting chokers. The choker was the lowest man on the totem pole, only one notch above the bullcook, who received the lowest pay of any man in camp.

Over the years, in diverse logging camps, Arne gradually worked his way up through various tasks on the rigging, until he became one of the most competent hooktenders on the B.C. coast. Early on in his career the men started to call him The Bull, and the name had stuck. Not tall, but extremely well built, he had a neck like a bull, and a voice to match. He possessed great physical strength, and was capable of lifting a man up with nearly out-stretched arms. But being strong and rock-ribbed were not The Bull's only admirable characteristics. He had as good a mind as God ever gave an earthly being, and he knew how to apply it to his chosen field — namely the rigging. So great was The Bull's skill that novices became utterly dumbfounded in his presence, whereas the professional could only marvel. As was fitting, The Bull had the choicest crew working for him. He never tolerated anyone for long who wasn't up to snuff — he fired such men as speedily as they came to the jobsite.

On the day in question, Arne's crew was yarding along the edge of a ravine. Steve, the yarding engineer known as Tightliner, was extremely proficient, one of the best operators to run a slack line show. He could tightline his cables like no other donkey puncher on the claim. In addition, he was fast, really fast in running the rigging out and back again. Steve would make the donkey scream in agony as he sent the empty rigging back out again for every new turn of logs. When pulling in a turn, dark blue smoke would belch from the stubby exhaust pipe of the yarder.

Standing on the worn-out running boards with his engineers' cap at a jaunty angle, Steve cut a dashing figure. Still, he was no man to trifle with. Brusque and impatient, he would clench his teeth together as his eyes followed the cables and rigging, his narrow lips pressed together tightly in his thin, pockmarked face. In addition, his eyesight was so keen that he invariably spotted the rigging just in advance of the signal from the whistle punk. This annoyed the whistle punk because his signal coincided with the already stopped rigging. The chokermen also disliked Tightliner, for not allowing them a single moment's reprieve all day long. The Bull, however, was fond of Tightliner, and so was the chaser in the landing, who gave him rare praise for the way he put down the turn.

The present setting The Bull was logging from posed a genuine challenge. The terrain was badly broken up by several deep gorges, with many nasty rock bluffs where logs were easily hung up. On such terrain the hooktender encounters a multitude of difficulties.

A further drawback to trouble-free yarding was the extraordinary size of the logs on this setting. They ranged in diameter from about four feet to eight feet, and had a corresponding tendency to hang up behind stumps and other obstacles. Of course, this was nothing new to The Bull. Untold times before had he logged this kind of land.

The entire crew struggled hard that particular morning. They had choked their first log using three chokers on a gnarly old fir butt log about six feet wide and forty feet long. Due to its awkward position in a creek bed at the bottom of a gorge, the fallers were unable to buck it into shorter log lengths. For a moment The Bull considered using dynamite to split it into halves. But then he reasoned that it would be less time consuming to do it his proven way, which was with the aid of additional cable and block combinations. To no one's surprise, it worked like a charm. The grand old log inched ahead slowly — ever so slowly — gradually getting clear of obstructions or moving around those that were in its way.

The whistle punk positioned himself at the edge of the canyon, well clear of the action, but still close enough that he could pick up signals from the hooktender. Ron, the rigging slinger, along with his two chokermen, scrambled out of the creek bed to get clear before the go-ahead-slow signal was sent to the yarding engineer.

With the help of extra blocks placed at the most effective locations, the desired purchase, which is a good, steady pull, was achieved. The donkey groaned against the strain of its colossal load, while overhead the cables hissed and twitched madly. Everything was strained to its uppermost limit, and an audible sigh of relief was heard from the men as one end of the log came steadily up and over the edge of the steep bank. From there on it was clear sailing.

While preparations were being made by the rigging men to lift the giant log out of the bottom of the creek, Slippery had to wait because there were no more logs to load out. It was just about then that I arrived at the landing, in tow behind Skinhead, the bullbucker. I had been chosen to buck the immense butt log into two shorter lengths.

As soon as I got there I unloaded my tools, comprising an axe, an extra long bucking saw, several wide steel bucking wedges, a ten-pound sledgehammer, a six-foot long measuring stick, and a whiskey bottle filled with oil. The cork in the whiskey bottle had a small hole drilled through it, out of which oil was squirted onto the saw blade, to overcome the friction created by tree pitch or sap, which tends to stick to the saw. Around the bottle's neck was a stiff wire, which allowed a logger to hang it within easy reach from the bark of a tree or log.

It must have been about ten o'clock by the time the heavy turn reached the landing. Having finished unloading my tools, I now waited for Ian, the chaser, to remove the three chokers from the big fir log. It was while I was waiting that I noticed Skinhead walki ng towards Slippery, who was standing on the front bumper of his logging truck busily dusting the green-colored hood.

"How's it going, Slippery?" asked the bullbucker.

Instead of answering with the usual "fine and dandy," Slippery straightened himself up, pulled out his brass-encased pocket watch, consulted it thoughtfully, and announced with a straight face:

"Half past nine and not a whore in the house is fucked."

In loggers' lingo, this was a most brilliant way of saying: no business.

I went to work without any further delay, and it took until well past the noon hour to pull the freshly sharpened bucking saw all the way through the immense log. Wisely, I had brought along my two-gallon waterbag.

Once I was finished, the oversized log, albeit now sawed in two, became the loading engineer's headache. First, he built a cradle by putting two forty-foot long logs of about two feet in diameter on each side of the heavy steel bunks. Next, the second loader, with the help of the chaser, put a strong strap around one end of the log, in order that the tongs could get a firm hold on it. Then the loading engineer lifted that end up, while Slippery backed his logging truck under it. Once one end was securely in the cradle, the strap was removed and put around the end which was still on the ground. Again, the loader lifted it as high as he could, while Slippery backed up his truck. The log slid neatly into its cradle, and I, along with the yarding and loading team, beamed with satisfaction to see that grand old fir log slowly disappearing downhill on the back of Slippery's truck.

The Gold Dust Twins

I have always had a great fondness for trees and rocks, both of which were an integral part of the natural surroundings in the Tyrol, where I grew up. In a creek near our home I remember finding a colourful stone which I admired for its oval shape, its water-polished smoothness, and its soft pink hue. Today I know that the stone I found was a relatively common pink granite, but my attachment to it was based solely on its inherent qualities, not the possible commercial value it may have had.

In my first year in grade school I traded this priceless pebble for a worthless horse tooth that belonged to an older boy from a near-by mountain village. Fritz tended to be cunning, and tricked me into a one-sided deal. That was the first time in my life I'd been taken advantage of, but I persisted in my rock collection and became what one might call a rock hound. Therefore it was only natural for me to explore and prospect the rivers and creeks wherever I worked on the B.C. coast, looking for semi-precious stones such as agate, garnet and quartz crystals.

One pleasant summer weekend in 1952, while prospecting one of the side streams off the main river about nine miles from Wakeman Sound camp, I found that a cascading waterfall was blocking the creek bed up which I was tenaciously struggling. In order to bypass the fall I had to climb several hundred feet up a steep, moist bank, fighting every foot of the way, over and under old windfalls and through dense underbrush. Sweat ran down my hot face, and the damnable horseflies bit me viciously on my back. Years ago an old-timer had advised me to tie a bell to my belt when prospecting, as the gentle chiming would warn grizzly bears of my presence; its clapper jangled less melodiously than usual as I fought my way doggedly up the bank. Nearing the top, I stopped to get my wind, and while I stood there gazing upward, I spotted a section of moss-covered roof.

Having striven up the last hundred feet or so, I finally reached clear, level ground. Before me stood an aged, weather-beaten and obviously abandoned log cabin. It rested among a stand of virgin timber, dominated by a vast forest of mighty trees, hundreds of years old, towering to the height of twenty-storey buildings, some of them twelve feet through at the stump. With the trunks of enormous trees for neighbours, the cabin stood as if in another world. No man had ever logged this forest. Like the lichens that grew on them, and the long moss that hung from their branches, these trees had been growing, dying and regenerating since the end of the last major ice age, some twelve thousand years ago. A few smallish red cedars among them had given way to great yellow cedars, many of which had aged into snags, but were impressive all the same. These ancient trees loomed larger than life, with their silver-grey bark, their enormous bulk and their widely flared and buttressed stumps. Yellow cedars grow slowly — it would be two centuries before they could be considered for harvest.

There were big hemlocks too, much larger than usually encoun-tered at this altitude. Their scaly bark contrasted with the narrow, vertical ribbing of the yellow cedars. Quite often these two species grow in close pairs, so that they almost seem to share a single stump. Some have cavities at the stump where a bear might find a place to spend the winter. Others have cracked trunks which provide homes for raccoons, owls and many other woodland creatures. Over all there lay a deep silence, a sense of tranquility and timelessness.

So far, I had seen only the rear portion of the cabin. The entry was located on the sheltered side, away from the dreaded southeasterly winds. Stepping around saplings and newly-grown seedlings from the surrounding trees, I walked to the side of the cabin, which was built from peeled red cedar logs. The roof came down low, and was made of red cedar shakes, now heavily covered with thick moss. Stopping in front of a narrow window, its panes covered from the inside by cobwebs, I tried in vain to peek through the glass.

At the entrance to the hut a lean-to rested against the cabin wall. It had served as a woodshed, judging by the splitting block and some cut firewood stacked against one side. Some tools (an axe, a crosscut saw, a pick and shovel, two short hand drills for drilling holes into rock, and a sledgehammer) lay forsaken in the corner, rusting for want of use. From the beams of the lean-to hung a wooden cage enclosed with screen wire, which must have been used for hanging meat.

There was no lock on the cabin door, only a latch, and the entrance was so low and constricted that I was forced to stoop as I crossed the threshold to get inside. On the outside of the door, which was made of splintery red cedar planks, someone had written crudely lettered words in white chalk: "The Gold Dust Twins."

Feeling somewhat apprehensive, I pressed the latch and pushed the door inwards — the rusty old hinges screeched fearfully. Standing motionless for a few moments, I surveyed the interior of the room. To the right, in front of the window, loomed a knotty table with an old-fashioned kerosene lamp on it. At the back was one bunk bed. Behind the door, to the left, stood a tiny woodstove.

Feeling bolder, I stepped fully inside the cabin, lifted my knapsack from my back, and placed it, along with my shabby rain hat, on the table. A comfortable bench and a footrest under the table made me relax immediately. Peering around, I noticed a faded calendar on the wall that dated back twenty years to 1931. On it was printed the name of the Alert Bay Supply Store, where prospectors, trappers and handloggers often bought their supplies when heading up the coast.

"Who were those Gold Dust Twins?" I wondered. "Where are they now, after all those years, and are they even still alive? What made them come here, build a solid cabin, lug equipment, supplies and even a heavy cook stove over such a vast distance, past unavoidable barriers, and then leave again never to return?"

I looked around more closely, and while I was doing so a bright ray of sunshine fell in through the window. There, on the sill, lay several dust-covered rock samples shot through with quartz veins. I examined and tested those specimens closely under my magnifying glass. Sure enough, I quickly noticed wee specks of yellow, and surmised that the rocks contained free gold. I hefted them in my hand to feel their weight, and felt even more certain that I was right.

Owing to the long depression of the early 1930s, and to the favourable pegged price of gold in those days (around thirty-four dollars an ounce), the coastal region experienced an influx of hardy prospectors. They panned for gold in rivers, streams and creeks, in every nook of the B.C. coast. Some prospected far up the mountains, looking for a telltale glitter, or still better — following traces in their gold pans. It was undoubtedly in such a manner that the Gold Dust Twins had reached this desolate place.

I sat there for a time contemplating, until I suddenly realized how quiet and still everything around me had become. The silence was so overpowering that I almost thought I could hear my own heart beating. On the table in front of me the coal oil lamp conjured up memories of my dear mother, lighting the lamp at dusk back home in the Tyrol. Still staring around the cabin I observed two shelves near the stove. Curious, I stood up and examined their contents: several tin containers with traces of provisions in them, a box of Eddy matches, a glass jar containing salt, and the meagre leftover from a bar of soap.

From what I could see, the cabin had been constructed very well, and with great care. Not one leak had sprung in the shake roof after all those many years. Also, strange as it may seem, there were no signs of mice, probably because the floor had been made out of heavy, tightly fitted planks.

One thing bothered me: an odd and pervasive smell that I was at a loss to define. How long ago was it since the last fire in the stove had been lit? Who were those men, and where did they come from? Those were the thoughts that raced through my mind as I ate the rest of my lunch. Finally I looked at my watch and realized that it was getting late. It was time to go, but I promised to return again in the near future. I picked up my empty knapsack and my prospector's pick, put my old hat on my head and stepped outside, closing the door quietly behind me. Glancing a last time over at the lean-to, I noticed a galvanized water pail, and one pair of big, hobnailed leather boots, size eleven or bigger, covered by mildew and mould. One of those twins must have had large feet.

Discerning an overgrown path in front of the cabin's entrance, I followed it out of sheer curiosity. Less than one-hundred feet away it swung to the right, behind a timbered knoll. There, built between four closely-spaced trees, stood an outhouse, minus the door. The path led still farther on to a little brook, and it was there that I saw my first real spring, gushing out of a limestone wall.

"So that's where they got their drinking water from," I mused. Taking off my hat, I bent forward and drank in deep draughts. The water was so cold that it hurt my teeth, but never before had I drunk such delicious water. I vowed to myself to come back soon.

Wondering where the trail might be by which the Gold Dust Twins left their property, I back-tracked to the cabin. Purely by chance, I spotted an old blaze on the side of a balsam tree. Indeed, this was the beginning of the blazed trail leading out. Occasionally, the blazes were hard to distinguish, because over the years the bark had overgrown the marks left by the prospectors' axe. The going was relatively good, with no windfalls of any kind to impede my progress, and after I had walked for about an hour the trail swung to the right in a north-westerly direction. There it crossed a creek, across which the old-timers had felled a tree to serve as a bridge. Looking south and up towards the treetops I could distinguish a V cut in the mountain ridge opposite from where I stood. "God only knows where this valley leads to," I muttered to myself, and proceeded to walk gingerly across the tree, high above the rushing water, taking care not to make myself dizzy by looking down at the swiftly running water below.

From there the trail followed the left bank in a westerly direction. Hiking downhill, the going was still good. Abruptly, the creek made a turn to the north, and so did the trail. Ahead of me, glistening between tree trunks, I could see the shimmering water of a lake, a splash of amber water lavishly decorated with yellow water lilies close to shore, the surface an effective mirror for the tall, surrounding trees. And that is where the trail ended. The Gold Dust Twins must have had a boat of some kind to get to the other end of the lake.

I had a suspicion that I'd stumbled across Goat Lake, which a timber cruiser in camp had been talking about not long before. Thinking about camp made me realize that it was time to head home. Taking my bearings, I struck out for home. Judging by the sun, I realized that it was already late in the day, and that I still had another seven miles or so to go. Moreover, I was getting tired, having been up since four in the morning.

Holding steady to my chosen course, I finally reached a branch of the main logging road. Dusk was upon me, and by the time I reached camp total darkness had set in, save for a starry sky above.

Tired, thirsty, and hungry from a long day, I entered the lightless bunkhouse and sat down at the edge of my bunk. Old Thom was still awake — he had waited for my safe return.

"Must be tired, eh?" he asked. "How did things go? Find anything to repay you for the mighty effort?"

Speaking quietly, I told Old Thom all about the day's events. Thom could only say:

"Strange, very strange indeed."

I slowly undressed and put myself to bed, my mind still dwelling on the mystery of the Gold Dust twins.

Tragedy at the Lake

Eventually, company engineers surveyed a road to the west end of Goat Lake, and in 1953 fallers felled the right of way for a logging road. Then followed the power shovel, compression drill, dynamite, pile drivers; in short, a small army of men who fought their way through heavily wooded mountain slopes, deep valleys and canyons.

Not long after the logging road was completed, men in camp took a liking to Goat Lake. Almost every weekend (except in the winter), loggers drove out to the lake in a company crummy to go trout fishing. Goat Lake is very deep, and the water stays cold even during a hot summer, owing to the fact that the creeks feeding it flow from high peaks covered with snow all year round. Rainbow trout and Dolly Varden feed in the creeks and lake alike, and it was a common sight to see men fly fishing from large rock boulders, or from trees that had toppled into the lake along its shoreline.

One of the men had the idea of building a small log raft to enable them to go farther out on the lake. Everything went well and there were no problems out on the water — they even built a sturdy guard rail around the raft. Once it was built, the boys asked Ed, the blacksmith, to make them a small stove, which they lugged onto the raft so they could fry the trout right when they caught them. Everyone enjoyed this immensely, and the raft was the center of much hilarity on those sunny summer outings. Up to twelve men would go on it at once, relaxing from many weeks of hard work. Baldy brought a short rowboat out to the lake to go fishing. Not many of the men liked the rowboat — it just wasn't as much fun as the raft.

One dreary fall day when the clouds were hanging low over the lake, and a Scotch mist lay over the water, Steve the Tightliner decided to go fishing in Baldy's rowboat with his eighteen-year-old nephew, Craig, and Nick, a friend. All three of them had come to the B.C. coast from the Prairies, where the opportunity for swimming had been rare — only Nick knew how to swim a little. They were the only ones on the lake that late fall afternoon — no one else felt any particular urge to be out on the water on such a cheerless day. But those three didn't mind the patches of fog, the low hanging clouds and the light drizzle.

Baldy used to leave the oars in his boat and tie it up at the lower end of the lake, close to where the logging road ended. Nick, Steve's friend, had brought along the fishing gear and carried it to the boat. Leaving shore, they rowed out near one of the streams that fed into the lake, which was known to be a good spot to catch lovely trout.

The water was calm, otherwise they could never have left shore, but the boat was tiny and crowded, and the men found it difficult to row. About halfway to their planned destination, Craig, who had never been fishing before, felt a sharp pull on his line and yelled for the others to stop rowing.

"What do I do?" he gulped.

"I'll give you a hand" declared Steve, and he stood up in the boat. At the same time, Nick leaned towards the gunwale, trying to grab the fishing line. This sudden change in weight distribution shifted the boat's center of gravity to the side, and in doing so it flipped Steve head over heels into the lake. A split second later Craig and Nick fell overboard into the ice-cold water. Nick thrashed around and managed to stay afloat, but there was no sign of either Steve or Craig. The little boat had capsized and was drifting upside-down in the water, the oars floating nearby.

Shock and panic set in and almost drowned Nick, but he continued to dog-paddle towards the shore. He had worn several layers of clothes, which helped in retaining some of his vital body heat, and luckily, he did not have to swim very far. Gasping for air, his teeth rattling from the cold, he struggled out of the water. The weight of his wet clothes almost dragged him back into the lake.

Nick looked back at Goat Lake once more in the hope of seeing or hearing his friends. The mist obscured his vision, and all was silent but for the dripping of water off the trees around him. Having lost his shoes in the water, he set out in his sodden wool socks in the direction of the crummy, already thinking about how warm the cab would be once he got the engine going.

When he reached the vehicle, Nick grabbed for the door of the cab, opened it and pulled himself in. His wet, cold fingers fumbled for the ignition key. It wasn't there!

"Oh Lordy, where's the key?" With a sinking heart, Nick realized that Steve must have put it in his pocket. There was nothing else he could do but walk back to camp. The soles of his socks were already torn off in places and his feet were sore. Frightened, shuddering with cold, he stumbled out of the cab and struck out for camp, a good seven miles away. The drizzle had turned into rain, soaking him anew and depressing him even more. Sharp rocks on the logging road had his socks in tatters in no time, causing his feet to bleed and ache. Darkness began to fall.

After a long and agonizing march, Nick saw the first glimmers of light from the logging camp. Lurching into the nearest bunkhouse he blurted out his bad tidings to the stunned loggers. As it was night, there was nothing anyone could do. The following day a party of men, along with an RCMP officer, drove out to the lake to investigate the drownings. No bodies were recovered at that time, but eventually they were found and shipped back to their next-of-kins.

With the drowning of the Tightliner, The Bull lost his best yarding engineer ever. Only the chokermen derived benefit from the tragedy — they were greatly relieved to be out from under the constant daily pressure of working with Tightliner Steve.

Over the years I spent in isolated logging camps, drownings became a sad fact of life. After one particularly tragic accident, in which several loggers drowned in the saltchuck, I calculated an average of a drowning per year over the time that I'd been logging. Most of these accidents were caused by overconfident or faulty reasoning. Sometimes, when women and children were involved, the tragedy took on extra proportions.

The year before my arrival at camp, a Canadian soldier returned to the coast of B.C. from overseas, bringing with him his new war bride from England. Eventually he found employment as a saw filer at Wakeman Sound, but his wife could never get used to the restricted, isolating life in camp. One day she and her four-year-old child disappeared. The ensuing search was intense, but in vain. Then late one spring day a timbercruiser, miles from camp, found a human skull washed up on the riverbank. The skull was handed over to the RCMP, who determined that it belonged to the English woman. The remains of the child were never found.

Following a glorious Indian summer in the fall of '53, there came a period of cloudy, rainy, cool and windy weather. It's the time of year when one dreary day succeeds another. These were the days, weeks and months that loggers dreaded the most. Christmas was still too far away to daydream about, and there was nothing, during this time, to look forward to.

On the job, the little-liked but necessary "Bone Dries" turned into steady companions for every logger. New or old, the "Bone Dries" were invariably stiff and wearying. As long as the newness of the fabric lasted they repelled the rain, but at the same time they held one's sweat inside. Later on, as they lost their uncomfortable stiffness, they began leaking like sieves, leaving one incessantly clammy or wet.

In such weather a chokerman's job turned into the worst job in the woods. As long as he stayed in action the misery was bearable. But when the turn of logs was headed for the landing, and while the rigging was headed back out again, there was nothing to do but stand around and wait. And while he waited, poised there on a gradient log, a stump or any other footing, all the pressure that his body weight exerted found its way to the ankle and toes of his lowest foot. Soon, he'd be shifting from one leg to the other for relief. Standing there damp, with hunched shoulders and cold, loosely hanging arms, he'd begin to long for a cigarette, but his hands and fingers would be too cold and wet to roll one.

There was little visual distraction, either: the other side of the mountain disappeared into a mixture of light mist and rain, both buffeted by the blustery wind. All one could do was watch with sinking heart, as the driving sheets of rain glided by without cease. Things were especially bad when yarding long roads, which was fine in fair weather but a real misery in foul winter weather. When there wasn't enough lift from the spar tree, the logs got dragged on the ground and covered with mud. Worse, the earth was torn up and the precious topsoil washed down into creeks, rivers, lakes or the sea. This was just one of the ways in which logging contributed to soil erosion.

Wherever one looked water oozed from the ground in small rivulets, which soon became larger as they converged on their journey down the slope. In the event that there was no witty fellow like Scotty among the crew to divert one from one's wretchedness, long-suffering silence became the rule of the day.

Not even the donkey puncher or loading engineer stayed dry in such dreadful weather, especially when the operating site was exposed to the awful southeast winds. Rain clothes were torn by jaggers sticking out from broken strands on worn or damaged choker cables, or on any other wire cables a man had to handle in a day's work. One's hands were often painfully pricked by those cursed jaggers; more torment on top of such unkind weather.

Once a jagger had torn the side of a pant leg, water invariably found its way downward. If the rip was bad enough one's feet were soon sloshing dismally inside their boots. After work, one poured out the water, then wrung out the wool socks before hanging them to dry. Looking down at one's white, waterlogged feet and toes, one often thought:

"Oh, what a miserable life this is!" And it was all made worse by the certain knowledge that the days to come would be no better.

Cold, wet and numb, the men were hardly aware anymore of the shrill signal tones, or the whining noise of the labouring yarder. The hours crept by slowly — an endless drag. Only when lunch hour approached would some vitality inject itself into the crew. The prospect of drying out somewhat by the open lunch fire provided a much-needed lift to the daily struggle for existence.

Shortly before lunchtime the rigging slinger assigned one or two chokermen to get a fire going. Normally a simple matter, starting a lunch fire under these conditions was a trying task. When everything was wet, one had to look hard for tinder and fuel, usually lichen, dry moss, cedar bark, or a dry stick or splint of wood, found at the underside of a large log. One fellow cut shavings with a pocket knife, bending over to protect them from the rain. Another fellow tried to light a match, frustrated by his cold, stiff fingers and the slapping wind. Other men came by with whatever they could find that would burn, while yet another cut several green-forked sticks with which to toast sandwiches, or roast pieces of garlic sausage over the hot coals.

While eating lunch everyone continually jockeyed for a better position around the open fire. Smoke from ill-burning wood, dampened down by cascading rain, tends to veer constantly in circles over the flames. With every new gust of wind, life is breathed back into the dying fire, which then gets fanned into a hellish blaze, sending live sparks everywhere, causing the men to shift anew around the lunch fire. Now and then someone would take off his logging boots, wring out the dripping wool socks, put them on again, and then hold his stockinged feet over the flames, to warm them up before forcing them back into the soaked caulk boots.

The moment the first whiff of smoke from the lunch fire drifted downwind, and the mighty roar of the yarder and the shrill sound of the whistle fell silent, a pair of ravens came into view, circling overhead and cawing loudly. The next ones to appear were the whiskey jacks, with several families all in one flock, fighting noisily among themselves for handouts from the lunchers.

Quite frequently there were blue jays as well, but these remained at a safe distance, waiting for their chance to steal from the other birds. Ravens do the same. They harass the smaller birds, steal their booty and hide it for later use. (Ravens remember very well the places where they keep a cache.) Bolder whiskey jacks will hardly wait for a man to open his lunchbox before they alight on his shoulder, trying hard to get a morsel. More daring ones will snatch the food from one's hand, or even from the mouth while one is taking a bite from a sandwich. In heavy rain all the birds looked bedraggled, and continually ruffled their feathers to shake off the wetness.

Sad to say, there were always certain men who enjoyed playing cruel jokes on the hungry birds, either catching them by their legs or trapping them in an open lunchbox. A sadist would put a crumb of bread on his open hand and wait for a whiskey jack to land on his fingers. Then he would close two fingers and hold the wildly screeching and fluttering bird by one or both of its legs. Worse yet, there were individuals who brought long, coloured ribbons from camp, in order to tie them around the captured bird's neck, so as to recognize it on following days. Those poor creatures, however, stayed far out of reach of them from then on. The tedious ribbons induced a drag on the wretched birds and impaired their flight. Such cruel, senseless doings only served to cause friction among the onlookers, whereas otherwise the birds would have enlivened a drab lunch period.

The turbulent storms coming in from the Pacific often follow one after another. The rain is heavy, and can last, uninterrupted, for up to ten days. During those times neither the sun nor the stars are visible for days on end. Sometimes, in between storms, the low, milky, but more often dark clouds may part for brief periods to give one a glance at a tiny piece of bright blue sky above, only to be covered over again by a new curtain of onrushing rain cloud. Even the spirits of the heartiest of loggers tended to succumb to the brunt of such foul weather.

By the time the men had finished eating, the bottom of an open lunchbox would be covered in rainwater. The men would reluctantly abandon the fire, gather up their equipment, and prepare themselves for a dreary afternoon of work.

Hank the Finn

Men working in the landing, like the chaser, head loader, second loader and, of course, the yarding and loading operators, congregated around their own lunch fire for comfort. The hooktender had his lunch wherever he happened to be at lunchtime, but most of the time he made sure he was in the landing for the noon break. The lonesome whistle punk always had to fend for himself, regardless of what the weather was like.

Towards the end of the day everybody on the rigging was soaked to the skin. Boots and clothes were muddied, and some men had large, ragged rents in the side of their pants, exposing the naked leg or thigh underneath. Porkchop Bill, the backrigger on the skidder, used to lament for all to hear:

"Oh Lordy, if my mother could see me in this great shape, she surely would weep bitterly for her only son."

Shortly before four thirty the yarding engineer blew the "slack off" whistle. This gave the chokermen just enough time to come off the hillside and head for the cold, open crummy. As they huddled on the wooden benches one could hear them say:

"Another day, another dollar."

By four thirty all was quiet on the hillside, save for the wind howling and whistling through the taut rigging wires. On the ride back the men endured the last agony of the day; cramped in their wet clothes in the cold, drafty crummy, while moist, muddy spray came streaming in through the wide open rear end.

On arrival, everybody jumped or climbed off the wagon, depending on how stiff he was from the long ride, then headed wearily towards his bunkhouse. Everyone, naturally, was looking forward to a warm bunkhouse, and hoping that the bullcook (whose job it was to light the hut's wood heater) had not fallen down on the job.

Cigar Oly, for example, was a rigging slinger who had fallen into the creek while changing lines. As he approached the bunkhouse, eager to get out of his wet clothes, he and his friend Jeff looked up to scan the roof and the chimney for signs of smoke.

"No smoke," says Jeff.

"What else is new," replied Cigar Oly. "The old fart." Which epithet he used to refer to the bullcook, Hank the Finn.

Pushing open the partly shut door, they stepped into the cool room to the sight of Hank the Finn, slumped on a pile of firewood next to the stove, a rifle between his legs.

"The bastard blew his brains out" declared Cigar Oly.

"Yeah, and he used my hunting rifle," mused Jeff angrily. "What do we do now?"

"Go get the super to come over here and have a look for himself," replied Cigar Oly.

Old George, one of the other bullcooks, happened to be walking by at that moment, and approached the hut with the intention of closing the front door, but when he overheard Jeff and Oly talking, he poked his head inside.

"Now, what do me old eyes see here?" he croaked in his broad Scottish accent, while adjusting his steel rimmed eyeglasses on the bridge of his long, red nose.

"You can see it as well as we do," retorted Jeff.

Old George stepped inside.

"I believe you boys could stand some heat in here, can't you?" With these words he began kindling the old wood stove, completely ignoring Hank the Finn on the woodpile. In no time at all, half the men in camp had come by to have a last look at Hank the Finn, who they all agreed had suffered from severe melancholy.

Loggers do know from long experience that trouble seldom comes alone. It usually brings one or more companions. What followed the suicide of Hank the Finn was not surprising to many of the men in camp. Hank's self-destruction took place on a Tuesday, in driving rain which had lasted for almost the entire past ten days. By Wednesday, to everyone's relief, the heavy rain diminished and the menacing winds abated.

Usually around the middle of October the first snowfall of the season would settle on the high, dark mountain peaks. The fall of '53 was no different in this regard. One morning we woke to breathe the new, raw air, and over the next few days some came down with colds, or even with pneumonia.

Shorty, the donkey puncher, who at that time was operating the yarder for Haywire, was suffering from a severe head and chest cold. On Thursday morning he felt so bad, he could barely drag himself onto the yarder's running board. But he hung on doggedly to his task, despite his miserable condition. Towards the end of the day, Shorty was seized by a severe headache, along with violent coughing and sneezing. He had just pulled another turn of logs into the landing, and Terry, the chaser, was in the process of unhooking the chokers from the logs.

During one of his violent coughs, Shorty's foot slipped off the brake lever. The mainline spilled towards the ground and part of the buttrigging struck Terry, breaking his exposed back. Terry was paralyzed for the rest of his life.

The next day, Friday, worse was yet to come. The weather was cooler, and while the rain and wind had subsided for the time, their place had been taken by a fog so thick that it loomed above us — no ray of sunshine pierced it, and even sounds were muffled.

The Bull and his crew were logging the highest show on the claim. As a matter of fact, a good portion of the back end was under snow already. Black Mike, as swarthy as his name suggests, had replaced the Tightliner as engineer on the yarder where Arne the Bull was tending hook.

Black Mike didn't like the present set-up under which they were yarding. For one thing, the ground was extremely steep and smooth. For another, the road bank was too abrupt and restricted, and he was having a difficult time landing the logs in such a manner that the chaser could safely and effortlessly unhook them. At that time they were yarding in timber from high above. To make things even more foreboding, the timber they were yarding was massive and incredibly heavy.

The Bull happened to be groping around in the fog and snow at the very back end, searching for a suitable stump to hang the haulback block on, his last tail hold on this horrible setting. Ha Ha Harry, who had the odd habit of finishing every other sentence with a funny little laugh, was the rigging slinger. He was having a very hard time spotting the rigging in the mist. For him, his three chokermen and the new whistle punk, the day was already becoming a nightmare.

Ha Ha Harry and his men finished choking a new turn of logs and advanced into the clear before sending the go ahead signal: three whistles. Buttrigging clanged, and the mainline pulled ahead with the choked logs in tow.

Ha Ha Harry could not see what was going on around him, but suddenly there was a different sound in the air — something was amiss. Acting on instinct, he told the whistle punk to blow one short whistle, meaning: stop all lines, followed by one long whistle, meaning: emergency.

Black Mike obeyed the signals right away, and was expecting further instructions from the rigging slinger. But nothing was forthcoming, apart from the continuous, shrill, piercing sound of the whistle atop his yarder.

Donald, a driver, had just hooked up his trailer to the tractor while parking in the landing, and was now busy connecting the air hoses for the airbrakes on his logging truck.

His back was turned to the hillside, and he was not paying attention to the high-pitched warning sound that came from the adjacent yarder. Perhaps he thought the whistle had stuck, as it sometimes did. Everyone else in the landing stopped what he was doing and raised his head in apprehension, straining to see through the mist, or to hear over the infernal din of the yarder and loading machine.

Ian, the chaser, had a hunch from the moment the whistle blew that a loose log might be on its way down towards the landing. The idea of seeking protection behind the butt of the big wooden spar came to him in a flash — which probably saved his life.

Colin, the head loader, and Doug, his second loader, were standing beside the loading machine, gesturing to Louis, the loading operator, to shut the engine down so they could hear what was happening.

Then, like the strike of a thunderbolt, there was a violent crash as the yarder was struck by a yellow cedar log about sixty feet long and thirty inches in top diameter. The impact was so tremendous that it nearly toppled the huge yarder over sideways. Black Mike was thrown clear of the running boards, and his left forearm snapped as he tumbled over several large rocks. From the yarder, the force of the blow was transferred to the spar tree via the mainline, causing it to rock back and forth violently.

Ian, who was standing at the base of the spar tree got the scare of his life. He was afraid the spar might buckle, and imagining the consequences made him freeze on the spot. Standing with his back against the butt of the spar tree, he had a side view of Donald, who was still connecting his air hoses, oblivious to what was going on around him. Black Mike yelled to get Donald's attention, but in vain. Suddenly a pecker pole of a fir shot out of the fog and struck Donald in the back, crushing him against the trailer reach and killing him. The grizzly sight nearly made Ian vomit.

Finally, Ha Ha Harry told the whistle punk to discontinue the emergency signal. Then Louis, the loading operator, jumped up onto the wrecked yarder and blew the dreaded accident signal: seven long whistles. One by one the men staggered into the silent landing. The last one to lurch down from the hill was the Bull. As Ha Ha Harry had correctly assumed, the last turn had dislodged some logs, which then started to glide down the steep slope with ever increasing speed towards the exposed landing.

"Look at the yarder," said Black Mike, while nursing his disabled and painful arm. "That tree must have come down the hillside with the force of a torpedo."

"Suffering Christ, what a day!" groaned the Bull. The tone of his voice indicated the enormous stress he was under. "It would have been better for some of us if we hadn't got out of bed." At long last he looked in the direction of the lifeless body lying on the gravel under the trailer reach.

"Poor devil, why didn't he pay any attention to the warning signal?"

"God only knows," said Ha Ha Harry.

"Not much we can do for him now," said the shaken men to each other. Louis brought a blanket from the yarder and covered what had once been a living flame, now gone, snuffed out like a candle.

The crew departed in silence for camp, there to report the dreadful account of the day, soon to become the topic of conversation in every bunkhouse. Some of the men blamed Hank the Finn, for having started the week out badly by committing suicide. Others blamed the fog, but this argument was shot down by men who could recall similar events taking place in bright sunshine.

Speaking from past experience, Highpocket summed it up correctly:

"There's precious little that one can do once a log, or worse yet several logs, get dislodged at once and shoot down a steep incline towards the landing below. They have a tendency to veer off course just when you think you've reached a safe place. Besides, a man can hardly outrun or outguess a runaway log, and to be honest, almost everyone gets scared in such a situation. I've seen men unable to run, frozen on the spot. I've seen others fall into uncontrollable laughter. And as far as Donald is concerned, nobody will ever know why he neglected to pay attention to the hazard whistle."

Blondie put it this way:

"There are many hazards associated with logging which must be accepted as part of the profession. An experienced and knowledgeable logger will recognize hazards and carry out his duties without being injured. But situations arise which are beyond anyone's control, and unfortunate accidents do happen."

Rats

It is said that every sailing ship has rats on board. Logging camps are no different, but the rats take the form of human beings. I met them wherever I worked during my many years in the woods. To co-exist with those types was trying, to say the least. None of them were great loggers.

At one time, in one of the O'Brien Logging camps at Stillwater, B.C., I saw the following inscription on the wall beside my bunk. It was written in pencil in small print, and read:

Heil Hitler. Sieg Heil den Fuerer der deutschen Volkes. Tod das Jude! (Hail the leader of the German people. Death to the Jew!)

Above this writing was a swastika, underneath it was a neatly drawn hangman's noose and rope. However, there were many things wrong with the inscription, which started me thinking. First, the swastika was drawn in reverse; second, all three definite articles were wrong; and third, the word "Fuhrer" was spelled incorrectly. This particular slogan had been in vogue in Germany from 1933 to 1945, but whoever the man was who had inscribed his feelings on the wall had never gone to school in Germany, since the message was written in broken German, and every German knew how to draw a swastika correctly.

I often wondered who this man could have been, and what had made him feel so strongly the way he did? There was no date beside it, and the bunkhouse was as old as the hill it stood on. I never saw anything like it in a logging camp, either before or after. It had a definite stripe to it, and that was rare for loggers, who had few political inclinations. Indeed, most of them held politics in utter contempt.

One early, frosty November day, with the onset of the first new cold spell, Old Thom, my first mentor at Wakeman Sound, went down sick with flu and diarrhea. Too ill to get up for breakfast that morning, he remained in his bunk, except for the frequent times when he had to make the long, painful walk to the toilet outside. Once the other inmates of the bunkhouse had left for work, the fire in the wood heater died out and the room he was now alone in became cold.

Old Tompkins, the aged bullcook, had also left the hut to do his chores outside. Shortly before noon Old Tompkins came back into the chilly bunkhouse. There, Old Thom asked Old Tompkins to wheel in some fresh firewood and light the stove anew. But nothing of the sort occurred. The old bullcook just sat down at the edge of his bunk, stuffed his pipe with tobacco from the pouch of a former pig's bladder, and puffed away on the short, straight stem of his old, chewed-up pipe. Old Thom got up on his weak, unsteady legs, and tottered over to the old man. Since Old Tompkins was, or pretended to be, hard of hearing (he was at that time well past seventy years old), Old Thom had to shout to make himself understood.

"It's cold in here, aren't you going to make a fire in the stove?"

Old Tompkins just ignored him. With no kindling and no firewood, Old Thom could not fire up the stove himself, even had he the strength to do so.

"It's maddening," thought Old Thom, "to be sick, helpless, shivering from fever, and so far away from the nearest outhouse." His legs were getting weaker, and he needed his long-handled splitting axe to steady himself on his repeated walks to the outhouse.

Old Tompkins was a peculiar, venomous little old man, but for some unknown reason, Dan, the super, had a soft spot for him. Instead of retiring the walking skeleton, he let him hang on to his dustbin, broom and wheelbarrow. None of the loggers in camp knew what kind of work he had done in his younger days, before he became bullcook. One thing, however, was known to all men in camp, he only picked up his paycheques once a year, normally at Christmas time. Some of the men speculated that he must have quite a large savings account stashed away in some bank.

Terrible Ted often bugged the old bullcook about his savings. One rainy, freezing cold winter day, Terrible Ted walked into the bunkhouse, where Old Tompkins and several other fellows, including me, were standing around the glowing stove, talking and warming our hands. Terrible Ted was in one of his exalted moods, and he began to pester the old bullcook:

"How about you lettin' me have some of your surplus money, eh?"

With one gnarled hand, the old man removed his pipe from his toothless mouth, spat on top of the wood heater, watched the spit sizzle on the hot iron surface, and declared:

"If I'd give you one million dollars, within one year you'd be either broke or dead. Too much money is no good for you — this way you might live longer." Terrible Ted begged to differ, and recounted some of his finer escapades, which had only been made possible by the benefit of a bit of good jingle in his pocket.

We can only speculate what motivated Old Tompkins to go to Dan, the super, and accuse Old Thom of threatening to kill him with his splitting axe if he didn't light a fire in the stove. This was cause enough for Dan, who had absolutely no use for Old Thom anyway, and he fired him on the following day. Old Thom had to take the next boat to town, despite the fact that he had not yet recovered from his illness. As I later found out from Old Thom himself, in addition to being fired he was also blacklisted. Being blacklisted is the ultimate punishment a logger can receive: Old Thom could never land another job in the woods. At his age, and without other skills, he was finished, doomed to a life of poverty. Before Old Thom left camp for the last time, he uttered a prophecy.

"The super of this rotten camp," he told us, "will eventually find himself fired and looking for a new job. As for this camp, God will burn it down and it will revert into oblivion. And Old Tompkins will not live another year."

A few years later I bumped into Old Thom on the streets of Vancouver, where he was living a dreadful, hand-to-mouth existence. Remembering the kindness he'd shown me on my first day at camp, and the unfair way in which he had been reduced to his present, pitiful condition, I helped the old man re-establish himself in Sointula, on Malcolm Island off the B.C. coast, where he outlived all his former tormentors.

And indeed, his prophecies came true. That same winter, while on holidays in Vancouver, Old Tompkins was hit by a car and died on the street. In time Dan lost his job, and in time the camp burned to the ground. Everything came to pass as Old Thom had foretold.

A big Russian man in his early sixties replaced Old Thom in the wood yard. Some of the old timers in camp knew this man from before, and said that his name was Big Nose Joe, on account of his grotesque nose. It was a stroke of luck that Big Nose Joe got Old Thom's bunk, right next to mine. Despite the tremendous difference in our ages, Big Nose Joe and I hit it off right from the start. Both of us liked it quiet in our part of the room. In addition, neither of us smoked, drank, or snored at night, all of which habits could create tension, or even trouble at times.

Big Nose Joe had a mania for cleanliness. He even avoided going to the toilet in camp, out of fear that he might pick up a disease. Instead, he would walk into the woods adjoining the camp to perform his calls of nature. Another bizarre habit of his was the way he cropped the grey stubble on his large skull with a pair of clippers and the aid of two hand mirrors. To shave, he used a straight razor which he honed on a soft, wide belt. With his cropped grey stubble, misshapen nose and penetrating green eyes, his appearance was intimidating, and even frightful.

Big Nose Joe's joy was endless when I once asked him to give me a convict's haircut, too. While busily clipping away on my thick, dark hair, Big Nose Joe cited all the potential advantages of having such an unusual haircut. In fact, I already knew all about it, since I'd been having my head shorn every summer. The haircuts became a habit, a most amiable arrangement between the two of us for as long as we bunked together.

Fire! (Part One)

Every year fire is set in the slash, usually in the fall, to get rid of the debris for next year's reforestation and to help prevent fires in the future. The process is called "slash burn," and is required by the provincial forestry department. To seasoned loggers it is a nuisance, and even a danger. To begin with, a burn can very seldom be successfully controlled — the flames often expand beyond the containment area and cause very costly losses in timber value.

It hardly needs saying that to achieve the best possible burn the slash has to be dry. Obviously the slash would be driest during the summer, but no man in his right mind would intentionally start a forest fire at the peak of the dry season. The next best opportunity comes in the fall, when the longer, cooler nights are followed by heavy dew in the mornings, and the occasional day of rain.

To the men fighting an out-of-control fire, the greatest adversary they have to contend with is the wind. On the coast, clear fall days are usually accompanied by strong north-west winds which subside by sundown. Yet the most feared winds, and the ones which do the greatest damage by dispersing the fire far and wide in a very short period of time, are the gusty breezes coming from the north, blowing all day long and often through the night. Those are the winds that loggers dread most when fighting forest fires. Sparks that are blown into standing timber quickly develop into flames, especially in over-mature old growth stands of red cedar and fir. When a burn gets out of hand, all able men in camp are called upon to help control the blaze.

Such were the weather conditions at Wakeman Sound in 1953, on the day the skidder and cold decker got trapped behind a fire break — a strip of standing timber between a logged off portion and an area that has only been felled and bucked. A small crew of rigging men had set out with torches earlier in the day to light the slash. By noon, the early morning fog had lifted and a clear blue sky was overhead. Unfortunately, the north-west wind had started to pick up strength, blowing harder by the hour. Soon it was apparent that the fire would spread into the standing timber in the adjacent fire break.

Word was sent to the skidder and cold decker to get their crew off the hillside and down to the landing — they were urgently needed for fighting the fire which was already burning out of control lower down the valley. The fierce wind had fanned the flames into a hellish blaze, and carried hot live sparks up to the tops of the giant old trees. There the dry moss and lichen caught fire, setting the treetops aflame.

From that moment on it began to be hopeless; the flames started to "crown," spreading from treetop to treetop. The enormous heat generated its own hot wind, which, combined with the strong northwester, carried the flames farther and deeper through the forest, devouring acres of lush greenery. Whatever game was there fled from the inferno. So did the birds and other small ground animals that could move quickly enough to escape. Few of them succeeded.

Knots of men stood around looking helpless. Yet something had to be done immediately to contain the fast-spreading fire in order to save the company's setting of felled and bucked timber, along with the heavy rigging and equipment on the other side of the fire break.

Blondie had his skidder crew well trained in fire fighting, and wasted no time in getting them into action. It was a good thing that he insisted on having the fire-fighting equipment checked daily, including the fire pumps, which were started every morning to make sure they functioned correctly. Every key man, such as Romolo and James, knew what was required of him.

A fast-running stream in a nearby gully was tapped for water; two fire pumps were set up and hoses laid to the fire line. The main hose was about four inches wide. At its end a "Y" coupling fed two small two-inch hoses, onto which one-hundred foot extensions were added as required. At the end of each hose two men worked as a team. One hosed down the flames, the other dug up the ground with a mattock or polaski, turning over chunks of wood, rock or other debris, so the soil could be wetted down to prevent the ground fire from creeping into the main roots of old growth trees. (Keeping the fire from creeping into the tree roots is important for saving timber, but even more important for saving lives. Once the root system is extensively damaged, trees can come crashing down without warning, endangering fire-fighters or loggers nearby.)

The strain on the men was enormous, and the twelve-hour shifts, day and night, made each and every one of them dog tired. Lack of proper sleep and good fresh air had its own consequences. There were no warm meals, only cold sandwiches and fruit juice brought out from the camp. Breathing became more difficult because of the ever-thickening smoke. Only days before the whole watershed had hummed with activity: logging trucks grinding up the steep grades, the mighty roars of yarders, the shrill sounds of the whistle punks, all quiet now. The eerie silence spread its ghost-like wings over valley and mountains. Only the steady buzz of the high-pitched fire pumps could be heard. Smoke enveloped the entire area and beyond as far as the eyes could see. To the fire-fighters, the sun appeared through the smoke only as a hazy ball.

The two men at the end of each hose worked together, spelling each other off as the grueling work wore away at their bodies. It was a tough, grim job. Quite frequently, the heat became so intense that their clothes and hair were singed. Inevitably smoke was inhaled, causing coughing and burning lungs. Their logging boots were soon ruined from the hot ashes and smoldering coal. The skin on their hands began to crack from handling the wet hose, which had to be dragged over burned out areas and was consequently black with ash and soot. Furthermore, the constant chafing of the fire hose on their legs, especially on the upper part of their thighs, made them clammy and cold at night.

Only once the fire had been subdued were the men able to breathe fresh air again. As we looked around, all we could see were black, skeletal tree trunks, their foliage completely burned away. Now it was time for nature to begin anew. The first vegetation to spring up would be the beautiful fireweed; its seeds, resembling cotton balls, get carried by the wind over long distances, and their arrival each fall is like a foreshadowing of snow. Fireweed thrives in the ash-rich soil of a burned forest, but it isn't long before other seeds from various evergreens follow, and thus life in the forest slowly starts all over again.

For weeks whiffs of smoke could still be seen rising from the smoldering snags and windfalls. These were difficult to put out, because the windfalls burn from underneath, and the snags have hollow pockets, where the wind can fan hot coal into new flickering tongues of flame. The out-of-hand slash fire which raced through the wide and long fire break was stopped just short of the skidder setting where the crew was presently yarding. Saving the setting took a stupendous effort by all involved, under the skilful guidance of Blondie. The super, Dan, was greatly relieved to have the skidder setting, along with the cold decker, safe once again.

Only now was there time for rest, and time to begin the laborious process of cleaning one's body and clothes. Stain from the wet charcoal residue enters every pore of a firefighter's skin. Its dirty black colouring remains for days — no amount of washing with strong soap can make the skin come clean at one time.

Poker

As the weather grew colder the best poker season of the year began. No doubt the adverse weather conditions had something to do with the increased gambling activity. With the days getting shorter, and as we headed into the final stretch of the logging season, the men inevitably became restless, and sought and longed for diversions more than at any other time of the year. Whether an occasional diversion or a serious vice, poker revealed a great deal about the characters of many of the men I worked with in the woods.

Siegfried was one of the best players ever to take a seat in the poker shack, despite the fact that he looked and acted just like any other greenhorn sent up from Vancouver. In 1951, Siegfried was a young man, tall, good looking, with an unassuming appearance. In Germany he had been an electrical engineer, but here in Canada he could not find work in his profession. Hence, he ended up labouring in the woods as a chokerman. It was not unusual for such men to end up in a logging camp, especially during the period after the second World War. It was said amongst Europeans: Brains not required in Canada, only muscles.

"At the foot of the mountain," Siegfried told us "the ascent begins." For a fresh immigrant, Siegfried spoke English well. He had no intention of becoming a logger; it was only a way station.

On his first day in camp, the new chokerman rode with the rest of the crew in crummy No. 9 out to the jobsite. Blondie introduced the new man to his fellow workers on the skidder. No one paid any particular attention to Siegfried, except for Red, who felt that he had seen this stranger somewhere before.

Siegfried felt similarly. He searched his sharp mind for the time and place in question. In a flash, it all came back to him.

"Yes," he said to Red, "we have met once before."

"But where?" queried Red, who was still befogged.

"Have you ever been in the Canadian Army?" asked Siegfried.

Red's faint spark of recognition erupted into a brighter flame, as he remembered a blustery day almost a decade past, during the Allied invasion of France, when Canadian soldiers were engaged in fierce battles with the Germans. It was then that Siegfried, a young officer in the Luftwaffe, became a prisoner of war. And it was then that he and Red had faced each other for the first time. Now, years later, fate had brought them together again in a distant country, but this time in peace and friendship.

Long after Siegfried had left Wakeman Sound he was remembered by the men as the ever-smiling lad from the Luftwaffe. In particular, he was remembered as a brilliant poker player — in the eyes of loggers a very uncommon and desirable ability.

As the years went by I saw many poker players in many camps, but the poker shacks remained largely the same. Gamblers like Yukon Jack, Silky Bill and Rene the Rat were known in camps up and down the coast — from Alaska to the 49th parallel and even as far away as the Yukon — as the slickest poker players around.

Occasionally, one or the other of these semi-professionals (they all held jobs while in camp) would arrive and fleece the suckers of their hard-earned stakes. The arrival of any of these men, called card sharpers by some disgruntled suckers, did enough to stir up the poker zeal in camp to a feverish pitch. And although payday came only once a month in camp, it had an insignificant effect on the poker activity, since the money more or less constantly rotated and changed hands among the active players.

There were loggers like Ely, however, who could only afford to play on paydays. On those rare days, right after supper, he would pocket his paycheque and head for the poker shack. Ely and I lived in the same bunkhouse, and I observed how he invariably returned less than an hour later, very subdued. As usual, he had lost his entire earnings from the past month in one short fling.

One year at Christmas time he was so flat broke he was forced to sell off his only worthy possession, a Gladstone bag, in order to pay for the fare back to town. And that only fetched him enough money to travel steerage, just as I always did.

Ely talked forever about making a trip back home to Sweden, which he had left nearly forty years ago. Alas, owing to his monthly poker passion, the trip remained a dream. Ely had another bad habit. Whenever he could afford a bottle of rye whiskey, which happened, thank God, only rarely, he and his partner Ben, another Swede, would get drunk on Saturday evening. Late at night he would get up, open the door of the stove and urinate into it. If the stove seemed too far away, he would relieve himself in some conveniently placed logging boots — never, naturally, his own. Ben, his drinking companion, had the filthy habit of urinating behind the inside of the bunkhouse door. Being a light sleeper, I almost always woke up and yelled at them. They would stop in the middle of their act, but then hurl drunken abuses at me. When sober, however, both were tolerable men.

In 1959, it was Gerry the Wild Frenchman who looked after the old poker shack in Camp A in the Nimpkish Valley. Gerry could be found there evenings and weekends, functioning as the official croupier, holding the bank with its coloured chips. Besides being responsible as dealer, he took good care of all the small amenities traditional at poker games. Unofficially, he tended to the bootlegging business in camp, a very lucrative sideline for him. Gerry had a discreet arrangement with one floatplane pilot, who would deliver the goods whenever he flew into camp to pick up outbound loggers.

Born in Quebec, Gerry was brought up by nuns in an orphanage till he was expelled from it at the age of sixteen. An accomplished raconteur, Gerry often kept his listeners spellbound, with incredible stories of what he had seen and personally encountered in the foundlings' home. In light of what is known nowadays, his tales no longer seem so incredible, but back then they seemed far fetched, indeed.

At the orphanage, said Gerry, the older lads were engaged in the manufacture of pine coffins, which were then stored in the basement adjacent to the nuns' storage quarters. It was there that Gerry stumbled upon Father Domingo in an intimate position with one of the younger nuns. The two were lying on an upturned lid amongst a pile of new-built coffins. Gerry was only twelve-years-old at the time, but he realized very well what the priest and the nun were up to, and lost no time in blabbering it to the other boys in the orphanage.

In time, Mother Superior heard the story, and found out who was spreading it. For his youthful blunder, Mother Superior punished Gerry by withholding certain foods, like the weekly apple, and by restricting his outing privileges, which she substituted with hard labour in the convent's fields.

One of Gerry's most incredible stories concerned the finding of baby skeletons. The orphanage needed enlargement, and one spring day the excavation for the new basement commenced with pick, shovel and wheelbarrow. To the workers' great surprise they unearthed in ever increasing numbers shoe-box sized skeletons. The best plausible explanation the nuns gave for those bones was that the orphanage had been built on the former site of a cemetery for small children. This was credible, but not good enough for Gerry and the grown up lads, who put two and two together and arrived at a different conclusion.

Later, during a similar expansion, an even greater number of infant skeletons were unearthed at the adjoining convent for girls. Some of the girls, said Gerry, were runaways, or were considered "loose," and had been sent to stay with the nuns to keep them out of further trouble. It was not surprising that the nuns stuck to the same explanation. Gerry often used to conclude his tall, colourful yarns by saying:

"There were mighty strange things done under the Quebec sun."

Gerry's fondness for girls showed up early in his turbulent life. Flattery, combined with his natural cheerfulness, aided him greatly in his conquest of women. Around the age of sixteen he successfully seduced and conquered the heart of a young, innocent nun. The choice of spots to consummate their desire was very limited, and they ended up in the same place where he had encountered Father Domingo.

In order to meet Gerry, the nun claimed that she needed to go to the storage quarter. Unfortunately for Gerry, on one of these infrequent encounters the Mother Superior also happened to make a visit to the storage room, and happened to hear giggling behind a heap of boxes. Her curiosity aroused, she came upon the two snuggled up in an open coffin. At first, said Gerry, she was startled, then she flew into a rage.

The next day the Mother Superior had him called up into her study. At first she "sweet-talked" him and tried to make him feel comfortable. Gerry, not realizing what the old creature was leading up to, felt increasingly confused. Eventually, she asked Gerry to sit up on the edge of the table and unbutton his zipper, so she could "blow on Gabriel's horn," as Gerry delicately put it. He refused to let her have the object of her desire, because, in his words, she was as ugly as sin. The situation was cut short when Gerry threatened to tell the outside world. The Mother Superior retorted:

"You may go ahead and do so, but who will believe you?" And with these words she dismissed him from her room. In retrospect, Gerry strongly suspected that she was in the habit of doing it with other boys, all of whom were too afraid to admit what was taking place. Soon after this incident, Gerry was expelled from the orphanage. With hardly a glance backward, he shook the dust from his feet and headed West.

Only a few years later he was working in logging camps on the coast of B.C. With a combination of ability and hard work, Gerry gradually worked himself up to the demanding job of chaser on a skidder. He was very well liked by all, and was the ideal man to run the camp casino.

Previously the casino at Camp A had served as a bunkhouse. Now it was a run-down shack, located in the farthest corner of the camp. The large skids of the sled on which the building rested had been all but destroyed by the ever–present carpenter ants. To make things worse, the rear skid had settled down into the soft ground underneath, causing the floor to incline sharply. The three short steps leading up to the door, which swung askew on its hinges, were worn thin in the middle from constant use. Weather-worn red cedar boards comprised the outer walls, and a thick carpet of green moss spread over nearly the entire shake roof. Dust-covered windows with cobwebs and cracked panes gave the old shack a dismal appearance. Three large, round tables, formerly wire rope spools, now covered with wool blankets, filled the otherwise empty room. Grouped around each table were six rickety chairs. Several erstwhile tobacco cans served as ashtrays. And for the convenience of those who chewed snoose, old fruit cans from the cookhouse served as spittoons.

Suspended from the rafters hung low over each table was an electric light bulb with a wide, green shade around it. Not in anyone's memory had it ever been dusted off or cleaned. Behind the door, to the left, a potbellied stove kept the gamblers comfortably warm in the winter. At times, when the going was heavy and all the chairs around the tables were fully occupied by players, a pungent tobacco smoke rose up over the men's heads. The heavy smoke enveloped the green light shades and escaped outside under the ill-fitting roof. Silky Bill only smoked cigars, and they had to be Havanas — there was nothing cheap about Silky Bill. One could smell the smoke of his cigars downwind from the poker shack, where he often gambled into the wee hours of Sunday morning.

Predictably, the poker shack acted like a giant magnet for curious spectators, predominantly young ones. They came to watch those diverse poker faces while standing back somewhat, trying hard to get a glimpse of the cards, which were held close to the gamblers' chests.

When the stakes were high, tension would grip the onlookers. Some of them were too timid to consider participating, or were lacking the necessary funds. Others would join in with wantonness, unable to control the onset of gambling fever. The outcome in most cases was predictable. They left the poker shack flat broke and desperate.

The seasoned poker players in camp were no less superstitious than poker players anywhere else in the world. Take Scissor Bill, for example. Never would he have considered sitting down to a game of poker without his trusty old wide-brimmed felt hat on his head, regardless of how oppressively hot it was inside the poker shack. Nor would he sit on any other chair but the one he claimed to be his own. Each gambler had his own peculiar habits, and most were hopelessly devoted to all sorts of superstitions in their strong desire to woo the ever elusive luck.

The Coffee Queen

If one were to consider an imaginary dividing line at the age of forty years, then on either side of that line the proportion of young men to old in any given camp would have been approximately equal. Roughly seventy-five percent of us were either single, divorced, separated, or living in common law. The remaining twenty-five percent were married, which meant either living long periods of time away from home, or staying in the camp's married quarter. No doubt the unusual circumstances under which loggers had to live and work greatly favoured such an unnatural lifestyle.

By far the greatest majority of loggers lived in bunkhouses. Just the same, hardly a logging camp, regardless of its size, ever existed on the coast of B.C. without a married quarter. For obvious reasons, contact between the men in bunkhouses and the families in married quarters was held to an absolute minimum. I can only recall one instance, during the late 1950s, in which sporadic contact was maintained over years among the single men in camp, and a woman living alone in the married quarter.

The Coffee Queen's husband (if she had ever been actually married to him), had worked as a handyman out in the woods, and was the sort of fellow who could double for almost any job on the rigging — provided he was sober. One summer day he simply vanished from camp. No one had seen or noticed him leave; he must have taken the boat out. Many years later he was observed in one of the various beer saloons in Vancouver.

The woman he left behind was now stuck in camp. Fortunately, there were no children involved. Out of respect for the suffering and distress she now felt, the camp super agreed to let her remain in the small company cottage she occupied. She in turn was now faced with the prospect of making an honest living on her own.

Word spread that she would do washing, sewing and knitting for a nominal fee. At first the response was far from overwhelming, but gradually business picked up, as the men began to appreciate the meticulous service she provided to all who called on her.

With the onset of bad weather, she occasionally served her customers a cup of good, hot coffee. The loggers, who were mostly coffee-loving Swedes, would seldom turn down such hospitality. Affectionately, the men in the bunkhouses began to call her the "Coffee Queen."

A queen she may have been in her own right. Her looks and appearance, however, were something less than regal. She was a tall, skinny, flat-chested woman with long, raven black hair streaked with grey. She possessed large, dark eyes, set far apart, and her nose, which resembled the beak of a bald eagle, hung over a wide mouth with thin, narrow, pale lips. When she talked, one couldn't help but notice that her mouth was toothless, save for one long, discoloured, upper front tooth. From the wrinkles on her high forehead, and at the corners of her eyes, one could tell that she had borne more than her share of sorrow.

What made up for all the Coffee Queen's physical shortcomings was the mild, soothing tone of her rich voice. As men will, the loggers teased her with questions like:

"Sweetie, how about you going to bed with me?" Whereupon she would answer affably:

"Of course not. Every night I look under my bed before I go to sleep to see if there's not one of you guys hiding there."

"Well, did you ever have any luck?" asked Gerry the Wild Frenchman.

"Don't get cheeky," replied the Coffee Queen, "or else I might break your neck just like this!" And she would snap her strong fingers loudly. Loud laughter followed her funny demonstration of self defence.

Old timers in camp used to say:

"Once the Coffee Queen starts to be good lookin', then it's time for a man to go to town to see the bright lights." How true!

Gunderson

Then there was Gunderson. Of all the unfortunate loggers I've known over the years, Gunderson's plight was one of the saddest. He was a towering grey-haired Swede, beset by physical misfortunes. His upper torso swung noticeably when he walked, due to the accident which had taken half of his left foot. With his size twelve right foot he could roll from heel to toe, but on his left foot he hobbled along with only a size seven boot.

Whenever I saw Gunderson lugging the heavy end of the two-man power saw along a steep hillside, sweat streaming down his large, well-shaped head, I'd call out:

"How is she going with you, Gunderson?"

The old faller replied with a deep groan:

"It got to go."

On Sundays, when the weather was warm, Gunderson sat on a bench outside the bunkhouse, rolling smokes from a tobacco can. Often he would take off his well-worn shirt, exposing his upper body and powerful arms, all of which were liberally sprinkled with painful looking white blotches. His broad fingernails were also affected, and appeared to be deformed. When I asked Gunderson what his ailment was, he replied that he didn't know, that it came and went. He began to sob, and told me that he too had once been young and handsome, and he had loved to see the girls in town.

The words "girls" and "town" made me think about the fact that I had not been away from camp for the last eighteen months. It was the late '50s, and to be quite frank, I had come to dread the day that I would have to return to the city. The wake-eat-work-eat-sleep syndrome, whereby time was told by the ringing of the gut hammer, and not by standard or daylight saving time, clasped me with iron hoops. Engrossed in my work, my weekend chores, standing for hours with a hand plunger over a washtub doing my laundry or patching torn work clothes, time went by in a measured manner.

Animals

It was in early November, 1959, that three most unlikely species of wildlife co-existed in close proximity to Camp N's yard: a tame deer, a young cougar cub, and a black bear cub.

By this time I was working in the Nimpkish Valley for the Englewood Logging Division of Canadian Forest Products (Canfor). The Nimpkish Valley, carved out by the Nimpkish River, was at one time an important travel route for Indians crossing Vancouver Island from Alert Bay to Muchalat Inlet. Canfor began logging operations in the Nimpkish in 1944, beckoned by towering stands of Douglas fir, hemlock and cedar. It was here that I spent the majority of my years as a logger, moving between Camp A, Camp N, Vernon, Woss and Beaver Cove camps.

Several months earlier, in June, a gravel truck driver by the name of Floyd picked up a faun. The faun was probably only a few days old — it cowered beside the road, fearing the noise of the loud truck, which was roaring beneath the weight of a load of road ballast. Against the advice of everyone else on the road construction gang, Floyd brought the faun back with him to camp. He raised it by bottle feeding, and it soon began to follow everyone around.

The faun grew up among those shaggy camp dogs which no one wanted to claim. They raced down the camp road and back again in a playful manner. Whenever a dog became too rough, the faun defended itself by slapping the attacker with one of its front hooves. The dogs learned quickly, and refrained from further roughness.

The faun thrived on the plentiful feed around camp, and it grew in a short time to be a comely young deer. One day somebody dubbed it "Susie," and the name stuck to it for good. At suppertime, Susie fell into the habit of following the men into the dining room, making the rounds there between the large tables. It would eat anything that was handed to it or left unobserved.

One day when the men returned from work, one logger found the bunkhouse door open and Susie curled up in his bunk. Before going out to work that morning, he had rolled himself a few extra cigarettes for the day, then left the open tobacco can on his bunk. Susie had tipped the can over, and chewed up the spilled tobacco. Some of the men would not believe it when told, so another tin of tobacco was held out in front of the deer. Sure enough, Susie fed from the new container too. Despite her familiar ways, Susie remained everybody's pet. She was the cause of many mirthful moments in an otherwise banal camp life.

The next animal to appear on the scene was the cougar cub. On a rainy, dreary day, Les, a timber cruiser, and Glenn, a company engineer, were both bent over a cruising map in the survey office which faced on to a marshy slough. Les happened to glance out of the window and spotted a cougar with two cubs streaking by. One of the two men had the crazy idea of giving chase. Storming noisily out the door, they frightened one of the two cubs up a nearby sapling. The other one followed its mother, who disappeared into the salmonberry bushes. On the spur of the moment the two fellows decided to snare the cub, which had climbed up to the first high branch on the young tree.

Glenn ran back into the shack to fetch a rope. Having fashioned a loop on one end, they lassoed the scared cub and pulled it down onto the ground. More dragging than leading, they got the cub to the camp. A young fellow by the name of Lars, the camp's freight and supply truck driver, happened to be standing right there when they tramped onto the yard with the bewildered, unruly cub in tow.

"Where the hell did you get that young cougar?" Lars queried. "And now that you've got it, what are you planning to do with it?"

This, it turned out, was a question that Les and Glenn had failed to ask themselves before setting out on their adventure.

"Well," said Lars, "if you guys don't know what to do with it, I'll take it."

For the first several days, Lars kept the captured animal in a small crate behind his bunkhouse. Later on he built a cage for it out of green wooden bars. Sitting there on its haunches, staring into the void with its spirit broken, the cub was a heap of misery.

To obtain the meat for its first feed, Lars had to go to the cookhouse and haggle with the overworked and cranky head cook. From the following day on he fed the cub deer meat, which he hunted himself. Susie, relying on her natural instinct, gave the wooden cage a wide berth.

Lars certainly had lots of nerve, the way he handled the cub. After work he brought it inside the bunkhouse, leading it on a short leash. Gradually, he gave it more freedom to roam near his bunk. One evening he decided he was going to trim the cat's claws. Putting on a heavy mackinaw coat to protect his body, he clipped the sharp claws with a pair of pincers while holding the animal tight with his upper arm and elbow.

No one in the bunkhouse felt at ease around the cub, or had any faith in Lars' ability to domesticate it. The smell of it was something else to which everyone objected. So back out into the cage it had to go again.

Ultimately, the entire camp came into discord over the captured cougar cub. Most men wanted to see the poor creature freed. Some felt that it made a fine pet, while others were indifferent. Lars' objective was to take the cat home to his parents' farm on the prairie, as soon as the camp closed around mid-December.

Shortly after the arrival of the cougar cub in camp, a black bear cub came literally hobbling into Lars' bunkhouse. I stayed on the same row, only two bunkhouses away from Lars, and I happened to be sitting outside on that late, bleak Sunday afternoon. I watched in fascination as that black teddy bear ascended the three low steps to the bunkhouse door, which had been left ajar. The bear stood with its front paws on the top step and its hind legs one step lower. It remained there motionless for several seconds, before poking its head inside and sniffing around inquisitively.

Somebody within noticed the bear cub. By the time I arrived I heard one fellow say:

"It must be hungry."

"Well, let's feed it," said Uwe, and he fetched his big thermos of milk. Uwe filled a cup and set it down in front of the famished creature. The bear put its snout into the mug and lapped the milk up as fast Uwe could pour it. Being fond of bears, I went over to the cookhouse to get some honey and jam from the by-now thoroughly disgruntled head cook. The bear, having finished with milk, honey and jam, crawled under the steps of the bunkhouse and promptly went to sleep.

Dusk comes early to Camp N in November, and although most of the men in camp dropped by, it was already too late to see the new arrival. The following day, the bear ate a hearty breakfast in the form of handouts from delighted, good natured loggers.

During the daytime the bear stayed close to the bunkhouse, completely ignoring the nearby cougar. Thanks to the excellent and ample food it received daily, it soon grew rounder and became bouncier and full of mischief. One evening Uwe said:

"I believe we have to tie this little rascal up — otherwise there might be trouble further down the road." After work the next day Uwe walked to the machine shop to see his friend Vic, a charge hand, about a long, light, link chain. To go with it, he needed a collar, for which he had no choice but to sacrifice one of his own leather belts. Since it was already dark outside, Uwe had to postpone the collaring of the bear till the succeeding day, a Sunday. Someone asked Uwe how he planned to restrain the cub long enough to put the belt around its neck.

"No problem there," replied Uwe, who was a big fellow. Sure enough, next morning at feeding time, while one man offered the bear a flapjack smeared with golden honey, Uwe stood behind the cub and fastened the collar and chain around its neck. Amazingly, it did not seem to much mind the harness, which Uwe tied to the base of a power pole next to his bunkhouse.

As it turned out during the following week, this was the worst move Uwe could have made. Right from the outset, the bear started to dig around the base of the power pole, to build what resembled a hillock. The mound grew higher every day, and as the bear jostled the pole the electrical cables shook all through the camp. Then the cub began climbing the wall on the corner of the hut up to the shake roof and down again, wrecking the cedar siding.

Fog Horn Bill, the camp super, came by one day to see what was going on. He didn't like what he saw. Bill told Uwe that either the bear had to go, or Uwe himself would have to leave on the next boat. Uwe had no choice but to load the cub into the back of a pickup truck and drive it far away from camp. The cub was doomed — one couldn't expect it to fend for itself during the coming winter.

The fate of the cougar was not much better. Shortly before Christmas that year, Lars left camp with the cougar on the boat for town. While he was waiting in the city for the next train back east, he walked the cub on a leash down Vancouver's busy Granville Street. Understandably, he was an instant sensation. The next day, the Vancouver Sun newspaper ran a short column in its evening edition about the logger and his cougar.

The trip on the train to the prairie passed uneventfully, because the cub had to stay in the wooden crate that Lars had brought along from camp. Back home on his parents' farm, he became the talk of the nearby farm community. One by one the farmers and their families came by to view the mountain lion from far away British Columbia.

Lars, unfortunately, could not think of any better way to tie up the cub than to string a clothes line between two high posts, which allowed it to run back and forth on a long leash. Such a set-up works well with a dog, which cannot climb up the posts; the cougar, however, did climb a post, and somehow managed to strangle itself. This, at least, was the word that came back to camp next spring.

Susie, as one could reasonably expect, was able to get through the winter months on her own. She had been browsing solidly since the time she was found, and had developed into a stately deer. When the camp opened up again in the early spring of the next year, the loggers returned to their jobs, and many wondered what had happened to Susie. Then one day, several miles out of camp, the driver of a crummy spotted a lonesome deer standing beside the road, and stopped to get a better look at it. Others were peeping from the open rear end of the truck to see what the hold-up was, until one of them yelled:

"It's Susie!"

All the men leapt out and ran towards the deer. Everybody wanted to pet Susie, and they decided on the spot to bring her back to camp. With the eager help of many hands they hoisted her into the rear of the old crummy, right in the middle of the men, and off they drove back to camp. Susie's return was greeted with great rejoicing, and she remained in camp till late the following fall. After that, no one ever saw her again. Perhaps she eloped into the woods with a handsome lover of her own species.

One of the many encounters I had with wildlife was particularly unsettling. My falling partner, Ken, and I, had left the crummy nearly in darkness as we set out to fall right of way. We followed the trail along felled and bucked timber. Above us, to the left, was a ridge about 200 feet high, which had the shape of a half moon. To our right was a marshy thicket.

The sun was still just a distant glow on the horizon when we were stopped in our tracks by the eerie howling of a nearby wolf. Another one howled from the far end of the ridge. Then several other wolves joined in — we were surrounded. Words cannot adequately describe the feeling one gets from being so close to the howling of a pack of wolves.

I had seen and heard many a timber wolf, but never so close up. In an effort to scare the wolves away, Ken banged a spare saw blade flat-side down on top of a stump. The wolves stopped howling. With some trepidation we continued onto the jobsite. We didn't realize yet that we had interrupted a hunt — the wolves had been closing in on a lonesome elk in the marshy thicket. The elk, by nature a shy and solitary creature, followed us to the job site and stayed in proximity all day. By the time we made our way back to camp the wolves had disappeared.

Axel the Scandihoovian

Like the dwindling virgin timber, so did my early falling partners depart. With few exceptions they had all been old enough to be my father, and I had excellent rapport with the vast majority of them. There was one man, however, who stands out vividly in my memory.

Axel the Scandihoovian was six years old when he came with his parents from Norway to Canada, and then to the coast of British Columbia. Axel was possessed of a remarkable intelligence, and he was fond of reading and reciting poetry. He could recite by heart all of the poems of Robert Service, the "poet of the Yukon." His favourites were "The Shooting of Dan McGrew" and "The Cremation of Sam McGee." While reciting Service his face would light up with a broad smile one could see a mile away.

Axel had a great love for the woods, which made him an almost unique head faller. While plumbing a tree with his falling axe he would hum as he deftly twisted the long handle to determine the lean of a tree. He had the uncanny habit of talking to a tree before cutting it down. He would tell a red cedar, for instance:

"Your wood is needed to shake a roof on a poor man's hut."

Even-tempered, and full of compassion for life in the forest, he was the ideal man for me to work with. I will never forget the day we found an entire raccoon family peeping anxiously down at us from the trunk of a large red cedar.

"Well," said Axel, "we'll have to give them time to evacuate their home." On the following morning the raccoons had departed, and Axel wore a smile.

Unfortunately, in the early 1960s, a tragic accident marred

Axel's career in the woods. Axel and Bjorn, the machine man, were doing the back cut on a tall yellow cedar tree which had quite a lean forward. Just at the most critical moment, when they should have continued sawing, that monster of a power-saw stalled on them. From the distance of three tree lengths away, I watched as the tree began to barber-chair. Bjorn, unable to get into the clear fast enough, was crushed by the splitting trunk of the tree. Axel tripped and dropped into a hole, which saved his life. Years later, worn-out and aged beyond his years, Axel succumbed to lung cancer.

Sadly, not all my partners were as agreeable as Axel the Scandihoovian. Some twenty years after Bjorn's death, I had the misfortune of teaming up with Packrat George. Packrat George was a raggedy looking man in his late fifties, with a nose shaped like the beak of a hawk.

In contrast to Axel, the utterly unreliable Packrat George was probably the worst falling partner I ever had. On one occasion he nearly snuffed out my candle, by dropping a tree over me while I was fuelling up my power-saw. I had just enough time to stand up and duck behind a large, red cedar, but I left my power saw behind, and it was crushed by the oncoming tree.

Stormy Weather

Nothing compares with the destructive force of the weather. Its challenge, especially out in the wilderness, is constant. Of all the fierce storms that batter the B.C. coast every year, every logger has one storm that stands out in his memory.

One such unforgettable tempest had a very subtle beginning in the early part of November, 1972. A high pressure system had been hovering over the remote parts of the B.C. coast, including the Nimpkish Valley, bringing with it a period of gentle weather. Soon, however, our halcyon days were pushed out by a low pressure system that moved in from the Pacific, bringing gale force winds and heavy rain.

The experienced loggers at Atluck Camp knew that a storm was approaching when the seagulls were observed flying inland to seek shelter. (Normally, this phenomenon occurs a whole day ahead of the storm front.) Next, the north-westerly wind became weaker, and ended in a lull. The short-lived calm was soon followed by a brisk wind blowing in from the south-east. Puffs of clouds began to spring up in the still fair sky, with more drifting in from the south over the imposing mountaintops. In apprehension, we braced ourselves mentally for the approaching storm.

On the following morning the eastern sky had an angry, dark red tinge to it. On our way to work that morning, several loggers trotted out the old adage:

"Red sky in the morning, sailor take warning."

Daylight was slow in coming, owing to the increasingly oppressive overcast. The sun could hardly be seen through the ponderous, dark clouds hanging over the horizon. Many of the workers had misgivings about the day ahead of them. Nevertheless, all crews proceeded on to their work-sites.

By starting time at 8:00 a.m., it was still semi-dark. Rigging men, fallers, as well as others, trudged through the gloom to their respective jobs. Gradually, the south-east wind increased, and men began to take notice of the mild air it was carrying along with it. Large, heavy, isolated raindrops began to fall. Men who were not already wearing their bone-dries were donning them now.

Old Fogie, the hooktender on a high lead show, was cursing at everything that morning. Nothing seemed to please him — nothing was going right. Of course, the bad weather was of no concern to him. He had outlasted countless gales in his many years of working on the rigging. Indeed, he had the appearance of a weather-beaten, gnarly old snag. Old Fogie was wont to tell the younger men:

"If it blows from the south-east, then it's not fit for man or beast — save for logger."

Slowly, the blustery wind brought driving rain along with it. In a short time, it was blowing up a gale. Saplings left standing by the fallers (because they were too small to be worth falling) were leaning over at a precarious angle; ones that were poorly rooted were being blown over by the increasingly strong gusts.

Weeping Willy, a rigging slinger on the haywire show, had one green chokerman under his care that day. Willy could sense that the lad was becoming rattled by the fearfully howling wind — it had even knocked him over while he was walking on a log. Near noon, Weeping Willy and his chokermen set chokers on two logs. Both logs in the turn were boom sticks, each sixty-seven feet long. After the chokers were set, the rigging slinger, followed by the two chokermen, positioned themselves approximately sixty feet uphill, to the side and at a right angle to the butt rigging. The rigging slinger then let the whistle punk blow "go ahead."

As the turn started into the landing, one of the logs jill-poked into a stump and swung sideways. Weeping Willy saw the log coming, and yelled to the chokermen to get further into the clear. As Willy turned to get out of the way, he tripped and fell into a hole, a happy accident that saved his life.

Ib, the alert whistle punk, had seen what was going to happen, and had taken it upon himself to stop the turn. In his estimation, neither the rigging slinger nor the chokermen were sufficiently in the clear, and he pushed the button for one short whistle: stop all lines! Unfortunately, the reaction of the otherwise wary donkey puncher was a split second too slow. He watched in horror as one of the long logs struck both chokermen down. Promptly, he blew the signal for an accident: seven long whistles. The bellowing wind and rain muffled the conversely shrill sound of the whistle atop the yarder.

Immediately, all activity in the landing ceased. Old Fogie, who at that moment was sizing up a new guy line stump, looked uphill apprehensively as he heard the dreaded seven long whistles. Wasting no time, he lumbered uphill as fast as his old legs would carry him. The chaser and others from the landing crew followed Old Fogie up the steep slope. The going was tough. Wind and rain forced them to stoop forward at an awkward angle. Grasping with both hands for roots or whatever there was to help pull them up, they struggled to the scene of the accident.

Weeping Willy had fallen headlong into a deep sinkhole. All he could recall was hearing a swatting thump behind him as the upended log slammed into the dirt, spraying him with muck. His foremost thought was:

"Are the chokermen all right?" But something within told him to be prepared for the worst.

Once on his feet again he found that his legs were wobbling. In addition, his hat was missing. With great difficulty he climbed out of the sinkhole, not bothering to look for his lost headgear. Only then did he become aware of the muffled accident whistle, and the feeling in his gut became a certainty. He could hardly make himself face those two hapless bodies lying on the ground in front of him. The wind had become even gustier. Willy steadied himself on a nearby sapling and began to weep bitterly, as the heavy rain washed the blood that was flowing from the mouths and noses of the fallen chokermen into the ground. Willy bitterly reproached himself for having failed to lead his crew far enough into the clear, a gross neglect which would hound him for the rest of his life.

Old Fogie rounded a rock bluff and came head on into the misery. Others came close behind him.

"Christ," yelled Fogie out loud, "why of all the hooktenders on this wide claim did I have to be the one to whom this happened?" A wet glimmer showed in his clear, blue eyes, and from the tip of his sharp, pike-like nose the rainwater ran in rivulets onto his grey-bearded chin. His heavily calloused hands trembled slightly as he lamented to the shaken men around him.

"It's a bugger when one preaches to them year round to get into the clear before blowing the go ahead. And to stay out of the bight all the times." Ron, the chaser, detached himself from the scene, and went back down to the yarder to get stretchers, and additional men for help.

Lunchtime passed but nobody felt like eating. The sky was getting even uglier, and neither wind nor rain was abating. Everyone was drenched, but the bodies had to be brought down from the hillside, no matter what.

Weeping Willy left camp, together with the mortal remains of the two chokermen, on the next boat out to town. For his failure to accept and carry out his responsibilities he had been fired. Personally, he showed no desire to stay on in the camp, nor had he any intention of working this part of the coast again.

On the same day that the fatalities occurred on Old Fogie's haywire show, a mudslide had blocked the main logging road, and a bulldozer and swamper were dispatched to the location. While en route, in the midst of a shrieking gale, the bulldozer operator had to drive his machine through a firebreak. As he neared the end of the firebreak, a large hemlock tree came crashing down from the upper side of the road bank. Its immense trunk fell right over the cab, killing the driver and pinning the bulldozer to the ground. What made this fatal accident so tragic was the fact that it could very well have been avoided.

During the previous spring, my falling partner, Art, and I, had felled the right of way through this particular, moderately steep firebreak. What had caught my eye at the time were the exposed patches of black slate rock. I reasoned that the soil in this area was shallow, and that the large trees that grew there could not be well rooted. I mentioned my concerns to Dribble, my bullbucker, and suggested that we fall all the timber far enough back so as not to endanger the road below, especially since this was going to be a main truck-hauling road.

In my opinion, if ever there was a deadhead of a bullbucker, then Dribble was the one. Dribble (so-called because he let saliva dribble from the corners of his mouth) put too much stock in his own, exalted position, and resented all and any suggestions from a faller. Predictably, Dribble gave me his standard reply:

"Management makes the decisions around here, and if you don't like it, you can fuck off or go to hell, whichever suits you."

Once the right of way left the firebreak, it led into a very steep mountain slope, where Art and I had to fall the tightest switchbacks we had ever felled before, over a mile up the mountain side.

I could see potential problems here, as well. What I wanted to do was fall all the timber inside the hairpin curves of the switchbacks, not just the standard, seventy-foot wide right of way. There were several good reasons for this. First, it would have facilitated the job immensely later on when the settings were going to be felled — the amount saved in broken and shattered timber would have been enormous.

Further, I could tell by the heavy lean of the trees that they were exposed to the strong, prevailing south-easterly winds, and I reasoned that the trees had a very good chance of being blown over, especially once an opening such as the right of way had been cut. Again, I mentioned my thinking to Dribble, who once again told me to mind my own job.

Work on the steep grade started during the late summer. Whenever the power shovel hit rock, which was quite frequently, the compression drill moved forward to drill and blast the rock out of the way. Now, working in the rain and high winds of the November storm, the power shovel and compression drill were nearing the end of the last switchback. Every so often the workers could hear a tree crash nearby. Branches were being ripped off, and came flying down the grade. Finally the shovel operator suggested to the driller and his helper that it was time to get out of there. All three men agreed and left for camp. On their way down they found the road blocked by fallen trees in the firebreak, and the crushed bulldozer operator. Struggling under and over the downed trees, they continued back to camp.

Days later they came back to find all the switchbacks blown over with trees. Once the windfalls had been bucked up into logs and the grade cleared, they were able to return to their equipment. A large, heavy fir snag had toppled uphill and landed square across the compression drill, demolishing it completely. A broken treetop had crushed the roof of the operator's cab on the power shovel. Those two operators, and their helper, were truly glad they had left when they did.

The whole upper side, and part of the lower side of the right of way through the firebreak had blown over during that storm. Entire root wads from the windfalls had simply peeled off the slate rock, exactly as I had foreseen. As far as I was concerned, Dribble had the dead bulldozer driver on his miserable conscience.

For the fallers and buckers, the day was a washout. Most never left the roadside, realizing that it would be useless to work against the weather. Even those fallers whose work-site was sheltered from the wind had to give up once it began to gust. They left the woods and started to drive back to camp, hoping to get under a dry roof. On their way in they were stopped by Andy the Cull, a side push.

He badly needed one faller or bucker, it didn't matter who, to buck out two trapped, loaded logging trucks, which had been hemmed in by downed trees. Both trucks had been driving through a greenbelt when one mighty gust sent trees crashing down in front of and behind them, forcing them to a halt.

None of the fallers or buckers on that crummy volunteered, so Andy the Cull commandeered me for the unpleasant and dangerous job. Andy and I had a mutual dislike for each other. Andy used to be a rigging slinger (and a poor one at that), before he got his job as a side push. Andy hailed from somewhere back east in Canada, but was of Scottish descent, a fact that he was notably proud of, especially when drunk.

Andy loved to talk, but he spoke with an unmistakable lisp, perhaps a result of his misaligned mouse teeth. What characterized him above all was his infinite urge for self-importance. On, as well as off the job, he acted in the same absurd manner as was depicted in the "Otto Knows Better" safety posters one saw at that time in logging camps on the coast.

Once, an old timer was spooling line on a yarder when Andy came up on him from behind.

"No, no," he hollered to the old rigging hand, "that's not the way to do it."

"Sonny," said the old rigging man to a suddenly sheepish looking Andy, "I've been spooling lines since before you ever gave your first yeller. So why don't you go behind a stump, sit down and jack off."

Since his arrival on the B.C. coast, Andy had done many kinds of work in the woods. It has to be said that he had not excelled at anything he did. Luckily for him, he met a supervisor whose thirst for rye whiskey Andy could quench. In return, he was given the lucrative job as a side push.

Having always been something of a loner, I was used to being disliked by men like Andy the Cull. One Sunday afternoon I was walking past the bunkhouse where Andy and several of his pals were drinking. Andy spotted me and immediately started in with a series of childish taunts. Encouraged by his drinking cronies, Andy insisted that I come and twist wrists with him.

"All right," I agreed, although what I really wanted to do was push Andy's ugly face in. "Let's see what you can do." We flopped down with our bellies to the floor. Andy was a short fellow, nearly as wide as he was tall. With his thick bow-legs, he did not walk, but waddled along in short strides, his arms swinging wildly alongside his body. A full, reddish-blond beard graced his visage, and his meaty nose resembled a round potato.

Andy showed a large, fleshy hand with tobacco-stained fingers, almost a paw, which I grasped with my own lean, work-hardened hands. Gradually, I put pressure on my opponent's wrist and forced it down. An embarrassed silence set in from the side of his boisterous drinking pals.

"You're not really much good at anything," I said, and with these brief words I got up and walked out the door. Andy never forgave me for the humiliation he received in the presence of his buddies. This then was the man who required me to do the job of cutting through windfalls in that gale.

I climbed down from the crummy, which left in great haste for camp. Andy supplied me with the necessary tools from his pickup truck, and I promptly went to work. To say it was wild would be an understatement, indeed, the storm had become devastating. All around me the treetops were dancing and circling in wide, angry sweeps. I was wondering how far they could bend before toppling over or snapping off in the middle. Every so often, a tree did come down close by. Both drivers crouched under their loaded trucks, convinced that this was the safest place around. Andy waddled around, shouting orders which everyone ignored. Undaunted, I kept cutting the downed trees as fast and as skillfully as I knew how. Andy the Cull was determined to get those loaded logging trucks out into the clear.

The moment a windfall was cut up into logs, the driver of the first truck climbed back into his cab and drove forward, pushing the logs aside with his big, steel front bumpers. Sometimes he used the weighty left or the right front wheels to push a log out of the way. Step by step, and with lots of luck, they made it safely out into the open slash. Both logging truck drivers let out a sigh of relief for having escaped alive from that witches' cauldron. For me, it had been one of the most demanding hours I'd ever spent on the job. The constant mental and physical pressure had taxed me to the utmost.

Weatherwise, things appeared to be getting worse. The velocity of the wind was increasing steadily. By the time I got back to camp, it was already dusk. Only then did I realize that I hadn't eaten any lunch that day.

Overhearing several men talking in the washroom late that afternoon, I found out about the toll that shocking day had taken on lives. It was my belief that all three fatalities could have been avoided, despite the bad weather. However, one fact must be restated again: loggers do not function nearly as well when they are cold and wet as when they are warm and dry. Wet, uncomfortable workers are more likely to have accidents, and are less able to scramble out of the way of danger. A dangerous sense of complacency tends to set in, and a man becomes reluctant to go that extra step for the sake of safety.

That evening, the entire camp was eerily hushed. A shrieking gale blew over the area and kept the men inside their huts. Most men went to bed early that night, each following his own train of thoughts. I lay awake, curled up in my bunk with my knees nearly up to my chest, which helped to relax my tired back muscles. Sleep that night did not want to come. My thoughts revolved continually around the same subject: The difficulty of getting men to think, reason, and act safely.

It had been as plain and clear as daylight that the trees at the upper edge of the road bank would blow over with the next windstorm. I wondered how Dribble felt when he heard the news of the bulldozer operator's death. Could it be possible that he was so indifferent, so detached, that it might not have bothered him in the least? Unfortunately, yes. It seemed quite possible. Outside, the storm was growing wicked.

Ever mindful about the wildlife, I couldn't help but wonder where the wild game retreat to in such bad weather. Do they know how to find the leeward side of the mountains? And with so many animals on the move, do the timber wolves come hunting?

In the not too far distance I could hear trees being downed by the high winds, and loud, splintering and snapping noises as entire treetops were ripped off. The wind blew so hard that it made the whole bunkhouse shake; the long stove-pipes from the chimney rattled ominously between the creaky roof rafters, the drumming rain sounded on the windowpanes like legion knocking fingers. With every fresh gust of wind the shake roof received a ferocious pelting.

Eventually, I drifted into a slumber. Then, sometime past midnight, I was awakened by a bone-chilling scream coming from the far end of the room, where a new inmate was having a really bad nightmare. Everybody woke up, and I heard one man tell another:

"It sounded like the squeal of a stuck pig — it sent a cold shiver down my spine."

"What next?" I wondered, curling up anew and pulling the cover over my head. And who could look forward to the next day after such a turbulent night? Nobody, really.

All early logging camps had one evil thing in common; if a man had to go to the toilet, he had to walk a fair distance to get there. Consequently, it was the prevalent habit at night to urinate outside the bunkhouses. In stormy weather like this, even such a deplorable

102

convenience was hampered. A man had to dress sufficiently before stepping outside into the howling wind, the driving rain, or the drifting snow, any of which could quickly shock a man wide awake.

Naturally, this was too much for some "sunshine" loggers. Such fellows solved the problem by standing in the doorway and letting go at random. Even so, there were obstacles. If the bunkhouse door faced into the wind then it was a trial just to stand on the threshold. To put it bluntly, most of the men just opened the door a crack and relieved themselves through it. Such habits did not pose problems on float camps, but the camps I worked in suffered from a noticable smell in hot weather.

For some men, the agony of the next day commenced even before they got out of bed. Such fellows had an extraordinarily hard time getting up in the morning, and were predictably late for everything else. Most of the older men were wont to rise early, but were frequently plagued by various afflictions. One might have a sore back, another suffered from recurring rheumatism, yet another might be nursing an axe wound. Hardly anybody was trouble free. A flask of "woodsman's liniment" was a common sight in the hands of an ailing logger, as he sat on his bunk rubbing parts of his aching body.

To dress for work every morning in such physical shape was arduous, almost like preparing for combat. And in a sense it was a constant battle with the elements, day after day, year round.

What I dreaded the most on such stormy mornings was putting on clothes that had not dried out sufficiently from the previous day. If one hung one's dripping clothes too near the red hot stove, they got singed. Too far away, and damp spots would be left around the shoulders, under the armpits or on the cuffs of the shirts. Naturally, all the good places around the stove were taken by the first one back after work. The most difficult things to get dry were woolen socks, and the vital logging boots were more or less constantly moist inside. To overcome the bothering clamminess inside the boots, it was helpful to wear two pairs of woolen socks, but few did.

As it turned out, the wind slowed down towards morning. By marshalling time it was calm enough that the fallers were able to drive out to their falling areas. Half of the large falling crew was needed that day to buck the windfalls which blocked the roads into logs. Strange as it may seem, the heavy rain had not abated, and showed no signs of letting up. Looking at the mess the windstorm had left behind in the preceding twenty-four hours, many a logger felt he was lucky to still be alive. Doubtless, those logging camps located along the surf-pounded headlands had absorbed the real brunt of the low pressure system which had moved in from the Pacific.

I was among the fallers who were able to go back to falling timber that morning. We were working in one of the steep valleys where timbered slopes reach far up the mountains, to heights where the sun reaches only briefly, or not at all on clear winter days. Little could be seen of the surrounding pinnacles, most of which were shrouded in dense rain clouds. The snow which had already fallen on higher elevations was now melting in the warm, Hawaiian rain. The combination of torrential rain and melting snow was causing the creeks to swell out of their ordinary channels.

Men were getting concerned. There was no way to shield yourself against such a steady downpour, and long before noon there wasn't a logger in the woods whose clothes were not drenched. The excessive weight of wet work clothes made any job in the woods that much more strenuous.

To get a lunch fire burning under such dire conditions was a trying job in itself. With the help of my two falling partners, I built a small fire several feet away from the base of a large, leaning, red cedar tree. Its inclined trunk served as a roof under which we devoured our lunches. Whenever one stepped away from the tree trunk, large drops of water made themselves felt, leaking down from a high canopy of thick branches. It paid to be careful when you looked up, or one of those heavy raindrops might hit you in the eye, and the sting would blur your vision for a time.

"What could be worse than this?" asked Art, hunching his wet shoulders, gazing fixedly into the flickering fire.

"Not much," we all agreed.

"You fellows know very well that life in the woods is a continuous struggle," replied Oscar, while taking a pinch of snoose from a soggy box with his big, strong fingers. "So, we might as well get back to work and slave away again for several more long, dreary hours."

One after the other, we stepped out from under the protecting tree and into the pouring rain. Scarcely anything was still burning from the sparse lunch fire. Almost all of it had been extinguished by the steady rain, long before we returned to our tools.

Around two o'clock in the afternoon, a scaler called Buttlog (named for his singular habit of scaling only the butt log of a tree, and estimating the rest) came hurriedly up from the road below, to call all the fallers and buckers off the hill. By this time, rushing water from the heavy rain and melting snow was raging down the creeks. It had spilled over the rocky banks, flooding the logging road alongside. One could hear from afar the mighty roar of gushing water and tumbling rocks, as huge boulders were swept down the steep creek beds. Of course, it took a little while until we were all off the hill, ready to drive back to camp.

We climbed into two crummies and set off, one behind the other, the first one driven by Buttlog, the second one driven by me. As far as the eye could see, the road ahead was already under foaming water. Soon Buttlog's crummy found itself in deep water, and not long after that, the engine stalled.

"What now?" clamoured the irritable men. Dirty brown water was rising up through the floor of the crummy at an alarming rate. In the driver's cab, Buttlog and his fellow scaler, Crazy Otto (so called because he loved the Crazy Otto records which one heard on the radio during that time), raised their already soaked feet onto the dashboard. For the time being, the men in the rear were safe.

I had held back cautiously before following Buttlog into the unknown, which turned out to be good planning. The water that was stalling Buttlog's crummy had started out only knee deep, but had now risen up to the wooden floor and spilled into the wide open rear, where the men were sitting on three long, narrow benches. Although already soaked to the skin, the men had no desire to take a chilly foot bath, and were standing on the wooden-planked benches waiting to see what would happen next.

As I stared through the rain I spotted a lonesome beaver cruising forlornly between the two crummies. It appeared confused, zigzagging back and forth along the torrent, but later drifted off into calmer water.

Meanwhile, several miles ahead of us on the road to camp, Burly, a bulldozer operator, was busy shoring up the road. Nels, the construction foreman, happened to come along to see how big the washout was. In passing, Burly mentioned to the foreman that the fallers had not come through yet.

"By gad," said Nels, "I'd better drive in and find out if the road is passable." Soon he knew why the fallers had been delayed. In front of him, the road and slash had turned into a large pond about half a mile long. Towards the far end, two unmoving specks were discernable.

"Must be the fallers all right," thought Nels, and he drove back to tell Burly to get them out of there.

In the meantime, the water rose steadily, so that those standing on the benches were ankle deep in the frigid, silty, gurgling snow water. No one was spared. All kinds of suggestions were offered but none of them made any real sense. Then someone spotted Nels' pickup truck, and we knew that help would soon be on its way.

The men realized that only a bulldozer could pull them out of their predicament, and soon Burly came driving backwards towards us in order to get the cable of the winch hooked up with the front bumper of the lead crummy. Since the water already reached above the top of the engine hood, the question had to be asked: Who would do the hook up?

The men were stiff with cold, and hesitant to come forward voluntarily. They glanced sideways at each other to see whether anyone was willing to risk hypothermia, knowing that the camp, a warm room and dry clothes, were still hours away.

Finally Ivan The Big Eater spoke up:

"Isn't going to be much wetter than what I am already."

He asked the men to hoist him onto the roof of the crummy. From there he climbed down onto the hood. Burly handed him a chain, and Ivan dropped down between bulldozer and truck to fasten it around the bumper. In order to do so, he had to submerge himself completely, and since he could see little underwater in the fading daylight, he had to work entirely by the feel of his hands.

Holding the chain in one hand, Ivan pulled the cable with its heavy hook and finally connected it to the bumper. With the help of Burly, he struggled up to the bulldozer, into which water was gushing from all sides. Ivan was a pitiable sight as he held on to the rusty steel frame of the cab's roof with his numb hands, the bulldozer rumbling full speed ahead. Once they were out of the clutches of the roaring creek, and all the water had drained out of the crummy, Buttlog undid the chain so that Burly could drive back to drag the other vehicle onto dry ground. Unfortunately, the water had now engulfed the other crummy as well, so Ivan stayed on with the bulldozer to perform his brave feat a second time.

Nels and Dribble, in the meantime, had rounded up a pair of crummies and drivers from camp, and had persuaded them to drive out and pick up the grounded fallers. All this took precious time. For each of the wet, shivering fallers it seemed to take forever. Some longed for a pinch of snoose or a smoke, but everything they had with them was soaked. Others, including me, just thought of getting rid of their wet clothes as fast as possible.

At about 6:00 p.m. the two crummies trundled into the silent, ill-lit camp yard, and the men hastened to their huts through the streaming rain. I stripped beside the stove, in which a roaring fire was burning, and hung my dripping clothes on the rafters near the wood heater. That evening at the supper-table, anyone with a grudge against Ivan the Big Eater had forgotten it — he had truly saved the wretched day.

Only after a day like the past one is a warm room fully appreciated. I lay awake in my bunk, lost in a myriad of thoughts. The downpour had still not ceased. As on the previous night, I listened to the drumming of the rain against the windowpanes and wondered what the new day would have in store. Would there be any change in the awful weather? Or was the worst yet to come?

At times, weather like that makes young and old alike feel dejected. I rolled over onto my side, closed my eyes, pulled the flimsy cover over my head to shut out the real world around me. With any luck, tomorrow might be better.

Unfortunately for all, the new day was just as bad as the past one had been. There were no signs anywhere of improvement. In apathy the men dressed for the day's drudgery in the woods. Breakfast was eaten faster and in greater silence than usual. It seemed as though everyone wanted to get the day over with as swiftly as possible.

One by one, loaded with downcast loggers, the crummies pulled out of the marshalling yard for their respective destinations. Yesterday's falling area was now inaccessible, and I, together with other fallers, had been designated to a different location. The road we took led along the shoulder of a very steep and rocky mountain slope. Where there were ditches, they were clogged by minor mudslides. Culverts were plugged by smaller logging debris, and rocks of all sizes littered the road. White, foaming water gushed out of every gully, or came cascading down the slopes and the sheer rock walls. Some of the rocks lying on the road were too heavy and too large to be removed by hand, and I was forced to manoeuvre around them as well as I could. Rounding a rock cliff at low speed, I came face to face with a house-high rockslide. Art, sitting beside me, swore that he had heard a rumble just before we arrived there, and some of the lighter stuff from the slide was still in motion.

I shut the engine off, and so did the two crummies behind me. One after another, men came to see what the hold-up was.

"Well, well, what do you know about that?" said Buttlog to the bewildered fallers. Crazy Otto climbed up the slide to see how extensive it was.

"It must be a good seventy to one hundred feet wide," he yelled down to us, "and who knows how long. There are boulders half the size of a bunkhouse."

At long last I ventured the unthinkable thought: what would have happened to us had we arrived here just a little bit earlier? Would anyone of us have made it through alive?

There was nothing else we could do but return to camp. The day was shot. Coming down the main hauling road, we met a crummy and two empty logging trucks also heading back to camp.

"What's your problem?" Buttlog asked the other drivers.

"Further up," they reported, "the main Cluny river has risen fourteen feet overnight, and the road is all under water. Fine thing, eh?" And with a string of maledictions we all drove in the direction of camp.

The road to camp passed over the long bridge of the main river. Oscar, the super, and his pile-driver foreman Charlie, were standing at one end of the approach to the bridge. They were looking intently into the boiling river below. To prevent the pilings of the bridge from being damaged or knocked out in high water, a steel cable supporting several boom logs had been strung from bank to bank. The idea was that the logs would catch and snare anything that came floating downriver in high water. Mostly what caught on the boom logs were uprooted trees or other logging debris that washed off the hillsides, and the system worked well up to a certain point. However, in this extremity the water level had risen too high, and the dammed-up debris was threatening the sixty-foot long center span of the timber bridge.

"Something has to be done quickly or we'll lose the bridge for sure," Charlie pointed out to Oscar.

"If someone cut the steel cable loose, the whole mess would still wash out under the decking of the bridge," declared Oscar firmly. "Where can we find a man with the strength and skill to do that?" he asked Charlie.

"Look behind you," replied Charlie, "there's part of your logging crew driving back to camp already."

Oscar walked up to the trucks, where the crews reported their troubles.

"Christ Almighty," he screamed out loud, "is everything falling in on me? God-damned weather! Before you guys drive away, I need one man with a helluva good axe to chop the cable which is holding the bag boom back. Otherwise, we'll lose the bridge."

"Take your pick from this keen bunch of fallers," retorted Buttlog. Oscar walked around to the rear of the fallers' crummy. He addressed us in his deep voice, with a deadly serious expression on his dour face:

"Can one of you men cut through a one-inch steel cable at the edge of the high river bank? Who's got the best honed axe here?"

"They're in all pretty fair shape on this crummy," stated Buttlog, who was standing behind Oscar.

"Well then, who's got the nerve and the strength?"

Big Gustav stood up and threaded his way through the crowded front of the truck. He took his sharp axe from the rack on the outside wall of the crummy and followed Oscar to the edge of the river bank. Oscar explained the situation and Big Gustav nodded in agreement. The rocks he was standing on were very slippery, and the sight of swirling whirlpools far below made him shiver. Should he lose his footing it would be the end of him for certain.

Concentrating solely on the task at hand, he assessed what he had to do to ensure safety for himself and still save the bridge from destruction. In order to swing the axe efficiently he took off his raincoat. With strong hands he gripped the axe and placed it at a forty-five degree angle on the spot where he intended to make the cut — luckily there was a log conveniently positioned beneath the taut cable. Then Big Gustav swung the axe high and brought it down with all the force in his powerful arms. With one single, mighty blow, he severed the steel cable, and with a gigantic swishing noise, the shored-up debris shot forward and safely away under the bridge. So mighty had the blow been, that the axe passed through the inch thick cable and still retained enough force to stick deeply into the log.

"Well done," said Oscar. He patted Big Gustav on the shoulder in recognition of his accomplishment.

No one ever expressed the thought afterwards, but it lay heavily on everybody's mind that if that key bridge washed out while we were at work, we would be completely cut off from the camp. It was a tremendous relief to know that the bridge had held and was still safe, thanks to Big Gustav.

As logging trucks and crew busses returned to camp from all directions, everyone had tales of similar calamities: washouts, mud and rock slides, or entire sections of road under deep water. Wind on the open sea and extraordinarily high tides had caused the main river to dam up for a long distance inland. In consequence, the logging road near the river leading to the log dump at tidewater could no longer be used, and all logging activity came to a forced halt. The heavy rain continued for days on end. This was a grim November for most loggers on the north and central coast of British Columbia, and was to be remembered for a long time to come.

Generally speaking, a severe winter storm on the British Columbia coast is often followed by a brief period of clear, cold weather. Cold air moving down from Alaska and the Yukon usually coincides with a high pressure system over the coast. For weary loggers, this makes for a much appreciated break in the weather. It is nice to see the sun in a cloudless sky again during the day, and at night to view the innumerable stars in a crystal clear firmament. Of course, the temperatures do drop; somewhat above freezing during the day, and at night several degrees below. This gives the swollen rivers and lakes enough time to drain themselves to a seasonable level. Fish such as steelhead take the opportunity to make their runs up the coastal rivers. But should the cold spell last too long, more than eight to ten days, the water level in the rivers drops drastically, making it hard, if not impossible, for steelhead to make their runs in rocky riverbeds.

In 1959, having managed to save enough money through frugality of habit and sheer determination, I purchased a piece of land overlooking Howe Sound near Horseshoe Bay. The land sheltered a small cabin, to which I would head during holidays, fire season and work stoppages. It wasn't much, at the time, but it was infinitely better than the run-down boarding houses of downtown Vancouver, and no-one could take it away from me.

CHAPTER 3

WINTER

Snow

With the onset of a cold spell in the late fall, a new anxiety beclouds the otherwise blue horizon of many a logger's mind. Extended periods of freezing, followed by snow, begin to make that white stuff "stick and stay," as loggers say. Experienced coastal woodsmen know how fast the snow can build up once it starts, and they also know the havoc it plays with logging activity. The problems start with the obstruction of hauling roads and other lifelines to production. In time, entire sections of felled timber disappear under the snow, making it difficult for the rigging men to work safely and efficiently.

Fallers, however, have problems of their own. To begin with, their ability to size up a tree before falling it is hampered by the blinding snowfall. And as a tree heels over and falls to the ground, it releases a dense shower of snow, momentarily impairing his vision. In these critical seconds, a faller may not see something that fell from the tree, such as a dead limb. These are the thoughts — and the realities — that destroy many a logger's enjoyment of a sunny winter day.

By the changing look of the sky, and even by the smell of the air, seasoned loggers can tell when it is going to snow. One November in the late '60s, while working from Canfor's Camp Atluck on the northwest coast of Vancouver Island, the men working on the bull gang under Pat, "the Mad Rigger from Rivers Inlet," were in the process of rigging up a one-hundred and twenty-five foot high spar tree. Handsome Roy, a second rigger, said to Brother John, the donkey puncher on the bull gang:

"I sure don't like the looks of the weather. Particularly the way the fair sky's turned grey. And there's the unmistakable smell of snow in the air. We'll be in for some tough slogging, come tomorrow."

"It's too cold for snow yet," answered Brother John (so called for his habit of addressing other men as "Brother").

"Just remember tomorrow what forecast I gave you," said Handsome Roy. And with these words he turned his back on Brother John and walked away.

Overnight the air became noticeably milder, and the temperature hovered near the freezing point. In the morning a massive overcast delayed the arrival of daylight by nearly half an hour. Work ought to have started at 8:00 a.m., but this morning there simply wasn't sufficient daylight.

Pat the high rigger, the Mad Rigger from Rivers Inlet, was getting edgy. He was standing at the base of the huge spar, searching the bleak eastern sky with his large hazel eyes. Finally he shouted at the men who were still standing indecisively around the crummy:

"Let's get goin', fellows, before we get all snowed under."

Reluctantly they fell in line. Brother John started up his donkey engine with an ear-splitting roar, and soon it was belching out clouds of black smoke from its stubby exhaust pipe. Pat donned his climbing irons, buckled his safety belt, and readied himself for the pass chain.

Standing there at six feet four inches and 230 pounds, Pat looked lean and tough. One had to be hearty to cope with his kind of work — way up on the lofty spar, in any sort of weather. When they were rigging up, Handsome Roy would sometimes help Pat place the monstrous Oscar blocks, some weighing half a ton, at the proper heights on the spar tree. In severe weather conditions, he would also spell him off.

On this dismal morning, Handsome Roy functioned as the signal man between Pat, who was high up in the tree, and Brother John, the lever man on the donkey. Brother John's job was to raise or lower the high rigger on the pass line, as required. The rest of the crew, under the guidance of Shakey Bill, was stringing out guy lines and notching stumps preselected by Pat, around which the guy lines would later be secured with track spikes.

Less than one hour after Pat had ascended the tall, wooden spar, an icy cold wind mixed with snow began to blow from the north. Doggedly, Pat kept on straining with the stiff, frozen cables and the cruelly cold iron of the guy line blocks. Wind and snow were pushing against him with ever greater force. Little icicles mixed with snow began to form in his short, black beard. His strong hands were taking severe punishment in the freezing wind, as were his size twelve feet. One wondered how long he could withstand the cold. His thunderous yells down to Handsome Roy were muffled and carried away by the intense wind. Only Roy, who was keyed into Pat's ways, could rightly guess the meanings of the garbled signals.

By halfway to lunch time, Pat had endured all even he could take. Brother John had to lower him down to the ground. Pat could no longer see, his eyes hurt so much from the stinging, needle-like snow. With numb hands, he unbuckled his gear and handed it to Handsome Roy, who spelled him off till noon. At lunch time, the men huddled around a wildly burning fire, trying frantically to avoid the swirling, acrid smoke. Not much was said apart from the usual comments about the hostile weather. Right after lunch, Pat returned up onto the tree for the final job.

Shortly before noon, Handsome Roy had hurt one of his hands when it jammed in a block, and was now warming it by the fire. Shakey Bill, an old rigging hand who bounced from one job in the woods to another, had been working with two chokermen and Frenchy, who was also a seasoned rigging man. Their job, that afternoon, was to fasten the loose guy line ends around the already notched stumps. Brother John would then put tension on the guy line with the aid of a line from his yarder. Shakey Bill, however, had inadvertently put one guy line end around the stump the wrong way, and when Brother John reefed on the line, it caused the tall wooden spar to rock violently. Pat was knocked around fiercely up on top of the spar. He yelled at the top of his lungs for them to lower him down.

Frenchy hooked the strawline up to the passline, and Brother John lowered Pat gently down to the snow covered ground. Pat's feet had hardly touched the ground when he scrambled in a mad rush out of the pass chain and came with giant steps, still wearing the climbing spurs, towards the unsuspecting Frenchy.

"You son of a whore," shouted Pat with his booming voice. "You motherfucker — I'll teach you a lesson!" Pat grabbed Frenchy like a block of firewood and heaved him over the road bank into the snow and rocks. Pat was so raving mad that he did not stop to ask what had gone wrong, or whose fault it was. Shakey Bill, fearing the wrath of the high rigger, lacked the courage to come forward and admit his error.

Both Frenchy and Shakey Bill were fortunate that Panicky Pete, the camp super, did not fire them the next day for their carelessness. Frenchy, who had been thrown with great force, did not land softly, judging by the way he limped back onto the road. Nothing more was said, and work continued on as if nothing had happened.

Unfortunately, the tale of Pat and Frenchy did not end there. Like Gerry the Wild Frenchman, Frenchy originated from Quebec, and he spoke with a very strong French-Canadian accent. Like so many of his countrymen, he was small of stature but agile in his movements. Because of his occasionally savage temper, he was called by some "the Wolverine."

In the wild, wolverines are cunning and vicious animals; even trappers fear to face them. Frenchy exhibited all of his namesakes' characteristics. Revenge had been on his mind for quite some time, but despite weeks of scheming, he had not come up with a suitable plan. He had even confided his problems to Fat Mike, the head loader, with whom he worked at the time. Then out of the blue an opportunity arose that was better than anything he could have ever thought of. Some time after being thrown across the road, the opportunity arose for Frenchy to become a second loader. He took it gladly.

Work as a second loader included, besides stamping logs with a branding hammer, removing and chopping off branches after the logs were stacked on logging trucks. While stamping and limbing the first load of logs of the day, Frenchy spotted Pat, the high rigger, at the far end of the landing. Without a doubt, Pat had come to place the mainline block in a new position near the top of the spar tree, and would soon walk by the very truck where Frenchy was working.

A limb, just the right size for his mean purpose, caught Frenchy's weasel eyes. He severed the branch with one blow of his sharp axe. Next, he positioned himself in the cradle of several long bunk logs (the bottom layer of logs on a logging truck). It was now or never. Putting the axe and branding hammer beside him, he watched Pat's movements like a cat in front of a mouse hole.

As Pat later affirmed, he was not even aware that Frenchy had been second loading at the landing. Besides, he had never given the fellow a second thought after that ugly incident with the guy line. Frenchy, standing in the shadow of the enormous logs, flushed with the sweet thought of reprisal. He hefted the branch, which measured about five feet in length and had the thickness of a large man's wrist. Holding the limb at the thin end like a baseball bat, he waited until Pat was within striking distance, then swung the club with both hands, bludgeoning his foe across the shoulders. Pat lurched forward, and Frenchy leapt off the bunk log onto the high rigger's exposed, bent back. Pat fell to the ground.

Luckily, Pat was wearing his Mackinaw coat, which reduced the brunt of the club and the bite of the sharp caulks in the soles and heels of Frenchy's boots. Without that heavy coat, the tissues and muscles on Pat's back would have been severely torn. As it turned out, the impact of the caulk boots merely lacerated his skin and left some strong bruising.

Pat picked himself up and looked around. In the distance, he saw Frenchy jump into Pat's own pick-up truck and drive away. Realizing there was nothing he could do about it now, Pat shrugged off the pain in his back and carried on with the job he had come to do.

As "Fat Mike" the head loader, recalled, everything happened so quickly that no one noticed anything. Only later, as Frenchy was running away from the landing, did anyone take notice.

In order not to raise undue suspicion in camp, Frenchy left Pat's truck parked beside the machine and tire shop and walked up to the time office. There he instructed the timekeeper to make out his time, because he had just quit his job. Two rigging men, who had been fired the day before by Panicky Pete, were also in the time office when Frenchy came storming in. The young rigging men could not wait for the steamer, and had ordered a seaplane to pick them up. It was a God-sent opportunity for Frenchy to get speedily out of camp.

Quitting, or getting oneself fired, was a daily occurrence in every camp. The only difference was the frequency with which it occurred, which varied from camp to camp. Panicky Pete, although in most ways a mighty camp super, was notorious for his indiscriminate firings. Pete had been a true "high baller" in his hay days as a hooktender, and he tolerated no nonsense from any of his workers. He used to bark at the rigging crew:

"On the ball or on the boat!" Other times he would shout: "Up the hill or down the channel." When he fired a man he always asked him if he had any friends in camp. If the answer was yes, the friends were fired too. Should he answer that he had no friends, Panicky Pete replied: "I'll get you a partner so you won't be lonesome on the boat to town."

Pete had no respect for "sunshine loggers" and utterly despised "dandies." When ordering a couple of chokermen from town, Pete would say:

"If they wear suit pants or carry a comb in their hip pocket, send me four."

These, then, were the kind of fellows that Frenchy joined and flew to town with. And from that time on, before hiring out into any new camp, Frenchy would ask at the hiring agency if the Mad Rigger from Rivers Inlet was working there. Frenchy was forever on the run from Pat, whether in town or in the camps. He was never sure where he might run into him, and realized very well the consequences of such a meeting. Eventually, Frenchy suffered just punishment for his dastardly action — Pat caught up with him in town.

Lee Wong

Once a year, Lee Wong, a Chinese tailor from Vancouver, would visit various camps along the sprawling coast in search of business. Lee's age was hard to tell: he might have been in his early fifties. Very polite and quiet spoken, he came in the evening, knocking on every bunkhouse door.

"Good evening, would any of you gentlemen like me to tailor you a suit or something else you may desire?" he inquired warmly.

"Well," queried Handsome Roy, "what have you got in line for a good quality suit?" Putting his small suitcase down on the bed beside Roy, Lee opened the clasp carefully with his slender fingers. Inside were samples of different materials, a neatly rolled measuring tape, and a black booklet and lead pencil, with which he took note of both orders and measurements.

Handsome Roy needed a suit all right. When in town he could never spare the time to go to a tailor — he was always too busy doing other things. Lee had just the right cloth, and once Lee was finished with the measurements, Roy made a small down payment towards the suit which would be ready for him when he came to town for Christmas. Lee Wong employed several industrious Chinese in his tailoring shop in town. Cloth of good quality, a moderate price and a comfortable fit, combined with reliability, gave him an enviable reputation. Loggers in the camps he called on used to say:

"One can depend on the old man like no one else in town."

All in all, it was a very satisfactory arrangement for isolated loggers, and helped the striving business of an honest craftsman.

For coastal loggers, November has always been irrefutably the bleakest month of the year. In the mornings the crews left the marshalling yard before first light; after work they returned to it in total darkness. With snow falling steadily in various amounts, depending greatly on the location of the logging operation, every completed day represented a battle with the hostile elements.

"You win some, you lose some," as loggers were wont to say.

After supper, some of the older men sat in silence on their bunks smoking pipes. Another might lie on his back with one foot raised upon the opposite knee, gazing straight ahead into the void, perhaps twirling his thumbs. Others again, talked together about logging in past winters, or about bygone Christmases. And the younger men naturally turned all their thoughts, hopes and desires towards the approaching holidays.

Not all of them, however, were looking forward to a forced lay-off. Those men who had just arrived in camp broke, were hoping and wishing that it would stop snowing so that logging could continue. But this season it was not to be. From early fall on, nature gave many hints of a tough winter ahead. There were lots of wild berries in the woodlands. Deer, as well as other wildlife, had their winter coats early, and had a good layer of fat on their backs. Squirrels had been busy gathering cones and storing them away in hollowed out tree trunks, or at the bases of old, large-rooted trees. Long before the leaves began to fall, it was plain to see for all who cared to read the clues, that a long, cold winter was approaching. Older woodsmen passed those clues along to the younger generation for future benefit.

By November of 1961, I had learned as much as I wanted to about the dangers of logging in the snow. It was then that Holger the Old Pro, a hooktender, had his yarder and spar tree sitting on a bench-like landing at the base of a rather steep slope. They were yarding fair lead about fifteen-hundred feet up the hill. Roughly thirty feet behind the tail block guiding the haulback line ran a logging road, the grade of which must have been close to sixteen percent. That was pretty steep for hauling logs in foul weather at the end of November. Nevertheless, they kept on hauling.

The Old Pro had been having qualms from the onset about those log trucks wheeling down the steep grade above his setting. He mentioned his misgivings to Three Finger Knut, another camp super, who in turn assured him it would only be for another day or so, since they were nearly finished with the cold deck pile.

Three Finger Knut was a tall, dour and gaunt-looking man in his late fifties. A former high rigger, he had driven his men mercilessly hard, and in time became one of the most ruthless camp supers who ever reigned over a coastal logging operation. Years ago, while rigging up a spar tree, his left hand had been crushed and he had lost two fingers — thus his nickname.

On that fateful day, snow started to fall about noon. As the previous night had been clear and cold, everything was frozen hard, including the bark on the logs in the cold deck pile. Holger instructed Stammering Joe, the rigging slinger, to keep an eye on the road above them, and to alert his chokermen in regard to the log trucks driving downhill behind their backs

In order for the log trucks to make the grade, the road had to be salted down first thing in the morning, and several loads left the cold deck pile before noon without any undue problems. Stammering Joe and his three chokermen watched those logging trucks all throughout the forenoon as they crept downhill with their enormous loads.

After lunch, the weather deteriorated noticeably, and the overall visibility on the hillside became drastically reduced. Objects in the distance appeared blurred, and every sound was muffled by the silent and thickly falling snow.

By early afternoon the long road leading down the steep grade had become too treacherous, and the log trucks stopped returning to the loader at the cold deck pile. Old Dad's truck was the last one to be loaded, and the last one to leave.

Hackle and Cackle, the two inseparable chokermen, were midway through the tedious process of choking a large fir log. As so often happens, the log was embedded in frozen ground, and no opening for the choker knob to pass through was available. Hackle and Cackle lay down on their bellies in the deep snow and began to dig a choker hole. With snowflakes drifting down steadily onto their exposed necks, the two began to curse as only loggers can.

Hackle was on the upper side and Cackle on the lower side of the large log. They were driving a tunnel from both ends, then meeting in the middle. Like moles, the two burrowed under the log with a sturdy stick in conjunction with their strong fingers. Stammering Joe and his chokermen had finished choking their log, and were waiting for Hackle and Cackle. Standing there with cold feet, wet and hunched over, Stammering Joe looked around for the whistle punk, who appeared indistinctly through the swirling snow.

"Wha' wha' what's taking so God damn long," stuttered Joe to Hackle and Cackle, as the two men strained to shove the clumsy choker knob through to the other side.

"That damn hole is tighter than a nun's cunt," replied Cackle.

Old Dad, in the meantime, was ready to leave with his last, huge load of logs from the thoroughly snowed in landing high up on the mountain. Ulf, the head loader, had piled up the largest logs he could find under the snow, and by the time he was finished, the load resembled a one-storey building. Old Dad was well aware that the logs had frozen bark, and that the snow would make them even more slippery. He started out gently on the unsafe road, and having rounded a switch-back, entered the long, steep stretch of road below which Holger and his crew were logging — a crew that included Old Dad's son, Hackle.

Like an enormous wooden torpedo, the peaker of the load, a

118

balsam log forty-one feet in length and eighteen inches in diameter, slid noiselessly off the log truck and rolled down over the road bank in the direction of the men below. Old Dad was not even aware that he'd lost a log. The soft snow acted like grease, making it skim sideways down the slope and over felled and bucked timber. As fate would have it, the log took course for Hackle and Cackle. Stammering Joe saw it coming — too late. He tried to give warning, but due to his speech impediment was unable to bring forth a timely sound. In horror, he watched Hackle disappear beneath the long log. Luckily for Cackle, the big log they were choking rested against two stumps on the lower side, which prevented it from rolling over him in response to the impact. Cackle realized at once by the ominous sound what had happened on the other side of the log. With much apprehension he scrambled to his knees, then steadied himself with his trembling hands and rose to his feet.

Stammering Joe and the other chokermen had already stepped behind the log to see if they could do something for Hackle, of whom only the lanky legs were visible. Stammering Joe was unable to holler for the whistle punk to call the signal for an accident — seven long whistles. In the end it was his chokerman who did it for him.

Down at the landing, everything came to a halt by the time the last of the whistle punk's seven blasts had blared from atop the yarder and been dispelled by the whirling snowflakes.

"What's gone wrong this time?" everyone wanted to know. Holger the Old Pro had a hunch, and promptly started to head up to the steep slope. Others from the landing crew followed Holger with a stretcher and several blankets. On the hike to the scene of the accident, Holger was thinking of the many logs one could see lying by the side of every logging road, having fallen off loaded log trucks while on their way to the log dump. Sooner or later, he reasoned, there would be a very serious accident if binders were not put on the loads.

Holger, a heavy-set man, was no longer the youngest hooktender around. For him, the going uphill in knee-deep snow was arduous. Sweat came pearling down his wrinkled forehead. He stopped to get his wind, and wiped the sweat off with the bare back of his large hand, wondering who had been hit this time. Scenes of appalling mishaps he had witnessed in the woods streaked through his weary mind. From behind, younger men were passing him and breaking trail. This made it easier for his old legs, as he was already pushing sixty years.

On arrival they met Stammering Joe and his crew, standing in dead silence. Snowflakes the size of silver dollars were descending around them. Holger asked for no explanations, he could see how everything had come about.

It was not by chance that Holger had stayed alive for so long a time in the woods, especially given that he had been setting chokers since the age of sixteen. Much of his longevity had to do with his attitude towards a safe way of doing things on the job. Looking down at the lifeless legs of the young lad, an unspeakable pain rose in Holger's chest.

"What a great waste of a precious young life," he thought. Hackle had a mother who gave birth to him in pain, nursed and raised him lovingly, and most likely in straitened circumstances. And then all the reason for her love and hardship was wiped out in a flash. How can one describe the suffering of a family which has experienced the tragic loss of a loved one from logging? One cannot. The best that can be said is that those left behind suffer emotionally, and often financially, for the rest of their lives.

Holger ordered the log on top of Hackle to be removed. Stammering Joe fastened a choker around one end, and it was yarded away by skinning back the rigging. Hackle's body was lifted onto the stretcher, covered with a blanket, and everybody gave a hand to carry him down the slope. Far off in the snowy distance a lonely raven seemed to hoot farewell, and nearby the rigging skidded to a halt as the men descended in silence with their burden.

What Holger had really been afraid of, and what one year later came to pass on the very same spot, was that a loaded log truck would fail to negotiate the curve in the switch-back and go over the side of the road, spilling the truck, and its entire load of logs, downhill. Fortunately the driver's side was opposite the tilting log truck, and the driver was able to escape in time. He was lucky to get out with just a broken ankle.

Not often, but perhaps once or twice during the winter season, the weather conditions get such that overnight the logging roads come to resemble skating rinks. The prelude to this is a period of several days when the ground is frozen hard, usually followed by an icy, overnight rain. For crummy and log truck drivers, such days start out as a nightmare. Some manage to get to their destinations, others don't.

Willie Boy, the log truck driver who walked with a swagger and a chip on his shoulder, would not venture out onto the icy road unless he had the sand truck right ahead of him. It was not unusual for Willie Boy to park his truck right beside the road, waiting to have it cleared of snow before he would dare to drive, while other, bolder drivers kept on trucking.

Matts, who drove the fallers' crummy, was one of those men whom nothing could perturb — not even a slippery November morning. Having driven almost two thirds of the distance to the worksite, he rounded a left hand curve in the road just a trifle too fast. Over he went, upending the crew bus, which landed on its roof in a brushy, shallow trench. It was a lucky accident, in that none of us were hurt.

Eventually another crummy came along, picked up the stranded fallers and transported them to their workplaces. For Matts, who was also my falling partner, the day was jinxed. Towards the end of it he slipped on the steep frozen ground and cut the top of his middle finger off with his axe. Brazenly he said to me:

"I wish it had been your finger instead of mine."

And then there was Iron Eric, that tough and stubborn old hook-tender, whose wild gaze and faraway stare scoured the world before him from watery, blue eyes. Once again it was a miserable winter day highlighted by a raging snowstorm. As always, Eric toted his double bit axe. Keeping his axe at hand was a habit, and Eric was one of those men who lived by habit.

"Habit is a powerful force," said Eric.

Behind his back, some men had guts enough to tell each other that Iron Eric was crazy.

Eric, along with several of his crew, was changing a quarter guy line from a tall spar tree to a new stump. All Iron Eric's chokermen were needed to carry the required tools: the Tommy Moore block, the sledge hammer, the claw bar and a bucket of rail spikes.

Eric had finished notching the stump he had chosen as a new guy line anchor. Now it was time for the guy line to be secured with track spikes. As he worked, Eric instructed the young man standing next to him:

"The guy line must be wrapped a minimum of two and a half times around the stump." He indicated the number and position of the spikes. "They must be adequate," he said, "to ensure that the guy line will handle the imposed loads."

They were now spiking the bottom lead line with ten spikes, to prevent the line from slipping until other wraps were applied. Eric held the ninth spike to the guy line and stump, ready for the young chokerman to drive it in with the sledge hammer. Billy struck the spike timidly at first, his fingers terribly cold and his hands feeling slippery on the wet wooden handle. Iron Eric pointed out that he'd seen ten-year-olds do better. Billy took a firmer grip and delivered a proper blow. Unfortunately, his hands slipped, and the blow glanced off the spike and crushed Eric's thumb. Blood spurted in all directions, leaving scarlet blotches in the fresh snow. Not a sound came from Eric. In fact, he was still holding the spike in position for striking. At the sight of the bloodied thumb, Billy's arms went limp.

"What are you waiting for," yelled Iron Eric, holding up his injured hand. "I've still got four more." Jari, a bolder, much tougher chokerman, took the sledgehammer from Billy's hands and with great force drove the last two spikes home. For the remainder of the day, Iron Eric poked his smashed thumb into the snow every so often to retard the bleeding.

"I'll never be that tough," said Billy to his fellow workers. He now understood why many older loggers have deformed fingers and thumbs, or split fingernails, and was playing with the idea of leaving the woods for good. "There must be a better way of making a living," he argued.

"If you're going to leave," said one of the older men, "do it soon. Once you've been in the woods for five years, you'll never be able to break away from it; you'll be doomed to always return to the woods, no matter what."

Screwy Louis

Shortly before Christmas it often became obvious that we could no longer keep on logging because of the sheer amounts of snow. Faced with the prospect of free time, men's minds began to wander towards far away towns. Screwy Louis, a volatile rigging slinger from the former "Timberline Logging" (a notoriously "haywire" outfit) had his two chokermen, the Garlic Brothers (they were great garlic eaters), all worked up over the prospect of having a jolly good time in town that coming Christmas. It was my second year in the Nimpkish Valley, and Screwy Louis and the Garlic Brothers were keeping the men in Camp A entertained by allowing their lively fantasies unceasingly free reign. In their exuberance, they hardly noticed, on the day in question, that the snowflakes piling up on their backs were slushy and heavy. Nor did they perceive the coldness which penetrated right through their clothes. Only when they stripped in their warm bunkhouse did they become aware of how soaked their clothes and boots were.

Screwy Louis, the Garlic Brothers, and five other young rigging men all stayed together in the same old dilapidated bunkhouse. On that particular winter day they all came in from the woods drenched and with chattering teeth. Soon, as usual, every square foot near the hot stove was taken up by dirty wet work clothes and logging boots.

After supper, the young fellows sat on their bunks smoking, belching, laughing and making plans for the expected shutdown. Most of them had been in camp since late summer or early fall, and they were eager and ready to break loose. Screwy Louis was looking forward to going on another of his "ego trips."

When in town Screwy Louis passed himself off to unknown loggers as an undercover RCMP officer. Being young, tall, not bad looking, and blessed with the gift of the gab, he may have been able to fool any number of strangers. But to the loggers who knew his bizarre ways from camp, he was simply, and without exception, Screwy Louis.

It wasn't long before the overheated bunkhouse made the tired fellows drowsy, and one by one they crept under their filthy blankets. Outside, the air turned cooler, and the snow began falling in light, dry flakes.

By nine o'clock, every light in the room was out and they were all sleeping and snoring in bliss. It is difficult to realistically describe the smell and stench inside a bunkhouse, with eight men together in one room, heated by a wood stove. Vapours rise from wet, dirty and sweaty clothes, socks and boots that stew in the torrid air near the stove, and all of this mixes with pungent tobacco smoke, body odour, and the unavoidable farting of men. That is how a bunkhouse smelled in the middle of winter.

At about midnight, I was woken by the sound of a frantic voice calling: "Fire!" I hurried out the door to see what was happening. Opposite the marshalling yard, I saw a bunkhouse in flames. Standing in the snow, stark naked and illuminated by leaping flames, stood Screwy Louis, yelling "Fire! Fire!" at the top of his lungs. In one hand he held a logging boot, in the other he clasped one wool sock, which he held high over his blonde head while screaming. Snowflakes were drifting down silently upon his naked body.

Someone inside the burning room knocked out a window. Grey smoke streamed forth, and along with it a fellow wearing only his shorts. Others made it out the door into the snow, most of them only in their Adam's suit. All escaped the acrid smoke and deadly flames unharmed, except the Garlic Brothers. The fiercely burning roof had caved in before they could reach the door, forcing them to escape through a gutted window, getting badly scorched in the process.

The bunkhouse had been constructed of red cedar boards, and all the lumber in it was so powder dry that it went up in flames like a torch. Clearly, the fire must have been caused by the clothes hanging too near to the overheated stove, especially the ones near the stovepipe, which can get red hot with a roaring fire in such an old wood heater. This singular calamity, for which all occupants were to be blamed, put a temporary damper on Screwy Louis' ambitions. When he finally did make his trip into town, he got embroiled in a fight and was killed in the process.

Town

With snow piling up relentlessly in the coastal area in mid December, the looming shutdown for those still-active logging camps became an increasing likelihood. Latrine rumours had it for some time that the outfit was just about ready to put the lid on its logging operation. Such reports injected a certain feverish activity into the otherwise blunted minds of loggers, who had slaved away in camp for the better part of a long logging season. Finally, the last day to be worked was officially proclaimed. At the breakfast table, one could hear men saying:

"Only three more days to go and then we're free."

Only people who have worked in isolation for any length of time can understand the intense longing one gets for outside social contacts. The age old maxim, man does not live by bread alone, is applicable to social contact as much as anything else. Whether young or old, everyone looked forward to going to town. Many of those loggers truly believed that they could make up for lost time, once they saw the bright lights of the city again. Of course, that was an illusion.

No one never recoups lost time. Out on the job, men's minds tended to be miles away from what they were doing, a deciding factor in many accidents. Evenings were spent rummaging through suitcases or bags for letters, addresses, phone numbers, or other items that might be needed in the city.

The last work day brought a smile — no matter how fleeting — to even the grouchiest old logger. Fortunately for fallers and buckers, the final day was always a short one, because the scalers had to tally up their scale sheets in time to submit them for the final payoff. Sometimes the rigging men got a break and were let off an hour early on the last workday. Such a boon depended entirely on the goodwill and disposition of the camp super.

A tall, lean man in his fifties, Three Finger Knut was known for his intense, penetrating stare, and for never giving an inch to his men. Out on the rigging the impatiently awaited slack off whistle was answered by a jubilant "Hurray, we've got it made!" as the men plodded through the deep snow towards the quiet landing.

Every donkey puncher put a tin can over the exhaust pipe of his engine to keep out snow and rain, as did the log truck drivers on their parked rigs. All at once the entire site slipped into tranquillity.

For those loggers who had endured and survived the endless battle with the harsh elements, another year of hard work, deprivation and grief had come to an end. Early Saturday morning the fire in the woodstoves was lit for the last time. Breakfast was served one hour ahead of its usual time, in order to give the hard-pressed cookhouse staff a chance to clean up and be ready to leave for town. Weatherwise, the day usually lived up to its standard, foggy fare.

Two barges towed by tugboats were required to transport all the men down the misty channel to where a coastal ship from Northland Navigation made a port of call. From there it was the same old route which coastal vessels always took for Vancouver, B.C. Sometime on Sunday morning, depending on weather conditions and tide along the coast, the vessel arrived in Vancouver harbour.

The loggers disembarked from the ship like swarming bees from a hive. They could not get away fast enough to meet their taxis, friends, relatives, or whoever else was there to meet them. Most of the men were unattached, and the majority of these headed for the loggers' hotels, such as the Blackstone, the Patricia, the Abbotsford, and many others in downtown Vancouver. Thrifty loggers, among whom I count myself, went looking for private places, or for housekeeping rooms where they could look after themselves.

Whenever loggers came to town, they invariably stayed at the same hotels (or "watering places," as they used to call them), where they could always find a friend, male or female. In addition, the hotel manager or the desk clerk would forward or hold a logger's mail, and look after his messages until he got settled.

A common practice for some loggers was to leave their good clothes at their favourite hotel. The clerk would send the clothes out for cleaning, and when the logger next returned, the suit would be there, cleaned, pressed, smudges removed. Over the years, a logger got to know his hotel manager so well that he could ask unabashed for credit on his hotel room, or borrow some badly needed money against his future wages. Predictably, such advance money (called a drag) was at all times the first debt to be paid once a logger was back at work. Cut off from the daily camp routine, the average logger was at a loss for things to do when in town for any length of time — especially during the wintertime. Only then did he begin to miss his accustomed surroundings and his fellow workers. Such a void had to be filled somehow, and, for a lonely logger, there was no better place to find company than the beer parlours. There he would find men who all spoke the same language: namely, logging.

Whenever two or more loggers sat down to talk, regardless of what the subject might have been at the onset, the topic always reverted to logging. No theme could hold a logger's attention for long, unless it had something to do with logging. Women and drinking were also fair subjects, but had to take second place to logging. Most of what they told each other was true, or at least had some truth to it. Certainly there were braggarts and exaggerators, but these only served to bring life, colour, and often drama into an otherwise monotonous conversation.

The men sat in the hotels, conversing as they would if they were in camp, sitting on a bench outside a bunkhouse, smoking and chewing snoose. In town the logging was done at the beer table, and the tall tales had to be taken with a grain of salt. For endless hours, young and old men alike would sit around the tables drinking beer, smoking and of course talking logging.

In those so called "watering holes," there would be no less than a dozen men at a large round table around noon on almost any day, except Sunday, and by late afternoon a throng of serious drinkers would be sitting at a cluster of tables. Those get-togethers served a multitude of purposes.

Besides providing a terrific setting for large amounts of drinking and quite a lot of swaggering, which gave the men a terrific boost to their egos, the watering holes were important places for making deals. Fallers would team up with newly found neighbours, and resolve to hire out afresh wherever a job might be. Others found women friends there — those who wished could pick up a gold digger or a harlot.

An established custom was for one man to order and buy a round of beer. Once the beer glasses were empty the next man would order a round and so forth, till the round had gone full circle. The only time a hitch developed in this process was when a free loader sat amongst the sportive beer drinkers, or when two adversaries had to step outside into the back alley to settle a difference.

Some of the craziest bets men can think of were made at those beer tables. One such silly wager would pit men against each other to see who could drink a glass of beer the fastest. Black Nic, a shrimp of a boom man I knew in the mid-'60s, was the undisputed winner of such stupid bets. He would tilt his large head backwards, open his mouth wide like a trap door, and literally pour a glass of beer down his spacious throat.

In such a manner the winter days, weeks and months would pass by for a logger in town, but finally the new year, and a new logging season, commenced with the call for loggers to return to work. If the fickle lumber market was on the upswing, the demand for loggers would be high.

Despite heavy snowfall, the logging camps in the coastal regions resumed operation and quickly shifted into high gear. Unusually good weather favoured the early start-up of logging along the coast. Logger hiring agencies had their blackboards filled with vacant jobs. Large companies and gyppos alike were crying for loggers. No longer could the thunder of hobnailed boots be heard on skid road. Beer parlours were empty of boisterous characters. Harlots, gold diggers and bootleggers had been deserted by their men.

Being of frugal nature, with spartan habits, I appeared to the others in camp to resemble Scrooge. Whenever I travelled on the boat from camp to town and back again, I used a small cardboard box as my suitcase. I always left my work clothes behind when I went to town, and I possessed precious little that I needed to take with me. All my items fitted nicely into this little box, which I tied together with a string and carried under my arm.

Around the end of January, sometimes early February, logging operations called all the loggers back to work for start up. Not all of the loggers who had been laid off before Christmas did elect to return to their respective camps. Some found new jobs elsewhere, others just weren't ready to struggle through deep snow so early in the new year.

The departure time of the coastal vessel was set for Saturday at 8:00 p.m. at Pier B in Vancouver harbour. Out of habit, I arrived there in good time. This gave me numerous opportunities to observe the arrival of loggers from the upper deck. I watched them stream on-board ship with their ponderous luggage. The loggers were easy to tell apart in a crowd of oncoming foot passengers. Most of them had already had a few drinks, which made it that much more difficult to walk up the boarding ramp.

As usual, the boat was late in leaving port. These delays were greatly appreciated by the inevitable last minute arrivals. During the course of the evening, congenial loggers from various camps met on board and enjoyed each other's company. Some got carried away in the excitement at seeing old friends again, and it often got a bit noisy as the night wore on. Just the same, no drunken brawls or other disturbances marred the night's voyage.

On Sunday afternoon the ship neared the bay where several of us were planning to disembark. On the wharf, two husky, potbellied tugboat operators were already waiting to take on men and cargo, all to be towed further up the channel to where the camp was located. Each tugboat towed a small barge, and orders were given that the men ride with the first tug while their baggage went along with the second. Such an arrangement was rather unusual, but the disgruntled men piled their belongings in a heap on the floor of the freight barge before we boarded the tug.

I walked onto the tug with my cardboard box under my arm, sat down, and held the box on my lap for the two hour ride. No sooner had the last man been accounted for, than the tug pulled away from the mooring while the last rays of the setting winter sun glittered on its wake. During the chilly, noisy ride, the air was filled with tobacco smoke and the smell of whiskey. Some smart Alec could not resist a snide remark about my stylish suitcase. In turn, I suggested to him that economy was a sign of both courage and determination, habits of mind he would be well advised to emulate.

Darkness had already set in when the tug tied up at the floating landing. Stiff from sitting cramped on the hard wooden benches, the men were eager to get on shore to stretch their legs.

Off in the distance, down the dark channel, the faint light from the second tug came into view. Not all of the men wanted to stay and wait shivering under the clear, starry night, so they left for their bunkhouses to light the stove and get some badly needed heat into the huts.

In time, a fellow came around to announce the arrival of the second tugboat, and the men wasted no time in walking down to the dock. To everyone's consternation, smoke was drifting off the freight barge. As they approached Lars, the tugboat operator, one concerned logger asked what the smoke was all about.

"I'll be damned if I know what you men have planted in there along with your gear," answered Lars. He pushed open the barge door uneasily; behind him hovered a throng of anxious loggers. Their worst fears were confirmed. Fire must have started in the baggage pile, most of which had burned or been spoiled by the smoldering fire.

Dismayed, the men returned to their bunkhouses — perhaps, they speculated, someone had dropped a burning cigarette on the pile. Not only did they lose all their gear and personal articles, they also lost all their indispensable rye whiskey. For some, the whiskey was the greatest loss and the hardest one to bear. Work clothes, logging boots and other items could be obtained next morning at the commissary. But not the whiskey.

In the days following, several fellows told me that I certainly had the right idea in carrying my box with me. I was the only one in camp who did not take a loss in that freak fire, and it was hard to feel pleased by these remarks, despite the hard times I had received from certain individuals over my particular way of doing things.

Back to Work

All able-bodied loggers returned to the camps. The first thing one noticed on arrival was the peculiar smell of the bunkhouse, an instant reminder of one's place in life.

Many of the returning loggers were nearly broke. It didn't take long for a big-spender to get cleaned out in the clutches of the town vultures. Most of the men were eager to leave town and return to camp, to fatten up, to get out of the hole and start work on a new stake.

After a lengthy absence such as winter shutdown, the first eight to ten days back on the job are the hardest to bear. Men, whether they admit it or not, do get out of shape while idle in town, and it takes time for them to become conditioned.

The initial week back in camp was tedious, until one slid into the daily routine of camp life. On those first evenings many men nursed some sort of ache or pain, and the majority went to bed early. All was quiet in the bunkhouse — unless one of the men had a drinking problem. As for safety on the job, vigilance was crucial until the men became mentally and physically tuned in again. Still, with the help of favourable weather, the break-in period was tolerable for most loggers.

It was very common, after the first week's work, for a broke logger to head for the time office and ask for a "drag." Bills had to be paid, or money had to be sent to a distraught wife who had little or nothing to pay the rent or feed the children. Others, like Spitfire Ed, who received a letter from his girlfriend Racehorse Mary, had to mail off a few day's pay. Gambling and playing poker were at their lowest ebb at such times. Gradually, things returned to the normal daily trot, everybody, including the heavy drinkers, feeling fine and comfortable again. Out on the job, the men worked doggedly in the deep snow.

In early 1968 my sister wrote me from Austria. She was playing the part of matchmaker, and suggested that I write a letter to a young woman she knew named Inge. I was in my late thirties by then, and in a position, financially, to contemplate starting a family. I put pen to paper, and Inge, in an answering letter, agreed to come to B.C.

Inge arrived on April 28 of that same year, and I took a week off work to drive my Volkswagen Beetle to Vancouver to meet her at the airport. There was little time to waste. Soon we were married, the cabin on my land torn down, and a home erected on its spot. Now I had something special to return to during holidays and shutdowns, and someone to miss when I set out for the woods again.

CHAPTER 4

SPRING

In Like a Lion

March, the month of wind, came in like a roaring lion with snow blizzards lasting for days on end. Spitting Pete, the old powder monkey, consoled his powder packer, Shithouse Joe:

"If March comes in like a lion, it'll go out like a lamb."

When building the sub grade for logging roads, it was Spitting Pete's job to blast the big stumps on right-of-ways so that the power-shovel following behind could dig them out more easily. Pete struggled patiently, removing the snow with a hand shovel from the base of stumps, then using an iron ramrod to punch a hole, into which he placed sticks of dynamite, the number varying according to the size of the stump.

A large spruce or fir stump required a whole box — one hundred and ten sticks of sixty-percent stumping powder, enough to split it apart or crack it sufficiently before the power-shovel could lift or dig it out of the ground. Keep in mind the enormous sizes of the stumps: they ranged up to eight feet in diameter and sometimes even larger, with thick, deep, heart roots which had to be excavated. It was Shithouse Joe's job to carry boxes of powder from the truck at the end of the road, or from the rear of the sled of the power-shovel, a distance of several thousand feet or more over any kind of terrain. Spitting Pete kept a good walking trail open, which was also used and appreciated by the right-of-way fallers returning from work.

Shithouse Joe was one of a kind. A big man in his middle thirties, Joe used to brag that he was built like a brick shithouse and not a brick missing. The men in camp would reply:

"Yeah, and you're full of shit too, aren't you Joe?"

Joe was an awful drinker, and would do almost anything for a bottle of rye whiskey. He was lazy by nature, and had other despicable attributes. In spite of his large frame, for he was well above six feet tall and weighed over 220 pounds, any determined fellow of only half his size could have floored him, because he was such a great coward. He scrounged drink at every opportunity, but would never share one of his own. On several occasions I saw him pull a bottle out of his big bag and suck on it when the rest of the men appeared asleep. Joe was really filthy when drunk; he would flop down on his bunk in his work clothes, go to sleep and snore loudly all night long. At times he wetted himself in his sleep, spreading an intolerable stench.

"Every good logger has a drinking problem," he'd say from time to time. The insinuation that he was a good logger, however, was far from true.

Joe was married to a woman he called Fenka, but the men in the camp who had met her referred to her as the "long-legged bitch," and claimed she would stuff Joe into the wood box if he didn't do her bidding. During one winter shutdown, Joe and Fenka paid Mike and his wife Olga a visit. Olga asked Fenka what she would like to drink. Fenka replied that coffee would be fine. Imagine Mike's surprise when he put a bottle of rye in front of Joe, only to hear him stammer:

"No, no, I'll have coffee, too, thank you."

Fenka confided to Olga, Mike's wife, that the first thing Joe did when he came home from a long absence at camp was drag her into the bedroom. This became known to the men in camp, and they began to ask Joe what the second thing he did was.

"Take off my pack sack," he answered, his small eyes twinkling in his fat face.

One summer night, around 1:30 a.m., Joe returned from the married quarters in camp, where he'd been drinking some potent home-brew. From afar, we could hear Joe singing with his good, powerful voice:

> *Way up the mountain I wander alone,*
> *Rye whiskey, rye whiskey, I cry —*
> *I'll drink you till the day I die.*

In this noisy fashion he staggered past the old bunkhouses, waking up dozens of angry men. Unable to get into his hut, he collapsed outside of it. Illuminated by the bright moonlight, he lay sprawled on the ground. I looked out the bunk house window, and saw a large, checkered dog which had followed him from the married quarters lying beside him, licking his hand. Towards morning Joe finally made it inside the hut and onto his bunk. Ultimately he had to move on, which was a relief to the rest of us. Nobody could get any proper sleep in a bunkhouse where Shithouse Joe snored so blissfully.

Of all the powder monkeys I've known, the one I remember best was Whispering George. I came to know George, who originated from Estonia, when he was well past sixty years of age, and living at Camp N. He was a medium built man, with a large head and a monstrous, bony nose, under which he sported a pencil thin moustache. His hands were large and gnarly, and he kept them cupped over each other when not in use. Once a heavy smoker, George had developed throat cancer. The treatment necessitated an operation, and he lived the rest of his life with an open slit under his Adam's apple. George loved to talk, but due to the opening in his windpipe, the best he could manage was a hoarse whisper. He was forever grinning and using his tongue to push the upper plate of his false teeth out of his mouth, which made him look grotesque.

George never had a mishap, and was considered by all who knew him to be a highly proficient powder monkey. In addition, George always had a good access trail built, for which quality alone every right-of-way faller loved him.

Whispering George had one strange habit of which I took a very dim view. He used to feed ravens on top of the stumps he was going to blast later on. At the end of a day's work he walked out of a right-of-way ready to light the fuses as soon as everybody was in the clear. For those ravens that lingered it amounted to Russian roulette, and predictably, once in a while, one of them was blasted up into the sky to the delight of some onlookers.

Eventually, Whispering George succumbed to cancer.

Hauling big, heavy loads in springtime is a treacherous occupation. Slushy, wet logging roads became heavily rutted. The drivers tried to avoid the ruts, but had to be extremely careful because the shoulders were soft. (Probably the greatest number of accidents on logging roads are due to soft shoulders.) To make things worse, there was still snow piled up on the side of the road, which left the driver in doubt as to how far out it was safe to drive.

Skippy, who I knew in the late '70s, was an old hand at driving gravel trucks. On the day in question he was hauling road ballast when he met a loaded log truck coming the opposite direction on a straight stretch of road. Skippy had a steep slope on his right side, which culminated in a deep box canyon. Ralph, the log truck driver, had a road bank of only several feet in height on his right side to contend with. Both drivers slowed down, preparing to pass each other safely. Unfortunately for Skippy, the road had a wide, soft shoulder, and three feet in from the outer edge of the road bank the ground was soggy. The moment Skippy swung out, his entire right side sank down and started to tilt sideways. By the time he realized what was happening, the driver's side was already high up in the air. It was too late for escape.

Years ago the sheer slope below the road had been logged off, right to the edge of the rocky box canyon. The fallers had left some scattered trees standing, because they leaned heavily down into the chasm and could not be retrieved. These trees now stood as the only barrier between Skippy's tumbling truck and the deep, narrow, water-filled gorge.

Skippy rolled about ninety feet down the slope, where his truck came to rest against two large, closely spaced fir trees. Miraculously, Skippy survived the mighty tumble, but not unharmed; he was thoroughly shaken, badly bruised, and cut from the splintering glass. Out of the corner of his left eye, Ralph had seen Skippy's truck leave the road. He stopped promptly, jumped out, and ran over to the crumbling edge of the road bank. He watched in horror, and then relief, as the gravel truck turned over on its side for the final time before coming to a rest against the trees.

Ralph descended the rough slope, over the trail of gravel the rolling truck had left behind. Fortunately, the truck had stopped with the driver's side up, and Skippy was able to crawl out through the smashed up door. Ralph assisted him in clambering back up to the road, where he put a compress on Skippy's bleeding head wound. Then the men drove to the log dump, where Ralph dumped his load before returning to camp for medical attention.

A few years later, in Atluck Camp, I met Gimpy the terror of the logging road. Gimpy was a log truck driver who exclusively drove big trucks. Anyone driving anything smaller than a six-wheeler dreaded to meet Gimpy on the road. A tall, dour, gaunt man in his late fifties, Gimpy walked with a pronounced limp, the result of a logging accident years ago. He was utterly unconcerned about other people's safety, and when he drove down the middle of the road, he refused to yield one inch to oncoming traffic. He had been involved in all kinds of road mishaps over the years, ranging from minor to very serious accidents.

Gimpy possessed the remarkable ability of always being able to shift the blame onto the other driver. One evening Gimpy was the last one to return from the log dump to park his truck. It was dark, and without sounding the back-up signal (two short beeps), he tried to back in alongside another log truck. What Gimpy failed to see was that the truck's driver was standing beside his rig with his back turned. Gimpy backed up, partly crushing the other driver. What saved this man from being killed was that the rear end of Gimpy's trailer bumped into the back of the other truck's trailer. The next day at the accident investigation Gimpy declared coolly that the other driver should not have been where he was. Gimpy' received a one-week driving suspension, whereas the other driver was off work for six months with a hip injury.

Another time, Gimpy rammed a mechanic's pickup truck while rounding a bend. This resulted in a head injury with multiple cuts for Clint, the ill-fated mechanic, who barely managed to escape before the pick-up was engulfed in flames.

Defensive crummy drivers kept a close watch on Gimpy's whereabouts. Only through forethought could drivers make sure they were off to the side when Gimpy came towards them. The worst place to meet Gimpy was in a tight switch-back. The driver of a crummy sighted Gimpy and came to a full halt alongside the road, although not as far to the side as he could have been. Still, there was sufficient room to pass, had Gimpy yielded a few inches to the crew bus. Never, however, did Gimpy slow down for anyone. He wheeled past the stationary crummy and ripped its left side open from front to rear. To the wonder of all, no one was hurt inside.

After realizing what had happened, Gimpy came to a halt and backed up towards the crummy. He yelled down from his cab and started giving abuse to the shaken driver, blaming him for not being far enough off to the side of the road. That evening, Cliff, the super, told Gimpy that he had had enough of his reckless driving: his services were no longer required.

Gimpy had been one of many cruel drivers who would not slow down for wildlife, be it a grouse picking up grit from the gravel road, an elk down at the river flats, a timber wolf or even a bear. Crummy drivers were the worst offenders, and deer the most common victims. Some very vehement arguments broke out amongst the men over such deplorable acts, especially when the chased creature had no way of getting off the road. Precipitous cliffs on one side and sheer drop-offs or deep waters on the other left no escape from a brutal pursuer.

Loggers used to, and still do, come into closer contact with wildlife than any other industrial worker. They ought to use discretion during these encounters, since men and wildlife alike share the same environment. The destruction of the last of the old growth timber deprives wildlife of sustenance, not to mention shelter from blizzards and gales in the winter, and from sizzling heat in the summer. There are few stands of virgin timber left, where groves of old, old trees provide homes for raccoons, owls, squirrels and many other creatures. Gone is the deep, mossy silence, the sense of peace and timelessness. The surviving species are driven farther and farther back into a rougher, more hostile environment, by the relentless actions of wasteful men.

Certain species cannot exist without the old growth timber. This fact was revealed to me one winter while falling a grove of old trees near a marsh. Having downed another forest giant, I proceeded to buck it into saw logs. Towards the top end on the third cut, I noticed that the sawdust was sticky as the cut went deeper. Once the cut was finished and the sawed log dropped, I realized that I had sawed right through a large honeycomb, about eighteen inches in diameter. No sooner had the bucked off log dropped to the ground than honeybees, woken from their hibernation, began to crawl out over the severed honeycombs. Several tried to fly in the bitter winter air, but fell into the snow. Slowly, in ever greater numbers, the bees came creeping out of both hollow ends. Their hive had been destroyed, and without it they could no longer exist. For aeons, their kind had lived here in the forest, doing what nature intended them to do. Without those old trees, their existence was endangered.

Birds, so vital in keeping forest insect populations at tolerable levels, cannot nest and survive without trees with hollow centers, knotty cavities or cracked trunks. When the old growth is cut down, an indispensable link in the natural balance is broken. Waterfowl, as well as fish, also feel the heavy hand of man. When lake shores and river banks are ruthlessly denuded, nesting and spawning areas are destroyed. Wanton waste, coupled with man's inordinate greediness, leaves its scars wherever loggers wielded their axes and saws.

March, known as the month of gusty winds, is the fiend of fallers. Unexpected changes in weather conditions lead to a variety of safety concerns. Heavy winds, particularly gusty winds, can blow over snags, loosen and blow down hanging limbs or other widow makers, and ruin a logger's ability to maintain directional control of trees being felled.

This loss of control can create hang-ups, widow makers and flying limbs, when the dry tops of falling trees brush standing timber.

March's snow conditions also present problems, by impeding the safe escape of a faller in an emergency; by falling from the limbs of trees in heavy clumps; by causing frozen and brittle limbs to break and fall through heavy build-up; by creating a thick cloud of snow when a tree is felled; and by covering the dangers of dangerous terrain.

When a faller's visibility is seriously obscured by fog, many hazards that are usually avoidable become invisible. In short, falling a tree requires a great deal more consideration than merely bringing it to the ground, and the month of March made it difficult to go about our business in safety.

Like everything else in logging, the basic principles for falling and bucking still apply today as they did eighty years ago. What has changed are the tools. In contrast to today's power-saw fallers, the old-time hand fallers worked with a crosscut saw, an axe, a spring-board, a squirt oilcan and a ten-pound sledgehammer, which they used to drive fourteen-inch steel wedges into the back cut of a tree to lift and force it against its lean.

Hand fallers worked in pairs with a bucker behind them, whose job it was to saw the felled trees into suitable log lengths. With the advent of the early power-saws, the same work system was upheld. Changing from crosscut to power-saws has not been an easy transition. The early power-saw had a five- or seven-foot bar, weighed about 150 pounds, and required two men to operate. Lugging them around, particularly on hillsides, was extremely hard work. Over the years, those cumbersome power-saws developed into today's modern, one-man chainsaws, which can be used for falling and bucking alike.

Gone are the days when a set of fallers (the head faller, the machine operator and the bucker) worked together as a team. Nowadays, each faller is on his own as he works his strip. Where it once took three men, now one faller alone does the same work. Production per man-hour is up, but the rate of accidents has remained unchanged. In addition, the quality of work is less than desired, partly owing to the ever steeper terrain being worked.

Matti and Jouko

I used to call such cliff-side falling strips the "goat shows." Every day for weeks on end I would be secured to a safe tree via a safety belt and a thirty foot long rope, while a second man had the enormous responsibility of looking after me while I dangled at the end of the safety line, tightening or slackening the rope in concert with my movements up and down the hillside. To fall timber at such lofty heights, with an ever present breeze blowing, required total concentration and prudence. More than once, before daring to clamber out onto a rock ledge to fall a tall tree, my partner would jestingly enquire whether or not I had made out my last will.

One pleasant, early spring day in late March, 1960, I was working as bucker with a set of fallers out of Camp A. Matti was the head faller, Jouko was the machine man. The two had felled a very large fir along the face. As it fell, it brushed a small second growth fir tree. Since the butt log, which was over six feet in diameter, was too big for my bucking saw, the two fallers intended to buck off the first log with the falling saw, which had a seven foot long bar.

Matti measured the length of the butt log to be cut and stood on top of the wide log, winding up his fifty foot measuring tape. His back had been turned towards the top end of the tree, which was in the direction of the fall. Jouko positioned himself below with the heavy saw, ready to start cutting. I was working off in the distance, keeping a close eye on the fallers, so as not to get too near them while they were falling timber. From where I stood I noticed that the sapling they had brushed was coming down backwards, headed towards Matti. I yelled as loudly as I could, but Matti was too slow to get into the clear. The tree came down on his head, knocking him off the log. Matti could not get up, and said that he could no longer feel his legs. In fact, he was permanently paralysed from the waist down.

Following Matti's accident, I had to double as both bucker and machine man, while Jouko did the head falling job until a new head faller arrived from town. Several days went by, and work proceeded as normal. Then, because he was being hasty, and not paying enough attention, Jouko had a tree sit-back on the bar, just as I was completing the back cut. Jouko had misjudged the tree's lean, and neglected to place wedges in the back cut as it was being sawed. The tree was now leaning backwards heavily, holding the saw blade tight, preventing wedges from being inserted. Jouko stated the obvious:

"She's tighter than a bull's arse in fly time." Jouko was left with two choices. He could use the bucking saw to fall the tree over backwards, or he could push it over by falling another tree into it. In both cases, the falling saw had to be disassembled first, wasting valuable time. Jouko decided to push it over with a tree from behind, which worked well.

A few days later, the same thing happened again. Since it was cumbersome and time consuming to take off the falling saw, Jouko suggested that I hang onto the handle bar of the falling saw and pull it back out of the cut at the moment the pressure was off. I refused to do it. It was something I had done before, but it was dangerous practice, and I was determined not to make a bad habit out of it.

"You're still single," joked Jouko, "whereas I have a family to look after. If you want to make a living in falling then you can't mind getting hurt."

"You're as crazy as a loon," I answered him. "Either we take the machine off or you hang onto the handle bar while I fall the tree into it." I stood my ground, despite the great difference in our ages. To tell the truth, I was positive I could do a better job of falling than Jouko had done so far.

The following weekend a new head faller arrived from town to replace Matti. Old Sam, the newcomer, was a hard working man in his late fifties, but he had the bad habit of jumping on top of the stump as soon as the tree had heeled over. He wanted to see whether the tree had "saved-out." In those days, fallers were all on piece work, and for broken or splintered timber there was no scale and no pay. The last time I saw Old Sam jump on a stump, the fir tree we had felled brushed another tree, and a short piece of limb, no more than eighteen inches long and six inches thick, came flying back at him, breaking his collarbone and dislocating his shoulder. Jouko and Sam left on the next boat for town, and I teamed up with a new set of fallers.

A memorable incident occurred in the same spring that Matti got hurt. For many days a lonesome raven had been attempting to enter the territory of another pair of ravens. Time and again the pair chased the intruder away, but he always returned, flying in just above the treetops. One day, however, the trespasser flew into the path of a falling tree, which killed the bird in mid-air. Even as the dead bird tumbled through the air, the defenders dove at it unrelentingly, so fiercely did they defend their territory. Only after the corpse had fallen to the snow did the victorious ravens fly away.

The Rites of Spring

Spring had finally arrived on the coast of B.C., and with the days growing longer the power of the sun increased noticeably. Flocks of Canada geese were coming back from the south, returning to their nesting grounds in the far north. At the same time the hummingbirds and swallows arrived. The bears had woken early from their long hibernation, and were combing the woods for food.

Leif, Gunnar and I were working together in the late '60s,

falling the timber for a right-of-way. Behind us worked the usual grade crew: powder-monkey, power-shovel and compression drill operators. Every day on their way back from work (fallers always worked a shorter day than the rest of the loggers) we walked by Hard Rock John, who was drilling with a jackhammer into a road cut.

"How's she going there?" asked Leif.

"Oh, she's a tough one," sighed John, resting one big leg over the jackhammer's handlebar, the usual grin on his dust-covered face. "This rock is harder than a whore's heart. If only this damn bear would leave us alone. For the last two days it has been trying to get into my drill shed while we're eating our lunch. But tomorrow I'll fix that bastard for good."

"How are you going to do that?" asked Gunnar.

"You'll see for yourself when you fellows come back from work tomorrow."

The next day, shortly after noon, Leif and Gunnar and I heard a loud explosion from the direction in which Hard Rock John was drilling. On our way out after work, we stopped to chat with the old man.

"How did you and the bear make out?"

"Go and look over there," he told us, pointing towards the edge of the road.

We walked over and looked down the bank. Hard Rock John had brought an extra lunch with him that morning, and at lunchtime he had placed it on a stump below the grade, put a few sticks of dynamite in with it and wired the whole thing up. Attracted by the smell of the food, the bear had gone straight for the stump. John waited for him, and at the very moment the bear put its head over the top of the stump he pushed the plunger. The explosion blew the bear's head into a dozen pieces, which could be seen scattered over the snow, and the entire area around the stump was stained with blood. At last Hard Rock John and his helper could eat their lunch in peace.

Hardrock John was not the only one bothered by bears. Fallers often complained that bears were raiding their lunchboxes, which they usually cached under windfalls until lunchtime. Such hiding places, however, were doomed to failure. Bears have poor eyesight, but an exceedingly good sense of smell.

Sometimes a bear would be waiting in the morning for the arrival of a crew, and some were so persistent that men had to take counter measures to safeguard their lunches. Often this was done by lowering their lunchboxes down into a hollow stump, usually a red or yellow cedar. When no such stump was available, the fallers hung their lunchboxes on saplings too thin for a bear to climb.

Bears often made nuisances of themselves in camps by breaking into the cook shack. They were particularly attracted to cook shacks after waking from hibernation, when the food on which they feed was scarce. The same circumstances occurred during the summer, if the berry crop was poor, or in the fall before the fish run began. Another ongoing problem arose when bears wandered the hills in search of a suitable tree to hibernate in. Such trees were fast disappearing, along with the stands of old growth timber in which they stood.

I had so many brushes with bears that it seemed like I was jinxed. Like the time I left my lunchbox on top of the third step outside the bunkhouse door, to be picked up on my way to the marshalling yard. Just as I came out the door again, I spotted a bear standing on its hind legs, holding my lunchbox in its paws. I yelled, and threw a rock at the bear, which was already making a quick getaway between the bunkhouses.

Bears were not the only animals to steal fallers' lunches. The wise old ravens even outdid the bears. Perched on the top of a tall tree, or soaring high above the ground, a pair of ravens would observe the coming of fallers, and no matter how carefully a lunch was hidden it was never safe from the keen eyes of those intelligent birds. Counter measures were necessary. Men would tie an old shoelace, or push a forked twig, through the clasps of their lunchbox lid, to prevent the ravens from opening the clasps.

In all my years in the woods, I never found a raven's nest, nor even the remains of one in a felled tree. Nor did anyone I know ever find one. I had an excellent rapport with ravens. Throughout much of the eighties, one old raven followed me from falling setting to falling setting, many of them miles or further apart. I used to feed it at lunch time with cheese, or morsels of lunchmeat. I named the lonesome old raven George, and in time it grew brave enough to come within yards of me to feed.

It was funny to watch the raven approaching. As soon as I stopped the power saw and headed for my lunch pack, the raven would come gliding in, landing on a nearby tree. From there it would lower itself to the ground, not far from me, and then waddle towards me, clicking its beak loudly, as ravens are wont to do. Once it reached a distance of several yards, George would hop sideways to within a yard or two of me and pick up whatever I had thrown to it. With its shiny black feathers, with their slight purple lustre, its enormous beak and massive sharp claws, it was a beautiful creature. Even after a lengthy absence from the woods, due to holidays, or to a strike in the forest industry, George always would locate me, wherever I happened to be falling timber.

One spring day a pair of young ravens appeared out of nowhere, and tried to force George out of his territory. For days on end they harassed the old bird. George, however, remained firm and stood his ground. In the end, the intruders gave up and flew away.

Since ravens mate for life, I decided that George must have lost his mate, and was now fated to a solitary existence. I felt compassion for the solitary bird, especially because I knew how close to each other mated ravens can be. I have often watched them show affection to each other, rubbing their beaks together and cackling loudly. I have seen a raven spot a kill on the ground, then call to its mate to let it know that there's food to be had. There are many lessons that human beings can learn from the behaviour of wild animals.

Fedor and Janus

About the time of year when the winter snow had almost all melted away, a young lad arrived in Camp N from town. The camp had filled with loggers, and there was hardly an empty seat available in the cookhouse. The head flunky had no other choice than to place the young lad at one of the fallers' tables, where one seat was still open. It happened to be the table at which Gunnar and I sat. Fedor had come to work as a chokerman, his first assignment in the woods. He was frail, skinny, and wore glasses. At first glance one could tell that Fedor was a bookworm.

He had come to camp in the hope of saving some money so he could continue his study of languages. Besides French and German, he studied Japanese every evening. One day at the supper table, Gunnar asked him in jest whether he would ever be successful. Fedor answered quite bluntly:

"Yes, but not in terms of money. And speaking of money, I could have more than any one of you fallers, because it's not what I make but what I save up that counts."

"Right," replied Gunnar, "all you need to do is hang in here and save up a bundle. 'Stick and stay, it will pay.'"

"By the way," asked Fedor, "when is payday in this lovely camp?"

"One never can tell for sure with those gyppos," answered Gunnar.

"What's a gyppo?" queried Fedor, looking around the table nonplused.

"A gyppo is an outfit that operates on a gin pole."

"What on earth is a gin pole?"

"It's a short spar tree used when raising a big spar tree or for loading."

"Well, well, very interesting, never heard of it before," said Fedor.

"You are still very young," replied Gunnar, "and you have lots to learn yet about logging."

"But I have no intention of ever becoming a logger," retorted Fedor.

"Many a man has said that before you."

Whenever Fedor asked for the tea at the supper-table, I would grab the searing hot spout of the large teapot and hold it in front of him so that he could grasp the handle easily. Fedor could never understand how I did this:

"Your hands must have a tremendous resistance to heat."

In fact, my palms and fingers were so heavily calloused that the hot spout did not bother me in the least. Unfortunately for Fedor he could not handle the rough job as a chokerman, and had to return to town. I had liked the bright lad, and missed him at the supper table.

Shortly after he left, another remarkable young fellow, Janus, came to work in the cookhouse as a dish washer. His large, dark eyes and prominent roman nose, along with his unusual name, gave him away as an Italian. Janus possessed a great voice, and he loved to sing arias from operas. Soon everybody called him "Caruso." On Sundays, while doing his laundry in a large tub, he consistently had an audience standing behind him, listening to him sing. But just like the famous tenor, Janus was the victim of terrible stage fright. He could not perform when facing his listeners, so he turned his back to his audience while singing. Thus fate precluded him from further opportunities as far as his brilliant voice was concerned.

Easter

On the morning of Easter Sunday the sharp sound of a rifle shot pierced the quiet air of the camp. Easter came late that year, and the weather in the Nimpkish Valley was already balmy. I was sitting on a bench in front of the bunkhouse, re-caulking and mending my torn logging boots. The sound seemed to have originated from the direction of Lefty's cabin.

Lefty, a trapper, lived in a log cabin near the outskirts of the camp. He had recently picked up a timber wolf whelp along his extensive trap line, and was rearing it on his own. Lefty named the pup Timbo.

News of the young wolf spread around camp, and made the

Author sizing up Sitka Spruce. Canfor Logging, Atluck Camp, 1965.
Courtesy: Erik Cook

Fallers with Crummy. Canfor Logging, Wolf Lake, 1974.
Courtesy: Erik Cook

Author bucking a large log at Atluck Camp, Canfor Logging, 1965. Courtesy: Erik Cook

Author removing undercut from a large Sitka Spruce at Camp Atluck, 1965. Courtesy: Erik Cook

children in the married quarters curious. That morning, a boy and a girl about ten years old took their family dog, an aged collie, and walked over to Lefty's cabin to have a look at Timbo. Lefty had tied the whelp to a long rope to prevent it from running off. The youngsters patted Timbo, while the old collie bedded down behind their backs.

Olaf heard the rifle report bouncing back from the nearby mountains and came out of his bunkhouse to see what had happened. Together, we strolled over to see Lefty, whom we suspected of having fired the shot. As we neared the clearing where he lived, we spotted two terrified children, a collie, and Lefty's tall frame dragging something heavy towards the lean-to beside his hut. Timbo kept charging furiously at whatever was being pulled along by his master.

Now we were close enough to see what it was all about. The old trapper, whose hair and beard were already grizzled, was holding the two hind legs of a mighty cougar in his strong, gnarly hands. On the grass where the cougar had been shot glistened a small puddle of blood. There was more blood on the poor collie, who had been clawed above the eyes by the cougar. Lefty's hunting rifle leaned against the side of the rough log cabin.

"How did you nail this one?" asked Olaf, gesturing toward the big cat.

"I just happened to come out to fetch me a pail of water from the brook," replied Lefty, "when I saw the cougar having a go at the collie right behind the children. I stepped back into the cabin and reached for the loaded rifle on the wall. It was a lucky shot — the collie and the cougar were going at it like cats and dogs. I could easily have missed it and hit the collie instead."

"Must have been the same cougar that's been dropping into camp to snatch up dogs," I ventured. The scene had reminded me of a summer day last year when Brent and I hiked to the river for a spot of trout fishing. A fat, black Labrador followed us from camp down the trail to the river. By the time we arrived at the fishing holes, the dog was nowhere to be seen, and no one in camp ever saw it again.

"Well, this one won't come prowling around camp anymore," Lefty assured us, as we looked at the outstretched animal, which had been shot neatly between its shoulder blades.

Some years later another Easter weekend brought a different source of excitement. Coola, a young native Indian who worked as a boom man, had Noosha, his girlfriend, come to visit him in camp. Coola and Henry the Humper (so named for obvious reasons), went down to the dock that afternoon to meet the boat. Along with Coola's girlfriend came the cases of beer and whiskey the two boom men had paid the boat's skipper to deliver. Henry the Humper, who had the build of an ox, lugged the booze into the bunkhouse which he shared with Coola and several other boom men. They were soon drinking heavily and carrying on, but as the hours went by the men became groggy. By nightfall, Coola and Henry had passed out on their bunks. Noosha was now alone with a few men who were anything but sober.

Soon word was travelling from door to door that a squaw was doing business. In no time a string of men had lined up outside Henry and Coola's hut. That night, Noosha took on at least ten of those sex-famished loggers. Coola and Henry slept through it all, and were none the wiser when they woke. Noosha left early the same day.

All the participants of that night's revelry received more than any of them had bargained for. Noosha bestowed on every one of her visitors a token gift of gonorrhea. In turn, Noosha found out later that she was pregnant. Coola quit his job on the booming ground after he heard what had gone on. Henry the Humper went right on living up to his reputation.

Rosie

Nowadays, homosexuality is an accepted fact. Traditionally, however, loggers frowned upon homosexuals, or "queers," as they called them. In camp, they were laughingstocks and the butt of bad jokes. The known or suspected gays in any camp usually worked in the cookhouse or as first aid attendants, and some were scalers. Among others, there was Rosie, who worked as a flunky in Canfor's Vernon Camp in Nimpkish during the mid-eighties. Everybody could tell from a mile away that Rosie was a homosexual, and, in fact, he made no great secret of it. He was a jolly type of a chap who no one could help but tolerate.

One ruse of Rosie's was to seek out men, normally fallers, who lay ill in camp with sore backs. With all the able-bodied men out on their jobs, Rosie prowled through camp looking for likely quarry. Then, entering the bunkhouse, he would smile and say:

"Hi there old boy, how are you today?" After which he would flop or sit down on the edge of the bunk, next to the ailing man. After b.s.-ing for a while, he would ask in his phony voice, which sounded neither like a man's nor a woman's:

"How about if I rub your sore back with a liniment?" While waiting for a response he would lick his red, fleshy lips with his tongue, roll his brown eyes and swallow nervously, his hands cradled in his fat lap. Rosie never tired of making passes and advances towards anyone in camp. Just the same, he was tolerated as a nuisance, and, as far as it was known, never made a conquest. In those days, loggers still preferred the real thing, no matter how hard up they were.

Sidewinder Rowley

Every season in the woods brought fatalities, and spring was no exception. I remember only too well the first falling fatality I witnessed, and the mild weather that made it even less excusable.

Following the end of the Second World War, jobs in towns were difficult to find, and the forest industry was the major employer on the coast of B.C. Consequently, not only those loggers who got discharged from the Canadian Armed Forces, but others who had never logged before, turned to logging for a living. Many of those men were insufficiently trained, a fact that accounts for the unacceptably high rates of serious and fatal accidents during those years.

It was a late spring day, and Sidewinder Rowley and his crew were working the strip next to the one where my partners and I were falling. Dewey the machine man and Don the bucker were brothers, working under the guidance of Rowley, whose ability as a head faller was average at best. Rowley and Dewey were doing the back cut on a balsam tree, two feet in diameter and somewhere near a hundred and twenty feet in height.

The strip Rowley's gang was falling bordered on an old burn. Experienced fallers know that the wood near a former burn tends to be brittle, an important factor which has to be taken into consideration. Rowley, in his slip-shod manner, made too deep an undercut in a tree he had neglected to plumb correctly. While sawing the back cut, the tree sat back and fell over, breaking four inches of brittle holding wood right across the stump. The butt of the tree drove the power saw into the rocky ground, and Rowley and Dewey just barely made it into the clear. Don, who had neglected to stay the minimum distance of two tree lengths from the fallers ahead, was crushed to death.

Those who had worked with Rowley were hardly surprised that his negligence had finally killed somebody. A rough and tough man with a deep, booming voice, he had once been my head faller, and we knew each other only too well. One snowy Friday several years before Don's death, Rowley and Steve, the machine man, had left the big falling saw and the rest of their tools at the base of a tall tree along the face of the setting. The tree had a heavy lean forward, and the snow was falling continuously. To the two fallers, the relatively snow-free ground under the heavy lean of that large tree appeared to be the perfect place to store the power saw. I placed my bucking tools under a great cedar windfall, mentioning to my two partners that the tree they had chosen was liable to pull over with so much wet snow piling up on its wide branches. Rowley told me not to worry, that the tree had stood like that for hundreds of years and would likely remain standing for another night or more. Nothing more was said, and the gang trudged through the snow out to the road, where other fallers and buckers were already waiting inside the cold crummy.

Over the weekend it never stopped snowing. By Monday morning, as we strained back to work through the deep snow, the entire setting could hardly be recognized. I had little trouble locating my well-protected tools, but Rowley and Steve could not find theirs. Try as they might, they were unable to locate the tree with the pronounced lean. An hour went by, and they still had not found their power saw. Meanwhile, I had finished bucking what was left over from Friday afternoon. Steve and Rowley were still floundering around in knee-deep snow, cursing and searching for their missing tools.

In the end it was I who located the root wad of the pulled over tree, under which the crushed power saw was lying. With great difficulty and lots of swearing, the wrecked saw was dug out, and another saw lugged up from the road far down below. All this took time, and when the scaler showed up in the afternoon there were very few logs for him to measure.

"No scale no pay" was the rule in those days.

Several days later the snow changed to freezing rain. Overnight the falling saw froze up. In the morning Steve could simply not get it started.

"We'll fix that!" snorted Sidewinder Rowley. He lit a gasoline fire, and turned the saw upside down over it. The engine caught fire instantly, and burned into a twisted heap of metal. We had something of a dispute over this incident, and consequently the gang split up.

Rowley, being a man who liked to brag, boasted how much timber he could fall in a day's work, and referred to himself as the "king of the forest." No doubt that sounded impressive to those who had never worked with him. Things went fine for a few years. Then one afternoon a large fir tree sat back on the bar, just as Rowley completed the back cut. First, the crew tried to lift the tree over by driving three long steel wedges into the back cut. One could hear far and wide the clear ringing of the steel wedges as the sledgehammer was applied. Nearby fallers nodded to each other:

"The Sidewinder is blacksmithing again."

But the effort was hopeless. Having wasted the better part of an afternoon trying to lift the big fir over, Rowley decided to allow the tree to fall backwards. Not bothering with a new undercut to make sure it didn't fall in the wrong direction, he and his partner sawed off the holding wood on the upper side using a bucking saw, and the big tree tipped over sideways.

Down below, my gang heard a mighty crash as the titan of a tree came crashing downhill towards us. No one was hurt, but we were all aware that our lives had been in danger. After work, my head faller told Rowley that there was no need for him to send down any more trees, since his crew was quite capable of falling their own. From then on, everyone was uneasy working below, or even in the vicinity of the Sidewinder.

A few days later Rowley had a similar incident, and at quitting time a fierce argument over his hazardous work practices broke out, as the fallers met on the road where the crummy was parked. Rowley and his partners left camp soon after that, but returned some years later to team up with Dewey and Don. Rowley was partially blamed for Don's death, and was fired as a result. He left camp on the next boat out, along with Dewey and Don's body.

About a year later, I learned that Dewey had been killed on the job in a freak accident. He had stuck his falling axe loosely into a log, and then bent over to pick up a wedge. The axe came unstuck, fell off the log and struck Dewey on the side of his exposed neck, severing his jugular vein.

Years later I met Rowley again in another camp up the coast. By then he was no longer falling, but his nickname "the Sidewinder" still stuck with him. He had had an accident while falling a tall snag — a portion of the rotten top had broken loose and struck him on his left shoulder. After a long period of recovery, he could no longer continue as a timber faller. Reluctantly, Rowley took a new job as a wood scaler, and sometime after was killed by a loose log that dropped on him from behind.

Sundays

Most camps on the coast took Sundays off. Much of the day was spent standing over a washtub with a plunger or a scrub brush, washing one's soiled laundry. Loggers seldom, if ever, washed their outer clothing. Their work pants became stiff with pitch, sawdust and oil. Some loggers called them "tin pants." Hardly a logger owned a change of work clothes. They wore one set ragged, then bought a new set from the commissary.

Sunday was also a day for fallers to sharpen their axes. Usually two men would go together, one man sharpening while the other rotated the solid stone wheel. Others wrote letters; some cut each other's hair. Logging boots were re-caulked, work clothes patched. But most of the older men rested or slept the entire afternoon. Some would sit on a bench in the shade of a bunkhouse, smoking a pipe or chewing snoose, telling each other endless tales of logging.

If the loggers were lucky, one of their number might have been an accordion player, willing to entertain them with a medley of stirring tunes. The setting for those rare moments of bliss varied little from camp to camp. As soon as the earth got warmer in the spring, or when the heat lessened in the fall, men sought out the sun, sitting on benches in front of the bunkhouses. During the summer men sat idle in the shade of a bunkhouse to cool off. More often than not several men, usually countrymen, sat on a long bench, conversing in low voices in their native language. Others just rested flat out on their bunkbeds.

The camp was at its quietest on such Sunday afternoons. Only the buzzing sound of annoying flies or the call of a far away bird of prey could be heard. It is difficult to describe the uplift of emotions when suddenly the sound of an accordion pierced the stillness. Some men listened pensively, others gave free play to their thoughts. The accordion player often just sat on the short steps of a bunkhouse, or stood with one foot resting on a step. Unfortunately, it was rare to hear a logger play an accordion in camp. A logger on the move had enough to carry without lugging an accordion along. And once in camp, where could he keep his beloved instrument? Usually right under his bunk, for all and sundry to see. That simple fact explains it all.

Sundays also gave me time to think about my family. My son Hans was born in 1970, my daughter Trudel in 1974. In my absence, they were raised most capably and lovingly by Inge. I usually managed to sneak home for a long weekend every three or four months, but other than that the only time I spent with them was at Christmas, shutdowns and fire season. Occasionally people would ask me why I didn't bring my family to the woods with me. I would answer: "There's nothing for their eyes here."

Camp life was rough, and the educational facilities for children were primitive, at best. I wanted my children to be well-bred, and to have the opportunities in life that fate had denied me. For this, I was prepared to make any sacrifice.

CHAPTER 5

SUMMER

Horseflies and Heat

Quite often an early spring indicates a hot summer ahead. Mild morning air is permeated with a certain fragrance which eludes description. Later on in the day, once the morning fog has lifted, a cloudless, deep blue sky, with brilliant rays of sunshine, heralds the imminence of a long, hot summer. The months of May and June are something of a respite in comparison to the rest of the year, and the men are not as likely to be taxed to the limits of their endurance by adverse weather conditions.

With the temperatures steadily rising, the months of July and August can get hotter than Hades on the coast of B.C., and are often the two most tormenting months of the year for loggers on the job. Experienced loggers keep a lookout for high flying swallows, or pairs of soaring eagles or falcons, all of which are sure indicators of a high pressure system over the coastal region. Accompanying westerly winds help to maintain high temperatures and low humidity, both of which are critical factors in a tinder-dry forest, where only a single spark is needed to set the woods ablaze.

Blistering heat was only one of the torments that summer brought, but its effects were varied and profound. For most loggers work was hard and sweaty, especially when temperatures reached into the high '80s (Fahrenheit) and beyond. Under such conditions, every piece of clothing, including one's woolen socks, became soaked with sweat. Dark sweat stains, left by suspenders that pressed down on a man's shirt, were visible on every logger's back. When there was not enough drinking water to quench one's thirst and flush the hot skin, sweat became salty and began to burn. Finally those salty rivulets would run down to the eye, stinging sharply and impairing one's vision. Other parts of the body stung as well, especially where rough clothes chafed against hot skin. Understandably, men grew desperate for water, which was simply not always available. Working on a hillside where there was no creek from which to fill an empty water bag was torture. At times the heat became so intense that it drained the body of its vitality. Despite the headaches and nausea which overcame heat-exhausted men, work carried on.

At lunchtime everyone desperately sought a shady spot, even if it was only the narrow shade of a log, just to get out of the searing sun. Seldom could the lunch pack be kept cool till noon, and few, if any men felt like eating warm sandwiches that appeared to have been cooked. Now and then a man handed over his lunch to the ever-present raven. After lunch the tools would be hot to the touch of the hand.

With the coming of summer weather, early shift is the rule of the day in coastal B.C. logging camps. To the uninitiated, early shift sounds innocent, but for loggers it's the beginning of a long period of torment. This is the time of year when loggers look hopefully at the sky, wishing for the rain which only months ago they had so abhorred.

With summer's short nights, work on early shift can begin at five a.m. Consequently, men had to get up by two-thirty a.m. to make their lunch, have breakfast, and be ready for marshalling at four. To get up at 2:30 a.m. is no easy task. Many a young fellow would refuse to rise at such an ungodly hour, sleep right on till morning, and then leave camp on the next boat for town.

The rest of us trudged through the dark towards the marshalling yard, the majority carrying a two-gallon canvas water bag to help with the sweltering heat of the coming day.

Before starting up, crummy and log truck drivers shone a light to check their engines for oil and water. Then the big motors roared to life. Drowsy men huddled on narrow benches swatted at swarms of pesky noseeums, and once the crummy was under way they were jostled and jolted mercilessly during the long ride to the worksite. Nothing much was said — the men sat tight-lipped with closed eyes, guarding against the road dust sucked into the rear of the open crummy. If the morning dawned without fog, bright sunlight would be warming the settings by the time the loggers arrived at their destination.

The first thing the men wanted to know was how much dew, if

any, was on the ground, and whether a morning breeze was in the offing to disperse the hoards of mosquitoes, noseeums and black flies, which have been known to drive normally implacable men into frenzies. These small, blood sucking insects are at their worst on muggy days, when the temperature is around sixty-five degrees, and the humidity around ninety percent. Cooler or hotter temperatures, or even a slight breeze, drive these smaller insects underground. But when the mosquitoes and noseeums disappeared, the larger horseflies and deerflies arrived to bite and torment the exasperated men.

Fortunate were those loggers who worked at this time of the year on the shady side of a mountain. They, at least, were blessed with a few hours in the shade before the sun rose high in the cloudless firmament.

But, pity those men who were exposed to the scorching rays from the very moment the sun appeared in the clear eastern sky. By 10:00 not one man could be found who was not saturated with sweat. Cool, clear water and a piece of shade, even if it came from a puny sapling, is what every logger craved. And even if water could be had, often there was no shade to shield one from the scorching sun.

Sweat ran down one's spine, over the back, down between the stinging and chafing buttocks and on further to the scrotum, dripping off into the crotch of one's pants. Hot, swollen feet begged to be released from the confinement of steaming, tightly laced boots. The tanned, dehydrated skin of old timers took on the appearance of wrinkled leather. There was no way of avoiding the searing hot air, nor of escaping the roasting sun.

Looking out over a setting or a distant slash, one perceived the rising heat waves and realized that the day would continue to get hotter. When a camp was located too far from the ocean to benefit from its refreshing breeze, men were nearly smothered by the oppressive air of the interior. A very distinct, pleasing smell, peculiar only to a dry forest, pervaded the entire logging area, but with every step moss, twigs and bracken crackled ominously, reminding one how dangerously dry the woods had become. Temperatures have been known to climb past one hundred degrees on very hot days.

Suddenly, out of nowhere appeared the devilish horseflies, assaulting a man from behind, biting ferociously, attacking while one's hands were too busy to fend them off. No matter how many were swatted down, there were forever more. Hours and days of misery passed by.

During early shift, supper was served around 3:00 p.m. The

cookhouse staff suffered no less from the sweltering heat than the loggers in the forest. Long hours of work were broken up into three parts of the day, with little sleep in between.

Only very late at night did it cool off somewhat, granting the over-fatigued workers a few hours of much needed sleep. With reduced food intake, little rest and few hours of sound sleep, a person's physical condition gets run down fast. The men tended to get irritable as well, short of temper, and quite simply wretched.

From 1936 until 1972 fallers and buckers were on piece work, getting paid only for what they produced. This contrasted with the remainder of the logging crew, who were all getting paid at an hourly rate. For a set of fallers to make fair wages, many things had to fall into place. More often than not, nothing was in their favour.

The factors involved ranged from the quality of the timber to be felled, the price paid per 1,000 board feet, the ground conditions, and, of course, the weather. The honesty of the scaler, compatibility of the crew, ability, endurance, perseverance, and the will to overcome adversity, all played an important role in being successful. And last but not least, the tools that one had to work with and the condition they were in were matters of great concern.

The most common contentious factor revolved around the scale. Some of the fiercest arguments I ever had in the woods were with scalers and bullbuckers over log scaling. I could demonstrate to the scaler that by simply changing the cut on log lengths one could obtain two different scales from a large, fast tapering tree. By bucking such a tree into short logs, one could get a higher scale than by bucking the same tree into longer sections, although the true total volume of the tree remained unchanged.

The bullbucker not only allocated the strips to be felled, but also arbitrarily set the price per 1,000 board feet that fallers would get paid for their hard work. Here again there was room for contention. Fallers who fought for their entitlement to a fair scale lived in constant strife with the bullbucker, check scaler and scalers. Where a bullbucker enjoyed the taste of whiskey, a bottle of rye from the hand of a faller would make all the difference to his earnings.

One particular incident from the mid-'70s is noteworthy. Hot Shot Jack was a bullbucker who had it in for a faller named Burke. Burke told Hot Shot Jack to get off his back, but to no avail. One day Jack went to check on Burke's work. Burke had had a mishap with a complex figuration of trees, and damaged his power saw in an accident that had partially been beyond his control. Jack walked in on him just as Burke was looking over the situation, spotted the damaged saw and fell into a rage. The veins on the sides of his scrawny turkey neck swelled as he screamed abuse at the already annoyed faller. Burke soon reached the limit of what he was willing to put up with, and hit Hot Shot Jack square on the jaw.

"Fuck her, Jack, she's a gunnysack," swore Burke. "I'm fired anyway, so I might as well do a good job on you now." Well over six feet tall with size twelve boots, Burke kicked Hot Shot Jack all the way back to the road.

Since I had been working next to Burke, I heard the commotion and observed the bullbucker's humiliating exit. Hot Shot Jack came stumbling over the felled timber, holding his hat in one hand while he steadied himself with the other on his scale stick. Blood trickled down his bleeding nose, and whenever he stopped to catch his breath, which was frequently, Burke booted him square in the rear end with his big, heavy logging boot. Many a faller had wanted to do just that to Jack, but had lacked the courage to do it.

The Grouch

On one of those warm, Sunday afternoons when we weren't lucky enough to have an accordion concert in camp, I decided to stroll down to the river by Atluck Camp for a swim. The path I followed led through one of those now rare groves of virgin timber. About halfway down I heard a murmuring voice off the trail behind some salmonberry bushes.

Curious, I stopped to investigate. I soon determined that the man behind the bushes was Grouch, the whistle punk from the skidder. Grouch was a short man in his middle thirties, who never talked to anybody in camp. He was notably reliable on the job, but exceedingly grouchy. He had one outstanding feature — his head, which boasted dark hair and Neanderthal bone structure. When Grouch spoke it was in a low, hesitant voice, and it was this that I recognized, even before I could see him.

Standing motionless beside a large tree, I peeked through the bushes. Grouch sat on a low, mossy boulder with his trousers down over his knees, facing the trail. He was stroking with determination at an enormous penis. His head was slumped, and his stubby, saddle-like nose and wide flared nostrils spread like a tent over his erection, which stood out like a miniature flagpole. As he stroked, he repeatedly uttered the following words:

"She's a hot one, she's a hot one!"

As quietly as I could, I stepped back onto the trail and continued down to the river.

The next day after work, I spotted Grouch in the washroom, washing himself out of a battered tin bowl. As I stepped into the shower I spoke out loud, so all the men in the room could hear me: "She's a hot one, she's a hot one!"

Grouch grasped the meaning of my words, threw the contents of his water bowl at me and stormed out of the building.

"What was all that about?" asked the astonished onlookers.

"Go ask Grouch," I replied.

They never asked, and I never told. Late in the fall of that year Grouch left camp, and I never saw or heard of him again.

Springboard Jack

Springboard Jack was slight of stature, but he had the head of a bulldog and a personality to match. Whether standing or walking his body seemed hunched, his head strangely tilted towards his right shoulder. Sometimes a fleeting, impish grin appeared on his face, and his large, tobacco-stained hands were forever clasping his scale stick.

I knew Springboard Jack, also known as "Wooden Shoe," during the '80s in the Nimpkish Valley. Many loggers had worked under his rigid rule, and no one liked it. Because of his self-righteous *I'm right and you're wrong* attitude, no bullbucker was more hated, cursed and despised. It was Springboard Jack's obstinate, counterproductive way, or no way at all.

Springboard Jack spoke very slowly with a sonorous voice, and used elaborate, long-winded words and explanations. What could have been said in three words he took pains to say in a dozen or more.

On occasion, however, he demonstrated a good sense of humour. He was fond of telling jokes, albeit crude ones:

"An old bull and a young heifer stood on top of a knoll," said Springboard Jack one evening across the cookhouse table. "They were overlooking a green meadow, where a small herd of cows was grazing. Looking down at them longingly, the heifer said to the bull: 'Let's run down there fast and fuck one.' 'No,' replied the bull, 'let's walk down there slowly and fuck them all.'" The joke was close to Jack's heart. His background was in farming, and at heart he essentially remained a farmer.

Arne the Bull of the Woods, an outstanding logger in his own right, was heard to say:

"Farmers never made great loggers."

Springboard Jack resented Arne for voicing his disparaging opinion. Nevertheless, many other men said worse, and there were numerous occasions when Jack narrowly escaped being attacked by a hot-tempered faller. Like the time, for instance, when he had a run-in with Wheeler Dealer John.

John, a slim fellow in his early forties, full of explosive energy, hated Springboard Jack with a passion. Unfortunately for Jack, John was no trifler. In fact, he possessed a sharp mind, and was always a step ahead of everyone around him. It so happened one pleasant fall day that John needed a new cutting chain for his falling saw. To avoid wasted time struggling with a worn-out chain, John radioed the camp at lunch time for a replacement. Later in the afternoon, Springboard Jack climbed the hill to where John was working.

"John," he blustered, "I've come to inspect the condition of your chain, to see whether you need a new one."

"You son of a whore," John shot back at the bullbucker. "I asked for a new chain, not for an inspection from you." Both men were standing on top of a tree that John had just felled. "Seeing as you haven't got a chain for me, get the hell out of my way or I'll knock that ugly wart right off the tip of your nose." John clamped his ear muffs down over his ears, started the power-saw, and moved towards the bullbucker, who backed off down the log and beat a hasty, undignified retreat.

Springboard Jack drove many skilled fallers from camp. It all led back to the fact that he was completely unsuited for his job in the woods. The only reason he lasted as long as he did was that he worked his entire life for the same company, a company that kept its share of deadwood on the payroll.

Only once did a faller succeed in disconcerting Springboard Jack, at least in the presence of a crowd. The faller's name was Fishhead, and although nobody knew how he'd received his name, it seemed to suit him. Fishhead was an inveterate joker with an unsavoury sense of humour, but in order to understand what he did to Jack, it helps to know what he did first to the Bunkhouse Lawyer.

Every morning before boarding the crummy to go to work, the fallers visited the saw-filing shack to pick up a chain-saw file, and other bits and pieces they might need for the day.

One morning Fishhead and a few other fallers had arrived early for marshalling, and were waiting in the saw-filing shack for orders from the bullbucker. Some of them sat on a long, low bench along the shabby wall, gabbing with each other or watching the wide entrance, through which the rest of the camp's fallers came lurching in one by one. Tottering in came a man we called The Bunkhouse Lawyer, an old-looking individual of about sixty years, who spent a great deal of his time in court, suing fellow workers.

Impulsively, Fishhead got up from the hard wooden bench, took a few steps towards the old man, and asked him how he was doing on that fine morning. Whereupon the Bunkhouse Lawyer replied unabashed:

"Without sex, what can you expect up here in this God-forsaken camp?"

Fishhead stepped up close to the Bunkhouse Lawyer, held his left index finger up to the nose of the startled old man, and said:

"Look at this here." At the same moment Fishhead made a lightning fast grab for the Bunkhouse Lawyer's crotch. A moment later Fishhead was laughing out loud:

"You son of a whore, do you always show up for work with such a big hard on?"

"Yes," retorted the Bunkhouse Lawyer. "And I'm mighty proud of it too."

Such behaviour was not unusual for Fishhead, who possessed the queer habit of grabbing men by the seat of their pants. We quickly learned not to turn our backs for long on Fishhead.

On the early summer morning when Springboard Jack got his comeuppance, most of the fallers from camp happened to be assembled in the saw filing shack. There was no particular reason why so many of them were there at once. Lengthwise through the middle of the shack ran a narrow, waist high counter, on which fallers picked up new saws and saw parts in the morning, and placed broken saws and parts when they returned from the woods.

Standing there at the counter, bent slightly forward to examine a badly damaged saw blade, was Springboard Jack. Behind him stood Chin Whisker Boyd, doing his utmost to egg on Fishhead to grab the bullbucker by his balls. Fishhead didn't need much urging. He stepped behind the unsuspecting bullbucker and grabbed him firmly by his scrotum. Someone blurted out:

"Now cough, you son of a bitch."

Fishhead relaxed his grip on the private parts of the startled bullbucker. Then he announced to the crowd:

"What a nice tobacco pouch Jack's long sack would make!"

The whole saw filling shack resounded with laughter. Being a good sport, which he could be at times, the bullbucker had a good laugh too, but after this episode Springboard Jack avoided Fishhead like the plague.

Fire! (Part Two)

From early spring on, all indications persisted for a dry, hot summer ahead. By July, weeks of rainless weather, along with steady, westerly winds, had critically dried out the ground in the woods. The heavy snow packs on the craggy mountains had receded, exposing the beetling slopes of folded rock. Foaming snow water surged through gut-twisting chasms and forbidding gorges, rushing to join with rivers far below. Steep, wooded slopes in different shades of green rose as far as the eye could see; scattered patches of snow still clung to pinnacles under an azure sky.

Here and there were the unmistakable signs of past and present logging activities. Narrow logging roads twisted through constricted valleys, crossed soaring log bridges. Clouds of dust trailed large log trucks and whirled away on the westerly winds. The moaning of labouring trucks throbbed through the peaceful air of the region, where for aeons the only loud sounds had their origin in snow or rock slides. Even worse was the roaring, high-pitched noise of the power-saws, accompanied by the air-rending crash of heavy timber. Once the power-saws were silent, and all the trees in a setting had been felled, the yarder would move in.

Hundred Percent Bill, a hooktender (with him, everything had to be one hundred percent, no less), had just moved his yarder onto a huge new setting. Most of the felled trees were Douglas fir and red cedar, and consisted of prime timber. Hundred Percent Bill had taken all necessary precautions. As always, he admonished his men to be mindful, and to minimize the danger of inadvertently starting a fire. By 7:00 a.m. the men were panting and sweating like horses in front of a plough. The old water bag passed from hand to hand among the thirsty rigging crew.

After lunch, at 9:00 a.m., Barber-Chair Fred, the rigging slinger and a former faller, spotted a whiff of smoke rising on a ridge where the haulback line touched the ground. Fred promptly blew the whistle for fire, one long and several short blasts. He repeated the signal, then stormed toward the landing with his men. Hundred Percent Bill had also seen the pale smoke, and likewise told the landing crew to grab the fire fighting equipment on top of the yarder. Dick, the donkey puncher, raced down the road to where the big fire truck with the huge water tank had been parked, and drove it back up the road, parking as close as he could to the point where the smoke came from. The crew frantically strung out the fire hoses, struggling uphill towards the now rapidly spreading flames.

To estimate how swiftly a fire will spread over a felled and bucked setting in dry weather, one has to know the strength with which the prevailing north-westerly winds blow during a high pressure system on B.C.'s coast.

Normally, the wind sets out with a slight breeze after sunrise, then increases steadily as the day goes by, usually becoming very gusty in the afternoon, only to subside once more after sundown. At times, usually coinciding with a full moon, the gusts never ease, but continue blowing incessantly day and night. Once a spark ignites the tinder in a setting, those strong, gusty winds act like giant bellows.

Looking up the steep slope, Hundred Percent Bill realized that he needed more men and fire fighting equipment than he had on hand. He sent a man in a pickup truck to get assistance from the nearest yarding and falling crew, miles away.

Long Butt Lars, my falling partner, and I, were among the men who came to help. Rushing out from the rear of the crummy, we took one look at the flaming hillside and realized how desperate the situation had already become. Driving up the bumpy logging road came Porky, the super, accompanied by his trusty side push, Windbag Sam.

Porky began shouting orders, and Windbag Sam led a contingent of fallers up the slope, dragging fire hoses over felled and bucked timber, trying hard to out-race the rapidly growing blaze. Our goal was to keep the flames from spreading farther up the hill, to save the remaining logs and standing timber.

Long Butt Lars and I were up front in the lead, our fire hose nozzle pointing towards the swiftly approaching flames. We stood there while precious minutes went by, anxiously waiting for the fire pumps down below to start pumping water. The devastating flames were drawing uncomfortably near. Only then did I grasp how serious the situation had become. Above us, the blistering hot noon day sun; in front of us a sheet of fire. Its fierce heat caused the skin on our faces to tighten, singed our beards and eyebrows. Live sparks, pungent smoke and hot ashes blew towards us on buffeting winds. Flames as tall as a man, ranging in colour from yellow and ochre at the base to deep red at the top, leapt towards us. I remembered a riddle from my childhood: What is this? The more you feed it, the hungrier it gets? The answer is Fire.

Still no water, and sparks from the fire were leaping behind us and igniting the ground cover. It quickly became obvious that we had to retreat speedily, or Lars and I would be trapped in that inferno. Dropping fire hose, we struggled frantically to get back into the dwindling clear. The two fallers who had been on the second hose had faced the same predicament, and were rapidly retreating before us.

Down by the siamese coupling, Windbag Sam was urging the men back down the hill — without water, there was no sense in staying in the way of danger. Somewhere on the line, one of several chokermen who helped to lay out the hoses had failed to connect two ends properly. In retrospect, the setting could not have been saved anyways.

Down below at the landing, men fought fearlessly to protect the yarder. Had it not been for the violent gusty winds, their efforts would have succeeded, but to everyone's dismay the donkey was quickly gutted by the devouring flames. Porky stood beside the big log truck with the huge water tank on its rear. Rivulets of sweat ran down his bald head onto his fat face.

"My aching back is killing me," he moaned — no great wonder with the spare tire he carried around his waist. Constantly short of breath, he may have suffered from asthma, which the pungent smoke was not helping. Having lost the battle on all fronts, Porky watched the flames race over the setting and spread into the standing timber. With the wind blowing harder than ever, sparks were carried up to the treetops, and from then on the fire started to crown. Blackened, overcome with heat, men stood helplessly by as the elements had their way.

More men and additional fire fighting equipment was on its way out to the hard-pressed fire-fighters. Every man in camp, except the cookhouse staff, had been conscripted to fight the blaze. Fresh sandwiches and newly filled water bags were delivered, and the battle with the flames was taken up in earnest. Slowly, from confusion emerged order. Despite his physical handicaps, Porky and several other cool-headed loggers got the men and fire hoses where they were needed.

To everyone's great relief the fierce blowing wind subsided after sundown, and with that the fire began to slow. Later that night half the fire fighting crew was sent back to camp for a few hours of sleep.

The following days were split into two twelve hour shifts. Long Butt Lars and I stayed out the first night falling burning trees. This sounds a lot simpler than it actually is. To fall a tree in a dense forest in daytime is tricky enough. To do so at night in a burning stand of timber is something else again. To begin with, it is difficult to determine the lean of a tree at night, and the faller can only make an experienced guess.

Snags are the worst things for a faller to work on, since they contain hidden defects not common to live timber. Special techniques and safety precautions are needed for their removal. But this is all rather difficult to achieve by flickering fire light. Trees and snags which had burning sections out of reach of the fire hose had to be felled, the burning parts cut out, removed, and hosed down.

This, then, was our job. I lugged the brute of a power saw and an axe, while Long Butt Lars followed behind with the canvas bag containing steel wedges, sledge hammer, fuel cans, and of course, the indispensable water bag. Usually the base of a burning tree or a snag was hot, and had to be hosed down before a faller could stand next to it. Occasionally, burning or smoldering bits and pieces came falling from above, striking workmen on the head or shoulders.

Long and endless seemed the nights, with only the noise of the water pumps and power saws audible in the burning forest. Infrequently, a mighty crash was heard in the darkness as a faller downed another burning tree. At one point during the dark night Fat Pat accidentally severed the main fire hose, leaving the firefighters with limp hoses in blackened hands. One man became lost in the darkness, fell over a cliff and broke his back. In the confusion, he was not missed till the end of the night. Shortly after dawn his two partners and a scaler were found fast asleep by Windbag Sam. All three workers were promptly fired.

As morning broke, the fatigued firefighters were overcome by a great desire for sleep and fresh, clean air. Sleep they could have, the relief crews were arriving, but fresh air was impossible. Over the entire valley, reaching up into the rugged ridges of the surrounding mountains, everything was enveloped in smoke.

Weary loggers fought such forest fires for days and often weeks on end. At the end of it they all had to throw their clothes and boots into the trashcans. And then, only days after the forest fire had subsided, a thunderstorm struck the hillsides. It brought the much needed rain, but it also brought lightning strikes. Once again, men were sent out to combat the flames.

What had once been a serene green valley, teeming with wildlife, was now a wasted landscape, reduced to ash and the black skeletons of burnt-out and tumbled trees. It takes decades before the scars of a devastating forest fire disappear, covered first by fireweed and bracken, then by lush deciduous trees, and finally by new stands of tall green timber. Inevitably, whether one likes it or not, fire is an integral part of logging.

The Law of Averages

And so it happened, in the middle of the summer of 1992, on a setting where the slash burn had run amok, that the law of averages finally caught up with me. Paul (my new falling partner) and I had just finished working in an ecologically sensitive area, where stream protection had been of utmost importance. We were ready for a new assignment. As Mel, the Woss Camp supervisor, drove us out to our new jobsite, he shook his head and smiled ruefully.

"You men won't like where I'm taking you. It's a fire burn."

"Great," I thought. "Another of those dreadful jobs that nobody wants to do."

When we got there, the setting was an indescribable mess. The slash burn from the year before had spread into green timber and ravished the better part of a steep, broken-up slope. As I knew from past experience, working in such an area is one of the most dangerous jobs a faller is called on to perform.

As was common safety practice on such dangerous jobs, Paul and I doubled up and worked together in partnership. In this manner we struggled for days on end, tortured by the searing summer heat and the acidic soot. It was hell on earth. Nearly done with the worst part, having slowly worked our way out of the ashes into green standing timber again, I came upon a very large burned-out red cedar snag. It was my turn to do the falling, while Paul, standing nearby, kept an eye on things that might endanger me while I worked at the base of the snag.

The burnt-out tree was well over six feet wide at the base, about forty feet high, and as wicked looking as any burned-out hollow snag can be. Having secured the area, I sawed the undercut, which went quite well despite the awkward position I was forced to adopt due to the snag's location on the steep, rocky slope. I finished clearing out the last chunk of undercut with my long-handled axe, and had just turned around to get in position to saw the back cut, when I was struck from above by a large piece of burned-out snag, which had dislodged itself for no apparent reason.

As Paul told me later, it all happened so fast he had no opportunity to give warning. Before he could even open his mouth the slab had knocked me downhill onto sharp rocks. I realized I had been hit, and felt a sharp pain all over my body. As I lay head-down in a twisted, prone position, I thought:

"So this is the end. What will they say at home?"

I was nearly crushed, but still alive, and with Paul's help I struggled back to my feet. I was bleeding profusely from several head injuries, and Paul needed all our field dressings to bandage the lacerations. My shocked mind began recalling the many instances where I had done the same for others. There had been cuts from axes — and worse, from chainsaws. Once a fellow had nearly all the flesh from one side of his face peeled off by a ricocheting piece of frozen tree limb. My nerves had been taxed to the limit by the sight of skin and flesh hanging from his face. I remembered the blood stain on the snow around us, as with shaking, frozen fingers I tried to assist my agonized fellow worker.

But this time it was I who needed help. I had always been so

164

careful, and so sure that I would remain uninjured. I had worked as a logger for over thirty years, and except for one broken arm ten years ago, I had never had a time-loss accident.

Young Paul was visibly shaken by my bloody appearance, and I was suddenly seized by the conviction that this was the end of my career in the woods. Fate had decided that I should lay down my tools just short of the mandatory retirement age of sixty five.

Despite terrible pain, I was determined to leave the site of the accident under my own steam. I put my trusty old axe and my crushed safety helmet at the base of the fateful snag, and proceeded to leave the woods, never to return. Paul and I struggled as well as we could up the hill to where our crummy was parked. There was a searing pain in my left lung, and I could not stop spitting blood. It was agonizing.

The accident happened on a Friday morning, around 9:00 a.m. The weather was overcast, with a light drizzle like scotch mist. Once we reached the crummy, Paul radioed back to camp and arranged for an ambulance to meet us at the foot of the mountain. He told the operator to call for a helicopter, because it was increasingly obvious that I was in very bad shape. Then Paul drove down the steep, rough road back to camp. Every bounce and jolt transferred itself to my wrecked body.

Back at camp, I had to wait for the helicopter, which was delayed due to fog. Eventually I was flown to the nearest emergency hospital, but the doctors realized that I needed special attention, and I was rushed by air ambulance to the City of North Vancouver. At 10:00 p.m. that night a surgeon went to work on my head injury.

While being prepped for the operating room, one nurse said to me:

"You're early tonight."

"No," I replied, "I'm late. It's been a good twelve hours since I was injured." Another nurse told me later on that the nurses initially thought I was an early "BBB" (Beer Bar Brawl) casualty, most of whom don't arrive in hospital until after midnight.

Following the surgery was a lengthy healing process for both body and spirit. Deep inside I knew how fortunate I had been. I had come very close to being another logging fatality.

The Shrine In Kyoto

During solitary hours, I often reflect on my life's work in the forest. Having labored for many strenuous, eventful years as a faller, one noteworthy occurrence remains fixed in my mind. It was the middle of December, 1989, and the operation was closing for the holidays. The next day nearly the entire camp, except for a skeleton crew, would leave for the journey back to Vancouver. As I returned from the woods on the last day of work, the bullbucker was waiting for me at the saw filing shack.

The bullbucker asked to speak to me privately, and once we were alone, he asked point blank if I would mind staying a few days longer for an "urgent" job. Without waiting for my reply, he began to explain why he needed me.

That afternoon three men in a rented van had arrived in camp, two of whom had flown in from Japan. The third was a Japanese Canadian who was employed by Seaboard in North Vancouver, and who now acted as interpreter. Canfor, my employer, was a member of Seaboard, a company that ships logs and lumber to Asia from the B.C. coast.

The two Japanese had come in search of four large red cedar timbers for a Shinto shrine. These were no ordinary timbers they were looking for. Seabord knew where such tall trees grew, which was why the Japanese had been sent to our camp.

One of the gentlemen was a structural engineer. He brought with him several rolls of blueprints for the shrine they were planning to build. The other, an elderly man, turned out to be a Shinto priest. Although I was as eager as the next worker to go home to see my family, something about the job piqued my interest, and I agreed to stay.

The next day the bullbucker drove me, with all my tools, out to where a stand of the tallest white bark red cedar trees still grew. Why white bark cedars? Because they are nearly free of branches up to a great height, and were thought to be ideally suited for the intended purpose. In addition, white bark cedars are less tapered than other red cedars, and would therefore make perfect corner pillars for the Shinto shrine.

Two factors had to be carefully considered: first, the enormous size of the cedar trees; second, the safest way of extracting them to the nearest logging road. Having arrived at the area where the most suitable trees were likely to be spotted, we began to search in earnest. Time was of the essence. It was mid December, 1989, and the timbers had to be at Seabord by the twenty-first of the month, when the freighter was set to leave port.

Once a likely tree was spotted, the sizing-up and scrutinizing commenced. The measurements of the requested timbers were large: no less than a fifty-four inch diameter at the bottom end, seventy feet long, with a minimum top diameter of forty-two inches (three-and-a-half feet). This meant that the tree had to be at least five-and-a-half feet in diameter at the butt, and approximately one-hundred and fifty feet in total height.

At that time of year daylight was at its shortest. Furthermore, a heavily overcast sky made it extremely difficult to look up through the branches of adjacent trees, to see how large the top part of the trunk was. Once the bullbucker and I agreed on a likely tree, I began to circle it, round and round, sizing it up for hidden hazards, meticulously inspecting its base for telltale signs of defects. Next I chose a spot for the tree to fall. This had much to do with the lean of the tree, unless it stood absolutely straight. A great deal also depended on the ground where the tree would fall. Both the tree and its bark had to be intact, so it couldn't fall on any hard surface, such as rock boulders, knolls, or old stumps. Only then, should the ground prove satisfactory, would I commence with the undercut, closely observing the out-coming sawdust, from which I could tell if the core of the tree was sound or rotten.

Next came the removal of the undercut and the moment of truth — only perfectly healthy red wood would suffice. Once the soundness of the tree had been established, the final back cut had to wait until later. Now was the time to prepare a bed for the tree to fall in. This was done by falling saplings crosswise along the entire length of the intended falling location. To further cushion the fall of the precious tree, large branches were used. It was imperative that the entire tree, right up to its top, remain intact. A break, even if it occurred on a spot beyond the required length, would extend, unseen to the naked eye, back through the grain in the trunk of the tree.

Having finished making a soft bed, I was ready for the back cut. Around me the forest looked gray and dismal — the smell of snow was in the air. In fact, at higher elevations, it was snowing already.

"Thank God it's not snowing yet," I thought, "or worse, blowing a crosswind." I could absolutely not afford to mess up, and such factors would have greatly increased the likelihood of problems.

While sawing on the back cut, I inserted wedges to prevent the tree from settling back on the saw blade. As I monitored the base where the cut was being made for unexpected developments, I again paid close attention to the outpouring sawdust.

Finally the tree heeled over, leaving the stump with only the sound of the holding wood breaking. Its fall into the ready-made bed was muffled — a good sign. The bullbucker and I watched the fall from our getaway path. We then scrambled eagerly back to examine the large stump for its worthiness. It looked good.

Wasting no time, I climbed onto the felled giant, checking to see if the trunk had been damaged, and whether any bark had come off, leaving unwanted bruises. Nothing untoward was discovered.

Heavy on my mind was the burning question: did the tree have the desired diameter at the required length? I measured out from the butt so the bullbucker could obtain the correct diameter with the aid of his scale stick: it passed. At seventy-five feet from the butt I cut the tree in half, again watching the outpouring sawdust closely. It had the very rich, dark red cedar look, and a good, fresh, strong cedar smell poured from the cut. The bullbucker and I heaved an enormous sigh of relief.

While we measured and sawed a D-8 bulldozer came rumbling up the logging road, followed by a large front end loader. Each had a swamper along for the ride. Their job was to extract the large, long timber, unscathed, and bring it to the logging road from behind standing trees. They were no less under pressure than I had been.

As they began their job, I picked up my tools and left with the bullbucker to search for the next tree. As I soon found out, it was slim pickings; one tree after the other was rejected. To save time, I skipped lunch. Besides, I was very aware of how much depended on my performance, and my appetite had all but disappeared. Try as we might, we couldn't find another appropriate tree. Daylight was fading fast, and we returned to the camp in a somber mood.

At the cookhouse that evening I sat alone. Only the second cook had stayed behind to serve the small skeleton crew. That evening I was plagued by the same nagging question: will we find the remaining trees within our time frame? The next morning nothing had changed as far as the dreary weather was concerned. Worried about our lack of progress, the bullbucker drove us farther afield. It was a good decision. I felled several more trees that day.

On the third day we needed only one more tree, which we found in a stand of tall cedars. Our chosen tree was very tall, but it leaned in the wrong direction. This meant that I had to use a hydraulic timber jack to push the tree over in the way we needed it to go. With the help of the bullbucker, who was an old pro when it came to handling timber jacks, everything went perfectly. (In fact, this tree was so large that I had to cut off four feet from the butt.)

Of the eight trees I had felled in two-and-a-half days, one turned out to be a reject and one was borderline in size, which left six good timbers from which to choose the four best candidates. All six timbers were hauled to a nearby abandoned landing, and laid out there for a final inspection by the Japanese visitors.

On the following day everyone who was involved in handling the timbers assembled at the landing site. Soon the van with the visitors arrived, and I watched two men alight from the rear of the vehicle. To my amazement, they unloaded a table and placed it at the edge of the logging road. With the help of the interpreter, the bullbucker conveyed the specifics of the timbers to the arrivals. Wasting no time in idle talk, the final selection was made. They went about their task meticulously, and soon picked the four best timbers on the ground.

A most unusual event then followed. The priest changed from his street clothes into his professional garb. From a flight bag he pulled a white linen table cloth to cover the table top. Next, he took out a bottle of sake, a small bag of rice, and what appeared to be a black prayer book. These were carefully laid out on the table. The priest then faced the dark forest on the hillside above him, looking up to the gray sky as if he were imploring forgiveness.

Everyone present formed a half circle behind the priest. A light drizzle, like scotch mist, descended from the grey sky, it was truly dismal west coast weather. The priest began reading aloud from his prayer book. He beseeched the spirits of the forest, and thanked them for their bounty. In between passages he would throw a fist-ful of rice and sprinkle the ground with sake. In time he blessed the assembled men, who stood awestruck by this strange ceremony in the woods.

Turning towards the four cedar timbers on the ground, the priest blessed them, and recited a prayer for each. I was struck by the respect given our land by a man of a different culture. His attitude stands out in my memory as a strong and painful contrast to the norm, especially today, when nothing seems to be sacred, nothing is venerated, and everything from nature is taken for granted.

Before parting, the priest handed me a brass Shinto amulet, with the exhortation to keep it close to me to avert evil spirits. On the same afternoon the four timbers were bundled up to protect them during the long trip on two large logging trucks to Seaboard. There the freighter awaited its precious cargo, and sailed duly on the twenty first of December to Japan. The timbers were a gift from Canadian Forest Products to the Japanese, and made excellent advertising for the coastal logging industry.

In turn, I received the immense satisfaction of having lent my hand to something meaningful that would last a very long time. Those remarkable trees did not end up at a saw or a shake mill, nor on the roof of a grand mansion down in California, where shake roofing is a status symbol for the rich.

Only one other time in my career had a similar job come my way. In the early '60s the Indian tribe of Alert Bay was planning to carve a large red cedar tree into a war canoe of ancient style. The chief of the band approached the Englewood Logging Division nearby for such a tree, which was duly granted. Englewood's head bullbucker asked me to scout with him in a stand of old growth timber. We found a majestic, five-hundred year-old tree. It was sound, all the way through, quite unusual for a cedar tree, which are (unlike Douglas fir) prone to ground fire. With great care the tree was felled, and later dragged out for transportation to Alert Bay.

What I observed during my life as a logger prompts me to say the following: logging seems to be an impossible task in a land where nothing seems to be impossible. The incredible harshness of B.C.'s coastal region mocks our plans to log those sheer slopes. All the same, expert loggers have always overcome every hurdle they've encountered. But it is also true that many have paid the ultimate price for their daring. Hence, there is no glory in a logger's life, only sweat and blood, and of these an endless river flows.

EPILOGUE

It took two years of physical therapy to recover from my accident. The pain was horrendous, and in all honesty I have no idea how I managed to recover. My head, shoulders and back had all been crushed, and even my eyesight was affected. I had multiple surgeries, including one to repair my fractured cheek bone with a small, stainless steel plate. Anyone seeing me now would never know the punishment my body has absorbed.

Inge and I continue to live near Horseshoe Bay. Our children are grown up and married. Trudel and her husband own a prosperous business; Hans and his wife are both successful lawyers, recently blessed with a baby girl. It could be said that logging provided for us well. But from a personal perspective, looking back on my life, and on the lives of the men I knew in the woods, the truth is a different story.

Loggers of Stewart-Welsh in front of bunkhouse at Myrtle Point, 1916.

APPENDIX 1

OLAF

Logging, like everything else in life, is in constant flux. Silenced forever is the yell TIMBERRR, which always preceded the fall of a tree. Never again will it take several men one or even two days to cut down a big fir or spruce tree. Gone are the crosscut saws, "the misery whip," and the long-handled, double bit axes.

Such axes were the western loggers' trademark from the 1860s onward; they had narrow blades which fallers kept razor-sharp. By chopping the right undercut, an experienced faller could line the fall so exactly that a two-hundred and fifty foot tree would land on a marker.

But before a faller did anything else, he had to plumb the tree, then choose its bed. Next, he had to cut a wedge out of the thick bark, so he could jam in the springboard to stand on. This allowed the faller to cut higher up on the tree, where the trunk was easier to cut, and yet might still be six to eight feet through. To work on a springboard, one needed good balance, the ability to chop precisely and (preferably) ambidextrously, a long saw, plenty of oil to overcome the friction of the sap, a ten-pound sledge hammer, and several fourteen-inch steel wedges to lift the tree against its lean. It took a long time to fall those huge trees, which could scale out up to 60,000 board feet of lumber.

Nowadays the art of hand falling is just about extinct, but the memory lingers in the minds of a few old-timers. My affinity for timber remains unchanged, and will last to the end of my days.

Years before the First World War a young lad from Norway came to the coast of B.C., destined to be a logger. His name was Olaf, and he later worked as a faller in many logging camps along the coast. For a Norwegian, Olaf was small of stature, slightly built, almost feminine in appearance, but he had great stamina, which compensated for his lack of height. Except for a long strand of blondish-grey hair at the top of his bony head, which frequently fell over his right ear, he was nearly bald. With his head invariably tilted to one side (due to a neck injury) he looked penetratingly at one with his deep blue eyes. When he spoke with his soft voice in a most beautiful English, one hardly noticed that he was of Norwegian descent.

Olaf possessed some remarkable qualities, such as an extraordinarily good memory and a good talent for painting in oil colours. Many of his landscapes were fit to be displayed at an art gallery. Because of such rare talent in a logger, Olaf became known up and down the coast of B.C. as the "artist." He was always cheerful, no matter how bad the weather was at work in the forest, no matter how fiercely the mosquitoes attacked in the summer time. His strong hands were constantly busy, and as he worked he hummed or sang old tunes of bygone times.

While having lunch by the open fire in the woods, holding the indispensable cup of coffee in both hands so as to warm his cold fingers, or cutting pieces of tobacco from the hunk he always carried while he worked, Olaf would relate from the past as he had experienced it. Every so often he would consult his ancient pocket watch to see if it was time to return to work; as the head-faller in the gang, it was his job to urge the others on.

"Well, it was like this," Olaf told us, "times were tough, jobs hard to get, wages very poor and conditions in the camps deplorable. Safety in the woods was unknown. If a man got hurt on the job, he had to tough it out till day's end when the crew returned back to camp. Before 1917, the year the Compensation Board was instituted, work did not stop when a logger was accidentally killed on the job. The body was laid to the side of the rail or road, covered with a blanket or a coat, and left there till the day's work came to an end and everyone rode back to camp. To make things worse, there were no provisions for the widow, children or other persons who depended on the workmen for a living."

Employer attitudes, related Olaf, were notoriously callous during the early decades of the century. Loggers were considered "scum of the earth," not only by their employers, but by other segments of the so-called "upper society."

Olaf once read once the following warning, posted on a wall in a logger's agency:

ALL FEES MUST BE PAID IN ADVANCE. DO
NOT ASK FOR CREDIT. EVERY MAN HIRED
HERE MUST REPORT WITHIN THE TIME STAT-
ED ON THE CONTRACT. NO FEES REFUNDED
TO DRUNKS OR THOSE WHO MISS THE TRAIN
OR BOAT. ANY MAN REFUSING TO GO WHERE
HIRED MUST FORFEIT ALL FEES PAID. NO FEE
REFUNDED IN ANY CASE, UNLESS YOU BRING
A STATEMENT SIGNED BY YOUR EMPLOYER.
DO NOT REPRESENT TO BE WHAT YOU ARE
NOT, AS YOUR EMPLOYER WILL SOON FIND
OUT, AND YOU WILL NOT GET ANY MORE
WORK FROM THIS OFFICE.

Olaf wrote it down, memorized it, and quoted it in later years at every suitable occasion. He also told of demoralized agents, who would sell a logger a job for a bottle of booze.

This situation changed during the Second World War, when loggers were hard to find, because so many men were enlisted in the Armed Forces. In desperation, logging companies hired men known as "mancatchers," who combed the hotels, streets, and beer saloons of downtown Vancouver. Age or fitness did not matter, as long as the individual appeared to be able to do some sort of work. Armed with sweet persuasion, good bribes of advance money and bottles of rye whiskey, the mancatcher rounded up his men and sent them up the coast to the hard-pressed camps.

During this period, the logging companies began forwarding transportation fares through the agencies to loggers returning to work in the logging camps. Since most of the loggers in town were more or less continually broke, this helped get the men back on the job, where they were sorely needed by their respective employers. Any man having obtained his hiring slip, along with his destination, was considered ready to go to work.

APPENDIX 2

THE HISTORY
OF THE IWA

The history of the IWA (International Woodworkers of America — the largest union in Western Canada), is packed with exciting drama; the drama of unrelenting struggles against powerful employers and anti-labour governments. It has been a constant and ongoing battle to win the right to organize, to bargain collectively, and to establish trade union democracy for the woodworkers, whose organization was born in the "hungry thirties," when men slaved for as little as twenty-five cents an hour in the woods.

The enslavement born of poverty and oppression, then endured, is now difficult to believe. Loggers worked long and hazardous hours for a pittance. Men who talked trade union organization in camps were hounded, persecuted and blacklisted out of employment. Reckless speed-up methods of production took a heavy toll on human lives.

The IWA brought loggers out of dark days of misery and degradation. The courage and stamina of those early trade unionists deserves the warmest tribute. It was the loggers of British Columbia who laid the foundations of the IWA as it existed from 1937 until September, 2004, when it merged with a much larger union, the United Steelworkers of America.

The rise and growth of the IWA can be fully appreciated only when one understands how difficult it was to organize the constantly drifting, loose-knit community of loggers. Most camps had three crews; one coming in, one working, and one leaving. A logger on the move was a hard man to talk to about camp conditions.

The loggers' bunkhouses were filthy and infested with bedbugs and lice. (The word "crummy" serves as a reminder of these days.) For the most part, camp food was very bad, and was served on battered tin ware. Clothes were dried in crowded discomfort around

175

the pot-bellied woodstove. Bunkhouses were badly lit and poorly ventilated. Washrooms were unknown. Men stood in line for use of wash basins, and found their own latrines in the woods. Each man packed his own blankets from camp, and was deducted fifty cents a day for the use of a rotten mattress, and for unappetizing fare on the cookhouse table.

In the dark, early days of logging, the industry killed two workers every week of production. A man who stated a grievance was promptly fired and sent "down the road." Holidays were seldom ever observed, much less awarded pay. The only vacations known were compulsory layoffs with no pay, at the whim of the employers. In the past, loggers were impoverished, exhausted and undernourished. They were the victims of poor grub, unsanitary camp conditions, disproportionate board rates and commissary robbery.

Loggers had to turn out to work under any conceivable conditions. Production, or "highball" as it is still called, was the order of the day, and safety practices, as we know them now, were unknown. Loggers were expendable, and if one was killed on the job, others scrambled for the available work. The loggers who survived were a hardy breed of men. But Vancouver's skid road was crowded with broken-backed, burnt-out loggers, who finished up in flop houses or charity hostels.

As hostile to change as conditions were, the misery of day-to-day existence in early camps was enough to make some loggers agitate for improvement. There was a desperate need for a union. Ultimately, victory came in 1937, the birth year of the I.W.A.

The merger of the IWA with the United Steelworkers of America in 2004 created the largest private sector union in Canada, with a national membership of 250,000, and a cross-border membership of some 650,000 workers. Although the IWA no longer exists as an autonomous body, it retains some vestige of its former self, functioning as the IWA Council within the United Steelworkers.

Daily wage rates for loggers
in the year 1936

Baker	$4.00	Handyman	$6.00
Blacksmith	$6.00	Hooktender	$6.50
Blacksmith helper	$4.00	High rigger	$7.00
Head boom man	$5.00	Second rigger	$5.00
Boom man	$4.50	Lever man	$6.00
Head brake man	$6.00	Loader (head)	$6.00
Second brake man	$4.50	Loader (second)	$4.25
Bullcook	$3.25	Loader (third)	$3.75
Car knocker	$4.90	Powder monkey	$4.50
Chaser	$4.25	Powder packer	$3.50
Chokerman	$4.00	Rigging slinger	$5.00
Cook	$6.00	Rigging up man	$4.00
Cook second	$3.50	Scaler	$4.75
Dishwasher	$3.25	Section man	$4.50
Dump man	$4.00	Section (foreman)	$4.75
Engineer (skidder)	$6.00	Steel gang	$3.50
Engineer (cold deck)	$5.75	Steel foreman	$4.75
Engineer (rigging up)	$5.00	Track walker	$3.30
Engineer (locomotive)	$6.50	Wood bucker	$3.70
Fallers and buckers	$5.00	Wood splitter	$3.70
Fireman (donkey)	$3.70	Watchman	$4.00
Fireman (locomotive)	$4.50	Whistle punk	$3.70
Filer (8 sets)	$5.75	Shop mechanic	$4.00
First aid man	$3.25	Steam/gas	
Flunkey	$3.25	shovel engineer	$5.00
Gas expert	$5.75		

- For board and blankets loggers were charged $1.25 per day.
- Work week: 48 hours / train crew: 60 hours.
- Estimated number of loggers employed in logging camps on the coast circa 1936: 10,000.

GLOSSARY

A-frame: An A-shaped framework used for yarding or dumping logs.

Anchor log: A log buried in the earth to hold a guy line firmly — also called a deadman.

Anchor stump: Stumps to which guy, or high lead, lines are attached.

Bag boom: Logs in water surrounded by boom sticks in a circle.

Back corner: An angle where a tail block turns the haulback line around a corner.

Back cut: Final falling cut. The back cut which progresses until the tree starts to fall in its intended direction.

Back end: At the back of a setting.

Back guy: The guy line which is back of the spar, opposite to the lead of the mainline or skyline; it takes most of the pull in yarding logs.

Back line: That part of the haulback line from the spar to the road line corner block.

Back spar: A tree rigged up at the back end of a setting to pro vide lift for yarding logs.

Bald-headed: Butt rigging sent back to the woods without chokers.

Bar or Blade: That part of the chain saw upon which the cutting chain travels.

Barber-chair: The configuration of a chair-shaped tree stump resulting from a tree splitting as it is felled; usually the result of poor falling cuts.

Barrel-swivel: A swivelling device used in the butt rigging.

Beads: Chokers.

Bed: The intended position in which a tree will be felled.

Bell: The socket which slides back and forth on the choker cables between the two knobs. The knob is hooked into the bell to choke the log.

Belly: The middle of anything. A slack in the cable, or a sag in a guy line.

Bight: Hazardous zone created by running lines under tension. Any section of a line between the ends.

Binder: A wire rope, connected by a cinch, placed around logs on a truck to prevent any of the load from spilling. Also called wrapper.

Block: A metal case (shell) enclosing one or more pulley sheaves, provided with a hook, swivel or gooseneck by which the unit may be attached to an object and used to change the direction of motion of a line. Blocks are described according to their use, such as guy line, corner, tail, moving, etc.

Block purchase: To use one or more blocks for mechanical advantage.

Blow down: A tree or stand of timber blown down by the wind.

Bridle: A method of choking a large log using two chokers. Also a method of tail-holding a guy line using two stumps.

Brush: Any kind of undergrowth.

Brush-out: To clear an area.

Buck or Bucking: To cut trees into log lengths; to make any bucking cut on logs.

Buckle: To bend under strain, as with a mobile spar.

Bug: A device carried on a belt used to transmit signals.

Bulkhead: A heavy barrier at the back of the cab to protect the driver of a log truck.

Bull block: A high lead block used on wooden trees for the main line.

Bullbucker: A supervisor of falling and bucking operations.

Bull choker: A large choker.

Bull cook: A man who cleans up bunkhouses.

Bull gang: a rig-up crew.

Bull of the woods: Logging superintendent.

Bundle strap: A length of wire rope with clamp, used for bundling log loads for transport in the water.

Bunk: The heavy steel frame or cradle assembly on logging trucks into which logs are placed.

Bunk house: Sleeping quarters for loggers.

Bunk log: Any log resting on the bunk; the bottom layer in load ing a log truck.

Burn: A burned over area.

Burr: Rough edge or mushroom effect on the striking surface of a hammer or wedge.

Butt: The bottom of a tree. Also, the large end of a log.

Butt hook (Bull hook): The heavy hook on the butt rigging to which chokers are attached.

Butt plate: A steel plate used in some butt rigging.

Butt rigging: A system of swivels, shackles, links and tags which connect the haulback and mainlines and to which chokers are fastened.

Cable cutter: A hydraulically, mechanically or physically operat ed tool for cutting wire ropes.

Cable logging: A yarding system employing switches, blocks and cables.

Caulks: Short spikes driven, or screwed into the soles and heels of boots to give sure footing while walking on wood or logs.

Chain saw: A gas operated power saw.

Change ends: To reverse a wire rope to equalize areas of heavy wear. Also, to swing a log around in the air, end for end, when loading, to get a better lay on the log truck.

Chase: Unhook logs at the landing.

Chaser: Worker who performs chasing duties at the landing.

Choke: To pass a line or choker around a log or other object and pull it tight.

Choker: The wire rope used to choke logs.

Choker hook: A sliding attachment; the "bell" on the bight of a choker.

Chokerman: A rigging crew member who sets chokers, some times called a choker setter.

Claim: timbered country for logging by a company.

Climbing irons (spurs): Irons with sharp spurs, strapped to the leg at the ankle and below the knee. Used by riggers to climb trees for topping and rigging.

Closure: Shut down for fire season, etc.

Cold deck: A pile of logs yarded and left for subsequent transportation.

Corner: The point at which the haulback line turns sharply.

Corner blocks: The haulback blocks at the back end of the set ting which change the direction of the haulback line.

Cull: A log of less quality than the lowest merchantable grade. Also, to reject a log, or throw away unwanted material.

Crummy: A vehicle used to transport workers to and from the woods work areas.

Deflection: Technically, the amount of sag at mid-point below a straight line drawn between the two ends where the rope is anchored or supported.

Diamond lead: Yarding past square lead, in the back quarter.

Dog it: To stop movement — set the dog on the drum.

Dog leg: To angle away from a straight line — crooked.

Donkey: A yarding machine.

Donkey puncher: A yarding operator.

Dutchman: A block arrangement used to pull a bight in a line to help land the logs (to hang a Dutchman).

Dutchman: Portion of the undercut not removed. Can change falling direction of the tree — very hazardous if improperly used.

Early Shift: A shift worked in the summertime when the fire hazard is high.

Extension: A line added to another line to make it longer. A 250-foot piece of straw line. A line added to a guy line to make it longer.

Face: Edge of area formed along standing timber as timber is felled.

Fair lead: Rollers or pulleys arranged to permit spooling in a cable from any direction. Also, the area between the two front quarter guylines.

Faller: A timber faller-bucker on the coast.

Falling: Process of falling timber.

Felled and bucked: Downed timber bucked up for yarding.

Fight hang ups: To change or reset the chokers to clear the turn being yarded when it gets hung up behind a stump or boulders.

Fire break: A stand of timber left between settings to slow down or stop forest fires.

Fire guard: A cleared trail around a fire made by machine.

Fire hazard: The relatively dry condition of timber in the woods.

Fire season: Usually spans from May 1 to October 31, or as long as the fire hazard is high.

Fire watch: A man left after work to watch for possible fires.

Flunkey: A table waiter and dishwasher in a logging camp.

Flying chokers: The number of chokers attached to the butt rig ging; e.g.: Fly two chokers.

Front end: At the spar tree, by the machine.

Gin pole: A short spar tree for loading logs.

Goat show: A dangerous place to work.

Grade: The quality of a log. Also, a completed base for a truck haul road. Also a hill.

Green timber: The uncut forest.

Ground: The terrain on which a logging operation is being carried out on.

Gut hammer: A triangular piece of metal which the cook or flunkey would hit with a chink of iron to announce mealtime in a logging camp.

Guyline: Wire rope attached to and stretched from a stump or ground anchor and a spar tree.

Gyppo: A small logging operator or contractor. Term is also used to define such an operation.

Handyman: A man skilled at various jobs around a logging operation.

Hang-up: Logs stuck behind a stump or other obstacle when yarding, also, rigging fouled in some manner so as to prevent logging, also, any kind of failure on an operation.

Hanging the rigging: Rigging up a spar tree.

Haulback block: A block through which the haulback line runs.

Haywire: Anything below normal standard; no good.

Haywire show: A logging operation without safety standards; a dangerous place to work.

Heel boom: Loading rig on a wooden spar tree.

High ball: Go ahead fast.

High lead: A cable logging system in which running line lead blocks are placed at the top of the spar tree to provide lift for the logs during yarding.

Hook tender: The man in charge of the yarding and loading crew.

Holding wood: The hinge of wood left uncut between the back of an undercut and the back cut.

Jagger: A broken strand on a worn or damaged cable; wires that stick out and tear hands or clothes.

Jill Poke: To punch against or make contact with. A protruding log, such as a log on a pile pushed ahead when struck by the incoming turn.

Kerf: The width of any saw cut.

Landing: The area where the yarder and/or loader are placed and the logs are landed.

Lead: The direction in which the lines run out from the yarder. Also, the angle the line will spool on the drums.

Lean: Outward slant of a tree in relation to its base.

Leaner: A tree which leans or is not growing perpendicular to the ground.

Line changing: Changing the rigging from one yarding road to another.

Load: To load logs, a load of logs, the stress placed on a piece of equipment or cable, to place dynamite in a hole ready to blast.

Loader: Any kind of machine used to place logs on a logging truck.

Logs: The cut sections of felled timber bucked into lengths.

Log dump: The end of the road where logs are put in water for further transport.

Log stamp: A branding hammer used to identify logs.

Mainline: The line used to yard the logs. It has a larger diameter than the haulback line. Also, the main road in a logging opera tion road system.

Man-catcher: A company representative whose job it was to induce loggers to return to camp.

Mat: Short lengths of logs for the pad of the spar tree to rest on. Also, a portable set of logs bolted or lashed together for a grade shovel to rest on when making roads.

Mattock: A heavy digging tool with a hoe blade on one side and an axe blade on the other, used for fire fighting.

Muck stick: A hand shovel.

Mud 'em in: To drag the logs when there is not enough lift from the spar tree.

Notch: A notch is cut in a stump to prevent the guy line or haulback strap from lifting off. The notch should lead to the top of the spar.

Old growth: Virgin timber.

Pass block: A light wooden block at the top of a spar tree, used to pull rigging up the tree.

Pass chain: A chain used to make a type of bosun's chair for a climber to ride in as he goes up a tree. Also, used to grasp the bight of a line.

Peaker: The top log on a load.

Pecker pole: A small tree or log.

Pile: A pile of logs.

Pile driver: A machine for driving piles.

Pitch: Sticky resin found in coniferous trees; sap. Also, steepness of a road on a hill.

Polaski: A light fire tool shaped like an axe.

Powder: Explosives used in blasting; dynamite.

Powder monkey: A worker who uses dynamite in logging operations.

Pull rigging: The work done by a rigging slinger.

Pump can: A five gallon water can with a built-in pump used in putting out small fires.

Purchase: To obtain additional pull by the use of lines and blocks.

Purchase block: A block used on rigging to obtain greater pull on a line.

Push: Any foreman or boss.

Quarter: An area within the setting, e.g.: front right quarter, back left quarter, yarding quarter, front quarter guylines. Also, area allotted to each faller.

Raise a tree: To set up a spar tree.

Raising guy: Usually the front quarter guys for the final raising of certain portable spars.

Reef: To pull hard, with the yarder throttle wide open.

Rig up: To set up a spar tree for logging.

Rigger: If "high rigger," a man who tops a spar tree and rigs it.

Rigging: Lines, blocks, hooks, chokers, etc., all the gear used in cable logging systems. Also, working on rigging jobs.

Rigging crew: The crew which handles the rigging in a yarding operation; the rigging slinger and the chokerman.

Rigging man: A logger working on the rigging crew.

Rigging slinger: The man in charge of the chokermen who spots the rigging and picks out the turn. He is responsible for the safety of the chokermen.

Road: The road along which logs are yarded to the landing. Also, short for skid road. Also, the truck haul road.

Root wad: The torn up mass of dirt and rocks caught in the root system when a tree is uprooted.

Running line: A moving cable in logging operations.

Safety strap: Strap attached to the guy line blocks at the top of the spar. Prevents the blocks from falling into the landing if the crown ring or shackles fail.

Saltchuck: Saltwater.

Set or gang: May consist of one faller who fells and bucks timber. Might be one faller and one bucker working as a team.

Set back: Occurs when a tree settles back opposite to the intended direction of fall, hazardous situation when the faller loses control of a tree.

Scaler: Measures each bucked log for number of board feet and grade.

School marm: A log or tree with two main stems instead of a single stem.

Scrub: Poor, unmerchantable timber.

Second growth: Young timber; the timber that grows after the mature timber is removed.

Second loader: Worker who assists in the loading of a log truck.

Setting: The area logged by one spar tree or cat.

Shackle: A clevis or heavy iron device use to hook rigging and/or lines together. May be a screw pin, Molly Hogan pin, or a knockout pin.

Show: A logging operation (high lead show, winter show, summer show, etc.)

Shutdown: A work stoppage for various reasons; road washouts, equipment breakdown, labour trouble, fire hazard, etc.

Siamese: A "Y" coupling for a fire hose, providing two outlets.

Side: A logging unit; the men and equipment needed to log an area (setting) of an operation.

Side push: The man in charge of an area of a logging operation.

Sidewinder: a tree which does not fall in the required direction while being felled.

Signals: Audible or hand signals used to direct the movement of logs in yarding or loading operations.

Siwash: A line not running in a straight line but bent around trees, logs.

Skidder: Used for skyline logging.

Skid road: Roadway along which logs are dragged.

Skin 'er back: go ahead on haulback, take the butt rigging back to the woods.

Skyline: Heavy cable hung between two spar trees with a travel ling carriage to haul logs through the air in rough country.

Slash: Debris left on the ground after logging. Also, a logged off area.

Slash burn: A fire set in logging slash, generally in the fall, to get rid of dangerous fuel before the next season.

Swamper: Helper.

Snag: Any dead or dying tree ten feet high or over.

Snoose: Chewing tobacco.

Spar: The tree or mast on which rigging is hung for any one of the many high lead cable logging systems.

Spark arrestor: A screen fitted over the exhaust to prevent sparks from escaping.

Spark chaser: Sparky, a fire watchman.

Spike bar: A claw bar used to pull railroad spikes.

Spiker: To stop anything.

Spike top: A tree with a dead top, usually with no branches.

Splice: To join ends of ropes on cables by interweaving strands. Also to join wire or rope in various ways; eye splices, long splices, etc.

Spool: A drum to hold cable; also to wind cable smoothly on a drum.

Spooling Iron: A metal hook used to spool line on a drum.

Spot fire: A small fire ahead of the main fire.

Spring board: Board old-time fallers stood on to fall trees.

Square lead: Right angles to the yarding machine.

Stand: An area of timber.

Strap: A short length cable with an eye in each end.

Strawline: A light cable used in rigging up, or in moving other cables or blocks. The smallest line on the yarder (mainline, haulback line, strawline).

Strip a tree: To take all the rigging off a spar tree.

Suicide show: A dangerous piece of ground to log.

Tailblock: A block used to guide the haulback line at the back corner of the yarding area.

Tailhold: A point of anchor for the dead end of a purchase line or rigging assembly. Also refers to the stumps the backline blocks are hung on.

Thread: To reef a line through blocks or a carriage.

Tightlining: To hold a line tight by braking or interlocking the lines.

Timbercruiser: A man who inventories volume and grade of standing timber.

Tommy Moore: A small block with a wide throat usually used with the strawline as a lead block.

Tongs: Scissor like hooks used to load logs.

Turn: One or more logs that are yarded to the landing at one time.

Twister: If a tailhold stump does not appear to be strong enough, it should be tied back to another stump, or stumps, by use of a length of line and a twister pole.

Undercut: Notch cut in tree to regulate direction of tree fall.

Up-end a log: To change ends of a log in order to position it for loading or piling. Also, to cause a log to up-end in yarding by coming in contact with an obstruction.

Whistle: A signal device for the yarding of logs, nowadays usual ly transmitted by a radio signal.

Whistle punk: Signalman. Transmits signals by electric buzzer or horn to yarding engine to indicate movements of rigging in yarding logs.

Widowmaker: A loose limb, top piece of bark, or anything loose in a tree that may fall on a logger.

Windfall: A blown down tree.

Woods: Timber country, logging area. "Bush" is also used to the same effect.

Yarder: a machine that yards logs.

Yarding: Pulling logs to the landing.

INDEX

Bold type = photo caption / *italics* = glossary entry

189

Tightliner Steve, 59, 66, 68, 73
tightlining, *187*
timbercruiser, 68, *187*
Toba Inlet, 12
Tofino, 10
Tommy Moore, 48, 124, *187*
tongs, 40, 44, 61, *187*
Trudel Knapp, 151, 171
tugboats, 11, 14, 125
twister, 54, *188*

U
undercut, 52, **145**, 148, 150,
  164, 167, 172, 181, 183, *188*
United Steel Workers of
  America, 176
up-end, *188*

V
Vancouver, 4, 5, 6, 7, 8, 9, 10,
  17, 19, 28, 37, 46, 76, 78, 82,
  87, 110, 116, 125, 127, 129,
  165, 166, 174
Vancouver Island, 6, 10, 11, 12,
  89, 111
Vancouver Sun, 93
Vernon Camp, 37, 89, 147
Victoria, 37
Victoria Public Library, 37

W
wage rates (1936), 177
Wakeman Sound, 5, 8, 12, 20,
  22, 37, 38, 47, 55, 62, 68, 77,
  80, 83
Weeping Willy, 96-98
Wheeler Dealer John, 158
Whispering George, 133
Whispering Swede, 42-44
whistle, 97, 119, 124, 156, 160,
  188
whistle punk, 32, 33, 38, 59,
  60, 71, 74, 75, 81, 96, 97,

118, 119, 156, 177, *188*
widowmaker, *188*
Windbag Sam, 161, 163
windfall, 62, 65, 83, 82, 99,
  101, 103, 140, 149, *188*
wolves, 94, 102
wood yard, 42-44, 78
World War, 10, 45, 82, 148,
  172, 174
Woss Camp, 37, 89, 163

Y
Yarder, 14, 32, 33, 34, 38, 39,
  48, 49, **50**, 51, 54, 55, 59, 70,
  73, 74, 75, 81, 97, 98, 100,
  113, 117, 119, 160, 162, 183,
  185, 187, *188*
Yarding, 14, 32, 33, 36, 38, 39,
  40, 58, 59, 60, 61, 68, 69, 71,
  72, 73, 74, 82, 117, 161, 178,
  180, 181, 182, 183, 185, 186,
  187, *188*
Yukon Jack, 83

Z
Zeballos, 10

Hancock House Publishers

Afloat in Time
James Sirois
ISBN: 0-88839-455-1
SC, 8.5" x 5.5", 288 pp.

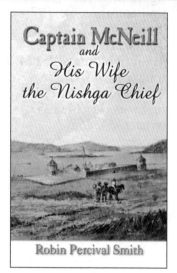

**Captain McNeill and His Wife
the Nishga Chief**
Robin Percival Smith
ISBN: 0-88839-472-1
SC , 8.5" x 5.5", 256 pp.

Dowager Queen
William A. Hagelund
ISBN: 0-88839-486-1
SC, 8.5" x 5.5", 168 pp.

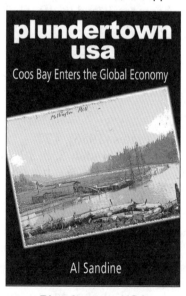

Plundertown USA
Al Sandine
ISBN: 0-88839-525-6
SC, 8.5" x 5.5", 176 pp.

hancock
house

Logging
Ed Gould
ISBN: 0-919654-44-4
HC, 11" x 8.5", 224 pp.

Big Timber Big Men
Carol Lind
ISBN: 0-88839-020-3
HC, 11" x 8.5", 160 pages

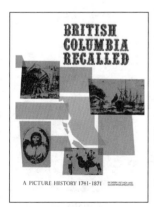

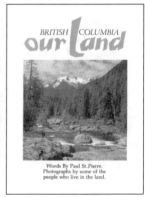

B.C. Recalled
Derek Pethick,
Susan Im Baumgarten
ISBN: 0-919654-12-6
SC, 11" x 8.5", 96 pp.

B.C.'s Own Railroad
Lorraine Harris
ISBN: 0-88839-125-0
SC, 8.5" x 5.5", 64 pp.

B.C. Our Land
Paul St. Pierre
ISBN: 0-919654-96-7
HC, 14" x 10", 160 pp.

hancock house

Look for all HANCOCK HOUSE *titles and ordering info at:* **www.hancockhouse.com**

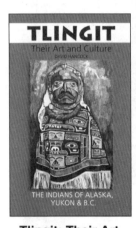

Tlingit: Their Art and Culture
David Hancock
ISBN: 0-88839-530-2
SC, 8.5" X 5.5", 96 pp.

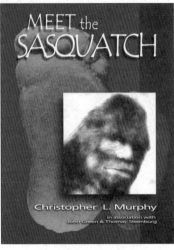

Meet the Sasquatch
Chris Murphy, John Green, Thomas Steenburg
ISBN: 0-88839-573-6
SC, 11" X 8.5", 256 pp.

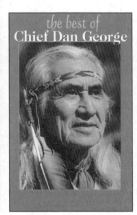

The Best of Chief Dan George
Chief Dan George, Helmut Hirnschall
ISBN: 0-88839-544-2
SC, 8.5" X 5.5", 128 pp.

Tlingit: Their Art, Culture & Legends
Dan and Nan Kaiper
ISBN: 0-88839-010-6
SC, 8.5" X 5.5", 96 pp.

Raincoast Sasquatch
J. Robert Alley
ISBN: 0-88839-508-6
SC, 8.5" X 5.5", 360 pp.

Bald Eagle of Alaska, BC and Washington
David Hancock
ISBN: 0-88839-536-1
SC, 8.5" X 5.5", 96 pp.